PRAISE FOR
101 Best Home-Based Businesses
for Women, Revised 2nd Edition

"What a gold mine of home-business ideas and resources! This book will save the reader countless hours of research."

> — Barbara Brabec, author of *Homemade Money* and *Creative Cash,* 6th Edition

"If you have ever wanted to work from home but needed some ideas, this book can provide just that—with its listing of 101 entrepreneurial ideas and vital information needed to make each enterprise a success."

> — Patricia C. Gallagher, parenting expert and author of *Start Your Own At-Home Child Care Business*

"Don't even think of starting your home business without first reading this comprehensive collection of home-business ideas that are perfect for the woman who wants to work from home."

> — Liz Folger, author of *The Stay-at-Home Mom's Guide to Making Money*

"Partners in Residence was born from ideas generated from Priscilla Huff's *101 Best Home-Based Businesses for Women.*"

> — Sharrie and Wil Thames, owners, Partners in Residence Home Inventory Service & Products

"I truly recommend this book for any woman who has the desire to work at home, running a business that would not only provide extra income but be one she would enjoy."

> — Sally Silagy, founder, Gardening Greetings

"This is a great overview of business needs and a great source for business resources. I'm certainly keeping it among my best books on business."

> — Maryanne Burgess, author of *Designer Source Listing*

Also by Priscilla Y. Huff

101 Best Small Businesses for Women

More 101 Best Home-Based Businesses for Women

101 BEST HOME-BASED BUSINESSES FOR WOMEN

REVISED 2ND EDITION

Priscilla Y. Huff

PRIMA PUBLISHING

For my husband and sons for their encouragement and patience.
A debt of gratitude also goes to the many women entrepreneurs who
talked with me about the starting and running of their businesses.
The information they shared with me was worth more than an MBA!

© 1998 by Priscilla Y. Huff

PRIMA PUBLISHING and colophon are registered trademarks of Prima
Communications, Inc.

Library of Congress Cataloging-in-Publication Data

Huff, Priscilla Y.
    101 best home-based businesses for women : everything you need
to know about getting started on the road to success / Priscilla Y. Huff.
–Rev. 2nd ed.
      p.   cm.
    Includes index.
    ISBN 0-7615-1651-4
    1. Home-based businesses. 2. Women-owned business enterprises—
Management. 3. New business enterprises—Management. I. Title.
HD62.38.H84 1998
658'.041—dc21   98-30181
                                                           CIP

    99 00 01 02 HH 10 9 8 7 6 5 4 3 2
Printed in the United States of America

Disclaimer: The business ideas presented herein are not a guarantee of
monetary success. The information is based on research, examples, and advice
from business experts, trade associations, and women business owners. Every
attempt was made to insure accuracy, and neither the author nor the publisher
can be held responsible for any errors or changing circumstances. All featured
businesses, franchises and business opportunities, publications, products, services, and suppliers are intended for information only. They do not represent an
endorsement on the part of the author or publisher.

How to Order
Single copies may be ordered from Prima Publishing, P.O. Box 1260BK,
Rocklin, CA 95677; telephone (916) 632-4400. Quantity discounts
are also available. On your letterhead, include information concerning
the intended use of the books and the number of books you wish to
purchase.

Visit us online at www.primapublishing.com

Contents

Introduction

From 1987 to 1996, according to the National Foundation of Women Business Owners (NFWBO), the number of women-owned businesses has soared by 78 percent. Today, women provide jobs for one out of every four workers at American companies—employing more people in the United States than the Fortune 500 companies employ worldwide.

The Small Business Administration's statistics show that twice as many women as men start businesses and that by the year 2000, over 40 percent of all small businesses will be owned by women.

Spokespersons for NFWBO also reveal that home-based, women-owned businesses in the United States number over 3.5 million and provide full- or part-time employment for an estimated 14 million people.

Each business that was profiled in this book contains most or all of the following details, depending on the information that was available:

* **Description of the Business**—Describes activities involved in conducting the business featured.
* **Start-Up Costs and Financing Sources**—Estimates what it will cost to get a business going and suggests financing options.
* **Pricing Guidelines**—Gives an idea of what to charge for business services or products.
* **Marketing and Advertising Methods and Tips**—Offers suggestions for attracting customers.
* **Essential Equipment**—Lists the basic materials you need to start the business featured.

✤ **Recommended Training, Experience, or Needed Skills**—Describes the knowledge or background needed, as well as tips for gaining experience.

✤ **Income Potential**—Estimates average earnings for the business featured.

✤ **Type of Business**—Lists whether it is an "in-home" or out-of-the-home" (meaning that you have a home office, yet do the work away from your home) business.

✤ **Best Customers**—Describes who will most likely use your products or services.

✤ **Helpful Tips**—Gives advice from business owners on what made them successful.

✤ **Franchises, Distributorships, and Licenses**—Lists of related commercial business ventures.

✤ **For More Information**—Lists publications, books, trade associations,* home study courses, business start-up guides, and other helpful resources.

✤ **Additional Business Ideas**—Lists related business ventures.

The home-based businesses described in this book are, of course, not the only ones you can operate out of your home, but they are some of the more profitable and highly recommended ones by the women who own them. This is not a get-rich-quick book; it merely provides an overview of certain home-based businesses and lists important resources that can be used to obtain more information. It is up to you to achieve whatever business goals you plan.

The women mentioned in this book are just a few of the millions of women who are working out of their homes, both part-time and full-time. You, too, can start your own successful business if you research the subject and make a commitment to persist until you make it happen. Good luck!

---

*Please note: Many associations *do not* have start-up business information, but, rather, they exist for membership networking. Whenever requested, please send a large, self-addressed, stamped envelope (55 cents)[LSASE] to insure a reply to your requests for information. Many associations are nonprofit and are staffed by volunteers.

Part I

Home-Based Business Considerations

❧ 1 ❧

Before You Start Your Business

Several years ago, Pam, a mother of two, quit her job as a book-keeper. "I liked my job but was tired of the looks I'd get from management if I missed work because one of my children was sick. Plus, after my expenses and child care, I was only clearing an extra $20 a week!" Pam decided to start her own bookkeeping service, which now grosses more than $35,000 a year. As thriving as her business has become, however, she is still able to arrange her workday around her first priority—her family.

Pam is just one of the millions of people who have launched home-based businesses during the eighties and nineties. Business experts estimate that 25 to 30 million people currently operate full- and part-time home-based businesses. *HOME BUSINESS* magazine (December 1997) stated that the Giga Information Group of Norwell, Massachusetts, estimates that by the year 2000, the number of U.S. households operating some type of income-producing business from home will increase to over 27 percent.

Women have begun working from their homes for many reasons: Although the situation is improving, high quality child care can be difficult to find and is usually costly; the need for both spouses to work in order to maintain an adequate standard of living is almost a necessity; and technological developments and advances in computers, fax machines, and other office equipment have enabled the average person to set up an affordable home office.

In addition, women learned in the seventies that they could neither do it all nor have it all. Trying to balance their careers with family obligations and relationships with their husbands just did not work—except for the few superwomen who had some magic formula to make it all happen! Many women were tired of climbing the corporate ladder, having to do twice as much as their male counterparts just to be recognized.

Instead of surrendering all of their goals and aspirations, women in the eighties began to use their education and previous work experience to start new ventures, many of which are still home-based today. This is not to say, however, that things are easier for the home-based business owner. The amount of time that is spent running a home business may well exceed the "normal" forty-hour work week; there can be endless distractions, including interruptions from family and relatives (which usually happen when you are in the middle of a very important telephone conversation!); and your customers may think that you are never closed and may call you at all hours of the day or night.

For example, Pam works about fifty to sixty hours a week, with approximately twenty hours of that time spent at various clients' offices. Her daughter is in school, but she still has to make arrangements to have her son cared for whenever she makes office visits. Pam says, "I try to work at the business when my son is in preschool. Luckily for me, I've just hired my mother to do part-time office work. This works out great because I not only have dependable help but also a built-in babysitter if one of the children is sick."

Although having a home-based business may lead to a more hectic home life, one primary advantage is the important element of flexibility, which is not usually found in a regular nine-to-five job. Home-based business owners can tailor their work schedules to fit their needs as well as their families' needs. They also have the freedom to work in their offices at any hour; to run their businesses according to their own personal philosophies; and to pursue any new opportunities that their businesses may offer.

Most people find that the advantages of having a home-based business far outweigh those of a "regular" job. As Pam says, "I'll never work for anyone else again!" Jerrie, who owns a gift basket business, takes her three-year-old son with her when she makes deliveries. She says, "I do not apologize for bringing my son. I believe that since so many women with small children are beginning businesses, people are just going to have to accept that children will sometimes help or accompany their mothers."

Home-based business owners (whose numbers are increasing every year) usually start at the top of the ladder. They are the presidents, the bosses, and the board-of-directors, all-in-one. In contrast to the relatively powerless actions of employees in most companies, every action that home-business owners take somehow affects their businesses. They are responsible for every aspect of their business, which includes financing and budgeting, marketing and advertising, dealing directly with customers and suppliers, keeping accurate records, and maintaining the production of services or products.

Many women entrepreneurs formerly worked in the corporate world and concluded that they could be more effective running their own businesses. Their job skills, honed while working for outside companies, greatly contributed to their successful private ventures. In fact, many experts recommend that you first work in a business outside the home that is similar to the one you would like to create.

To some people, running their own "company" becomes overwhelming, and they go out of business in less than a year. For those who persist (often working at other jobs while supporting their fledgling businesses), the rewards are great. As you will discover from the examples listed in Part II, women business owners have a distinct pride in themselves and in their accomplishments—something that few other jobs had given them.

What types of businesses are run from the home? In the past, women babysat or ironed and mended clothes or made crafts from their homes to earn "pin-money," yet they were not considered business owners or entrepreneurs. At present, however, home-based businesses are as varied as any list of established businesses. They include everything from catering to clowning, from garden consulting to cleaning. Take a look at any community bulletin board and you can see endless advertisements for a multitude of small businesses, many of them home based.

The businesses that are featured in this book are owned and run by women. Some are full-time and some are part-time, depending on the type of business and the time each woman has to put into it. This book can also help men who are interested in becoming entrepreneurs, because today jobs are performed interchangeably by men and women. I chose to focus on women's home-based businesses because so many women are seeking alternative ways to balance their careers with their families and personal goals.

By featuring the women's businesses I have chosen, I am hopeful that women who have been hesitant to start a business might now be encouraged to go ahead with their ventures. For this reason, too, I have tried to be realistic in describing each business. There are no get-rich-quick stories here or magic formulas for instant success, only actual facts about real women working very hard to establish and run their own businesses.

Many of these businesses are service-oriented, because this type of business usually requires less start-up capital than others. Dr. Geoffrey Kessler of the Kessler Exchange, a research bank of information for small businesses (see the various sources for research and information in Part III, for more information), says that service businesses are among the best types to start now.

According to his report, "Service needs for the 16 + million busier and busier two-income (or three- or four-income!) families will mushroom. So will those for the burgeoning number of single-parent and single-income families. The elderly and the affluent people of the world will be more numerous and wealthier than ever before. They, too, will want more services."

What is a service business? It is one that fills a need in your community. How can you determine what people need? Listen! If you hear people saying over and over, "I wish there were someone who could help me . . ." or "I hate doing . . ." or "I wish I could hire someone to do it for me!" there might be an opportunity to create a lucrative service-type business.

Once you have an idea for one or two businesses, see how many similar businesses are offered in your community. If there are others like the one you want to start, think of how you could improve or interpret such a business in your own special way. You could offer better rates or better hours, target a wider (or smaller) age group, improve customer service, or offer door-to-door delivery. The next chapter goes into more detail about how to choose the best business for you.

Questions to Ask Yourself Before You Start

Where Will You Work?
Where you work will depend on whether your service involves going to your customers' homes or offices or their coming to you. With a cleaning business, for example, you (or your workers) will be going to clients' homes; but if you have a tax or financial service where your customers come to you, you will need adequate parking spaces and a home office, preferably with a separate entrance (or one that can be shut off from your house so that your customers do not hear the cartoons your children are watching, or, worse, their squabbling!).

Your home office may be a corner, closet, room, or other space that can be used exclusively for your business. Pam's office is in her dining room, but she has plans to remodel her garage into an office. She says, "I'd like my office moved where I can shut the door on it at the end of the day. Whenever I walk by [my dining room] now, I'm reminded of work."

Setting up an office—in no matter how small a space—will help establish your business as a serious venture to yourself and your family. If you plan to have your business be more than just a hobby, your work area will have to look professional. Determine what basic equipment you need, and purchase it new or used. You can always upgrade later as your business grows (and it will, if you are determined enough!).

Installing a separate telephone line for your business (with an answering machine or service or voice mail) is almost a necessity if you have a family. Just one teenager can tie up a phone for hours! You will lose valuable business if your customers cannot reach you.

Having your own office or space will help you to set in your mind that you are "going to work." It may take some self-discipline, especially at first, to walk away from household distractions, but, in order to succeed in your business, remind yourself to save that wash, or tape that TV program to see later, after your business is closed.

Is It Permissible to Work from Your Home?

Before you open for business or begin to advertise, check with your local authorities about laws and restrictions pertaining to home businesses. Honey, who owns a silk flower business, first checked with her township. She was given permission to open a home business as long as customer traffic and deliveries did not become so heavy that neighbors would complain. Honey says, "I also went to my neighbors to tell them what I was planning to do. They said they would not mind and thought it was a neat idea. One even gave me some orders!"

Your state may have regulations and licensing requirements for running certain businesses, such as catering; caring for animals, children, or the elderly; or operating a beauty salon. Check with your state department of health or social services, or call your local state representative or senator to get a listing of state agencies that issue small business licenses.

Your regional Small Business Development Center (SBDC) will also have information about your state's business regulations. (See "Government Resources" in Part III.)

Who Should You Talk to Before You Start?

1. A good accountant can be worth his or her weight in gold! He or she can show you how to set up a workable bookkeeping system and keep vital records for tax purposes. Two women who run a party business have this to say about their accountant: "We send him our quarterly statements, and he tells us how much money we are making and if we should even be in business!"

2. A lawyer who specializes in small business matters is a valuable resource. He or she can legalize your business name (even though you can do this yourself) and can give counsel on steps to take to protect yourself and your business from possible lawsuits.

   If you can only afford one hour of a lawyer's time, take it. Even a brief appointment may be beneficial and could help to prevent costly legal mistakes in the future. Good legal advice can give you the peace of mind you may need, especially if this is your first business venture. As your business grows, you can always hire a lawyer for more information.

3. A licensed property and casualty agent can evaluate your business insurance needs. These agents, unlike accountants or lawyers, usually do not charge a fee. They are given a percentage of the policy premiums that you pay. Start with the agent who handles your homeowner's policy. If he or she cannot help you, ask for a referral to another agent who can.

4. A growing number of financial advisers and home-based business and professional practice consultants provide services for individuals and small businesses. They can help set up your business by advising you on how to find start-up money, by helping with the bookkeeping, and by suggesting ways to manage and expand your business.

5. Of course, you should do some of your own research before you hire any expert's services. Check with these sources first:

   + The local chamber of commerce
   + Local women's business club(s)
   + The state association of insurance agents
   + The state bar association
   + Your bank
   + The local library for county business and professional directories
   + Other women with home-based businesses

   Talking to women who run home-based businesses may be your best research source. These women can recommend the services of professionals who understand and have had experience in helping home-based business owners. It will pay off to look around for the best people to help you. Remember to ask all of the questions you can think of before you hire any experts. If you are not satisfied with their services, try someone else. After all, it is your business and you know best what goals you want to achieve.

What Kind of Insurance Does a Service Business Need?

According to independent insurance agent Kathy Delp, "It depends on the type of business. For example, you may need more liability coverage if you have customers come to your home office, additional insurance to cover equipment if you produce a product, or insurance covering accidental breakage or damage if you work in clients' homes."

She recommends that you check your homeowner's policy to see if it contains any personal business coverage. After you decide what you want covered, your agent can modify your present policy with an extension to adequately cover your business needs. If your present policy cannot be extended, your agent can recommend a company that will offer the additional coverage.

Kathy Delp also believes that it may be best to ask an independent insurance agency about business coverage because they deal with many insurance companies. An independent insurance agency, which has flexibility because they're not affiliated with just one large company, can recommend the best carrier at the best price.

Insurance for your home business should be expanded as your venture progresses from its start-up period through increased growth and eventual stability. Check with your agent to make sure your insurance covers at least three major areas: crime and disaster prevention; accident prevention; and liability prevention. If your car, truck, or van will be used in your business, check with your agent to make sure you are properly covered.

Study your business insurance policy—know what is covered and to what extent—before you launch your business. Keep copies of your policies in a safe place. Also, keep a listing of your agents and their phone numbers close at hand so that you can easily call them if the need arises.

Will You Work Alone or with a Partner?

This is a good question to discuss with your attorney. He or she can tell you the advantages and disadvantages of a sole proprietorship (a business owned by one individual) and a partnership (a business owned by two or more persons).

Three out of four businesses are sole proprietorships. If you start a business by yourself, you are the sole proprietor. You make all the decisions; you decide which direction your business will take; and you benefit from any related tax savings and, of course, all the profits. In other words, it's your "baby."

As with a baby, though, a sole proprietorship is also the full responsibility of the parent (owner). You have to pay all business debts, and anything you own can be subject to liquidation if you cannot pay off the debts. You have to learn to handle every aspect of your business. You should have plans in place in the event that you die or become incapacitated.

Most of the businesses in Part II are sole proprietorships, and their owners have loved the challenges inherent in these business ventures. If they were uncertain how to handle various aspects of their businesses, they went to people who could help them or figured out their own methods through trial and error.

A partnership has the advantages of combining the skills, expertise, and capital of two or more persons. Partners share the responsibilities and the costs. Whether you and your partner have been friends for twenty-five years or have just met recently, you should have a written, legal agreement drawn up by your lawyer. Why? Unfortunately, two-thirds of all partnerships dissolve, many due to unresolvable differences between the partners.

The owners of one of the businesses in this book had difficulty holding their partnership together. The partnership of the two women, who had been friends ever since childhood, worked well until one of them got married. The husband was jealous of the time his wife gave to the business, so, to placate him, she put in less time. Her partner became resentful that she was doing all the work. The married woman dropped out of the business to start another one with her husband. As a result, the women's friendship has never been quite the same!

A lawyer can draw up a partnership agreement containing information such as how much each partner invests; division of salaries, duties, and responsibilities; participation of each partner in the profits and losses; what happens if one partner wants to sell out or dies; and other details to equally protect each partner's interest. A partnership must be based on trust, but people are only human and a legal agreement can help prevent future hassles if you go your separate ways. (See "Legal Structure," page 26.)

How Much Time Will You Need for Your Business?
Whether your business will be full- or part-time is, of course, a factor. Regardless of your choice, it is better to start small and grow with your business than to take on a full-sized endeavor—unless you are completely prepared to do so. Careful planning will save you time in the long run. There are scores of books and motivational tapes that can help you manage your time. Here are some basic time-management tips:

* Keep a record of a week's worth of day-to-day activities to see how many free hours you have daily.
* Set your priorities. Family, business, and volunteer work should each have its place. You may have to cut down on your volunteer efforts or settle for a less-than-perfect house, but you will need all the extra hours you can find to get your business started while still having time for your family.
* Make goals and set tentative deadlines for meeting them. Decide what steps it will take to reach each goal and schedule them, one-by-one, on your calendar.
* Sit down with your family members and tell them what you are going to do. Tell them you love them, but you are going to be busy starting a new business and would appreciate all the help and understanding they can give. They'll probably be enthusiastic about your new job until the morning comes when you've forgotten to do the "white" wash. If you involve your family in your business from the beginning, they will be less apt to feel resentful.
* Be realistic. Remember that everything will take longer to accomplish than you expect. Be flexible and learn to make the most of whatever blocks of time are available during the day, especially if you have a family. One divorced mother of four

has her own wallpapering and painting business. She says, "I work four days a week, leaving one day for errands or family matters. I let my customers know that my family is first in my life and that there may be interruptions from time to time. If they cannot handle that, I will refer them to someone else."

✤ Get organized. At the beginning of each month, one mother, who has a basket and chair caning business, marks down her and her children's activities in different colors on a calendar. She writes down due dates for long-term projects (both hers and her children's), so that things are not neglected until the last minute. She laughs as she says, "If anyone ever stole my calendar, I would be lost! It would be far easier to replace a TV or a VCR than it would be to remember everything that has been scheduled and written on that calendar!" She also plans a month's worth of meals for her family, so that she doesn't "have to think when making the weekly shopping list."

All schedules are subject to unexpected changes, of course, whether due to family illnesses, weather conditions, car or appliance breakdowns, or any of life's other unforeseen mishaps. But with a home-based business, the owner often has the advantage of being able to work around these crises.

If you are a woman with children, you will have to make the most of your free time. Keeping your office or work area organized will help you to save time in picking up where you left off, whether to start a meal or take your turn car-pooling. Write a note to help yourself remember where you stopped. Periodically, file your papers to help keep your office in order.

A tip from the magazine *Home Office Computing* says that if it takes you longer than a minute to find something in your home office, you should take a few minutes to reorganize. The old adage "Time is money" applies even more emphatically to a home business, because any time that you waste takes money from your own pocket.

Will Your Business Be Full-Time or Part-Time?
Unless you have substantial savings put away or someone else to support you, starting a business full-time is usually not the

best way to go. Many of the women business owners featured in this book are still working part-time in their businesses. Others went full-time at the point that their part-time businesses warranted it.

According to the SBA, millions of people work at home part-time. Many of them work for other companies, but the number who are working for themselves is increasing every year. Working part-time in your business will give you time to learn how to run a business. You can take courses as needed or else work in a similar business to get the experience and know-how you will need in your own. Working at home part-time in addition to your regular job will also enable you to save money to invest in your new business. Plus, in some cases you can maintain your health benefits. With the present health care crisis, you need health insurance, especially if you and your spouse are self-employed. It only takes one severe medical crisis to bankrupt an uncovered person or a family! [Note: There are business associations such as the National Association for the Self-Employed (NASE) that offer health insurance for small business owners.]

Your business will dictate when it is time for you to go full-time, though you may decide that you still like it just part-time. Either way, it's your decision, and you will have to decide what's best for you.

**Will Your Business Be an "In-Home" Business
or an "Out-of-the-Home" Business?**
Some home-based businesses involve out-of-the-home work, such as landscaping, cleaning, and entertaining. Others involve more "in-home" work, such as writing, handicrafts, upholstery, and computer businesses. Many require that you both travel to see customers and then do related work in the home office, such as in a bookkeeping service.

Be aware of the percentage of time that your chosen business venture will necessitate in-home or out-of-the-home work. Knowing this will help you decide certain matters, such as the items in your wardrobe (whether they must reflect a professional image or can be functional work clothes), your child care needs, your home office hours, the staffing of your office when you are away, and other needs of your business.

How Will Your Family Be Affected or Involved?

As I mentioned earlier, discuss your business venture with your family. Let them know how much you need their support. Consider the following:

❖ *Expect an adjustment period.* Your family may have a hard time accepting that you really *are* working from home. They may interrupt you at any time, even when you have an important business call. Let them know that you are always there for them but that you have to do your work, too. It will take time to find the right balance between your family and business obligations.

❖ *Emphasize the positive.* Let your family know that you are flexible—you now have the freedom to arrange your business hours so that you can be a classroom mother or take summer picnics, and so forth.

❖ *Involve your family whenever you can.* Linda Pack, a freelance photographer, often takes her ten-year-old son on assignments whenever he is home from school. Linda says, "Justin acts as my assistant, carrying my tripod and camera bag and getting extra film for me. Sometimes, he even gets into the photos, like when I photographed a local herpetologist for a magazine article. I needed a shot of the man showing his snakes and lizards to someone, so I used my son. Justin got to hold a twenty-five-pound python and a large iguana and now he has pictures to prove it!"

If family members want to help out, give them responsibilities they are capable of handling, such as answering the phone, collating papers, or even creating designs or logos for brochures or pamphlets. JoAnn, who has a painting and wallpapering business, hires her high school age daughter to help her in the summer. She lets her younger children paste paper that is ready to be hung.

If you have infants or preschoolers, it may be difficult to run a home-based business without help. Some women pay babysitters to come into their homes to watch the children while they work. Others barter sitting time with friends who are home with their own small children. And some women work when their husbands come home.

It's not easy to have a home-based business and a family, and at times you may feel you are performing a crazy juggling act. JoAnn says, "My business has helped support me and my family and I feel good about what I do. My children are proud of me, and I know I can be there when my kids need me. Need I say more?"

Some other helpful tips for working at home with children are:

❖ Make sure to spend some exclusive time with your children each day—even if it is just to listen (with no interruptions) to the events of their lives.

❖ Hire a teenager or a mature adult to come over to participate in a craft or an activity with your children an hour or two a day or several times a week so that you will have a concentrated block of time to work.

❖ Trade time with other home-based working moms.

❖ Be flexible: remember, being an entrepreneur gives you the option of arranging your hours according to the demands of your family as well as of your business.

For More Information

Business Insurance

Insuring Your Business—What You Need to Know to Get the Best Insurance Coverage for Your Business, by Sean Mooney. 1992, Insurance Information Institute Press, New York. (212) 669-9250. $22.50 + $2.50 postage and handling (New York residents add 8.25% sales tax).

Protecting Your In-Home Business (brochure). Independent Insurance Agents of America (IIAA), 127 S. Peyton St., Alexandria, VA 22314. (703) 706-5407. < http://www.independentagent. com > Send an LSASE for information or check the consumer section of their Web site.

Home Business and Family

The Complete Idiot's Guide to Starting a Home-Based Business, by Barbara Weltman. 1997, Alpha Books, Indianapolis, IN.

How to Raise a Family and a Career Under One Roof, by Lisa Roberts. 1997, Brookhaven Press, Moontownship, PA.

Mompreneurs: A Practical Step-by-Step Guide to Work-at-Home Success, by Ellen H. Parlapiano and Patricia Cobe. 1996, Berkeley, New York.

The Stay-at-Home Mom's Guide to Making Money: How to Create the Business That's Right for You Using the Skills and Interests You Already Have, by Liz Folger. 1997, Prima Publishing, Rocklin, CA. < http://www.bizymoms.com >

Organization and Set-Up

135 Easy Ways to Increase Revenue and Reduce Expenses: A Guide for the Business Owner (booklet) by Bill Perry. 1998, Organizing Solutions, P.O. Box 1373, Dept. PS, Havertown, PA 19083. Send $5 (U.S. currency or International Money Order) and a self-addressed, double-stamped, #10 envelope to Organizing Solutions.

Home Office Design: Everything You Need to Know About Planning, Organizing, and Furnishing Your Work Space, by Neal Zimmerman. 1996, John Wiley & Sons, New York.

Organizing Your Home Office for Success, by Lisa Kanarek. 1993, Penguin Books, New York.

The Home Office, by Candace Ord Manroe. 1997, Reader's Digest, New York.

The Home Office & Small Business Success Book, by Janet Attard. 1998, Henry Holt, New York.

Recycled Office Furniture
Business Product Industry
(703) 549-9040

Provides names of the nearest recycled furniture dealers in your area.

ɘ 2 ɘ

Choosing the Best Business for You

Do You Have the Right Personality for a Home-Based Business?

Many financial experts note that successful small business entrepreneurs have certain characteristics in common. How do you compare to their findings?

☐ Are you an independent-type person, not afraid to go in one direction while others go in another?

☐ Do you believe in yourself? When others ask, "Why?" do you ask, "Why not?"

☐ Do you know how to set goals toward an objective and persist until you have achieved them, even if you make mistakes along the way?

☐ Are you well-organized? Can you juggle numerous projects simultaneously? (Most women and mothers do this all the time!)

☐ Do you have experience and/or knowledge in the business you are pursuing? If not, are you willing to take the time to learn the needed skills?

☐ Do you know where you can get professional help in running your business? (The resources listed in Part III can be a start.)

☐ Were you or one of your parents ever self-employed before? Many people have a fear of starting their own business. Those who have grown up with self-employed family members usually understand what it means to run a home-based business.

☐ Are you a good money manager? Are you willing to start small and expand as you go along, instead of overextending your business before you become established?

☐ Do you have good people skills? Even though you work by yourself, you may be in the business of satisfying other people's needs. Do you have the ability to understand, communicate, and deliver what each customer wants?

☐ Are you flexible and adaptable with your business goals? Many entrepreneurs start out in one direction with their business, only to go in another, unexpected direction later. Successful business owners are wise enough to recognize a promising trend and follow it.

☐ Do you have the energy, drive, and patience to make your business work? The SBA estimates that the average small business takes one to two years even to show a profit. Most likely you will have to make time for your business while trying to maintain your other activities (another job, family matters, etc.). You may end up working many hours over the "normal" 40-hour-a-week job!

How Do You Decide Which Business Is the One for You?

Think hard about what goals you want to achieve and what is important in your life. Then write them down. Visualize what you see yourself doing six months from now, a year from now, and five years from now.

If you don't have a definite idea of what type of business to start, assess your skills and interests to narrow your business choices. Filling out the following chart on pages 22–23 may help you determine which business is right for you. If you need to, copy the chart onto a wide piece of paper and fill in your responses.

1. **Jobs**—List all the jobs you've ever held. Include part-time jobs and jobs you held while you were in school.

Education/Training—If you needed a degree, certification, or special training for any of your jobs, list them here. Having credentials can help establish you as an expert or a professional to your customers. Print your credentials on your business cards and promotional materials if they apply.

Deborah Schadler's bachelor of science and master's degrees in education and her ten years' teaching experience were the basis for the successful tutoring center she began from her home.

Achievements—This is the time to brag about what you accomplished in each of your jobs! If you increased sales, started a new product line, organized a new program, or were responsible for any other important achievement, write it down. This process will help you analyze your strengths and give you more self-confidence as you list the results of all your work.

Skills Acquired—On-the-job training can be as valuable as completing courses in the same subject—in fact, even more so, if you are able to transfer those skills to your business. Why? Because you have had first-hand experience and have seen what works and what does not.

What You Liked Best About the Job. Why? You may have hated a job but not everything about it. If you add up all the things you liked about your jobs, you may get a better picture of what you like to do. It usually follows that if you like what you do, you will work harder at it—and thus the better chance you will have to succeed in your business.

2. **Volunteer positions**—Just because you were not paid does not mean you did not accomplish something. Volunteering your time shows dedication and direction of purpose. Write down any volunteer positions you've held and fill in the columns as you did with your paid jobs.

Women have traditionally been the volunteers in communities (which is one of the reasons they have been willing to work for less than men) and often have been responsible for starting organizations. School parent-teacher groups, family support groups, and church committees are commonly directed by women. Fundraising, organizing support, and leading the groups are just a few of the many tasks that an active volunteer contributes to an organization. Skills acquired and achievements made in your volunteer work are just as significant as those acquired in a paying job.

3. **Military service positions**—Relate any military experience, training, and education you've had to civilian occupations.

4. **Hobbies**—What starts out as a hobby for some people often turns into a full-time business. One woman made custom lampshades as a hobby, then turned it into a part-time job. When her husband was injured in a car accident, she was able to increase her business to full-time to cover their expenses until he recovered.

5. **Interests**—Write down your interests and examine them to see if you have the knowledge to adapt them to a service business. In selecting a business, feel free to think up new and different businesses or a new twist on a standard idea. One woman developed a sewing service for the physically disabled, after a disabled friend requested clothing that would be easy to take on and off.

Sometimes our interests can lead us into related hobbies or work. For example, Linda always liked to take pictures. As her interest grew, she read everything she could on photography and, of course, kept taking lots of pictures. She later went to work at a photo store and also took a night photography course. Now a mother of young children, she has a home studio specializing in children's portraits and takes freelance photos for businesses and writers. Linda says, "I love being able to earn money doing something I enjoy!"

Remember, don't be afraid to brainstorm for business ideas and to search for your particular niche. You just might find yourself in a business that is both special and successful!

	Education/Training	Achievements
Jobs		
Volunteer Positions		
Military Service Positions		
Hobbies		
Interests		

Skills Acquired	What I Liked Best About the Job. Why?

For More Information

Books

Finding Your Niche, by Lawrence J. Pino. 1994, Berkley Publishing Group, New York.

Finding Your Perfect Work: The New Career Guide to Making a Living, Creating a Life, by Paul and Sarah Edwards. 1996, J. P. Tarcher, Los Angeles, CA.

The Pathfinder: How to Choose or Change Your Career for a Lifetime of Satisfaction and Success, by Nicholas Lore. 1997, Fireside, New York.

Which Business? Help in Selecting Your New Venture, by Nancy Drescher. 1997, Oasis Press, Grants Pass, OR.

❧ 3 ❧

Your Business Plan

Taking Care of Legalities and Other
Pre-Opening Business Matters

Discuss starting your business with experts—your lawyer, accountant, bookkeeper, insurance agent, business consultant, and financial advisor, as well as local, state, and federal agency offices that oversee business practices. Because laws for home-based and small businesses vary from town to town, county to county, and state to state, you need to follow the proper steps to avoid possible future legal conflicts.

Networking with other home-based women entrepreneurs can also be a great help in obtaining start-up information. Some cities, counties, and states have organizations or offices specifically funded to help women get started in their own businesses. Do your research—there may be more resources out there than you thought!

Selecting a Business Name

Experts suggest using a word or words that describe what you do in your business name. For example, "Karen's Custom Cushions," lets the prospective customer know that Karen, the owner, will do just what her business name says: sew custom-made cushions for chairs, outdoor furniture, benches, and so forth. With Deborah Schadler's Teach Me Tutoring Service, you assume that students who need help with their studies will use her services.

At the same time, it is wise to have a name that is not too specific and can cover a number of related services. Often a person starts a business in one direction and then finds an opportunity to go into another. For example, with the Teach Me Tutoring Service, Schadler began tutoring high school students who were having difficulty in certain subjects. Today, she has expanded her services to include coaching students to qualify for scholarships; offering a reading-readiness summer camp; teaching English to new citizens; helping newly promoted company executives improve their grammar and writing skills; and helping brain-trauma patients relearn basic reading and writing in a local hospital's rehabilitation center. If Schadler had named her business "Schadler's Algebra Tutoring," technically she would only have offered remedial algebra instruction and would thus have closed off other business opportunities.

When you decide on a name, register it with both your county and state officials. This registration—also known as DBA, "doing business as"—protects you from someone else using your name for their business (assuming that the name you picked has not already been registered by someone else) and permits you to conduct business using that name. Contact your county clerk's office and your state business office for the procedure. You can then open a bank account, cash business checks, arrange for a separate business telephone line, and so forth, under your business name.

Legal Structure

Your business will fall under one of the following legal structures:

* ❖ A *sole proprietorship* is a business that is owned and operated by one person. It is the least costly way—in terms of registering and legal fees—to start a business.
* ❖ A *partnership* is a business formed by two or more people. Because many partnerships dissolve, it is best to have legal agreements drawn up by your attorney in order to prevent unforeseen business disputes.

❖ A *corporation* is a more complex business association, in which the business becomes a legal entity in itself, with powers and liabilities independent from the persons who own it. It is much more likely that your home-based business will take one of the other two forms.

Permits, Licenses, and Resale Tax Number

Depending upon where you live and the kind of business you will be conducting, you may have to get a permit, a license, a resale tax number, or all three in order to operate. Locally, check with your city, town, or borough regarding the zoning and other regulations related to a home business. With county regulations, contact the office of your county clerk.

The business identification numbers you must have in order to conduct business include the following:

❖ A *resale tax number*—if you sell any product to consumers, most states require you to collect sales tax. Your resale tax number is also your tax exemption number, which allows you to buy supplies wholesale without paying sales tax. Contact your state department of commerce to get a number and sales tax filing procedures.

❖ A *tax exemption number*—if you sell products wholesale only, you do not need to collect sales tax, but you do need a tax exemption number, which also allows you to buy wholesale supplies without paying sales tax. If you sell wholesale, you must record the resale tax number of the shop that buys from you for your tax records.

Establish a Business Bank Account

When you are ready to open for business, you should also open a business bank account. This will keep your start-up money and income earned separate from your personal account. If your business is not a corporation, you will need a Social Security number or a federal employee identification number (if you plan to hire employees) from your local Internal Revenue Service (IRS) office. If you are the sole proprietor of your business and do not employ others, your Social Security number can be used as your federal identification number.

Talk to other women business owners in your area and ask about the financial institutions they use and why they prefer them. Shop around and compare the services of a number of banks and see which one best fits the needs of your business.

Your Business Plan

Just as you need a map to help you find the route to an unknown destination, you need a plan to help you determine which direction(s) to go in order to get your business up and running. Your first plan should estimate your goals, expenses, and how much you will charge for your services, as well as show how you intend to attract and keep customers. After you actually begin your business, you will find that you must revise your plan yearly or even monthly as your business grows.

There is no right or wrong way to create a business plan, but you do need to write it down. Putting your plans on paper takes your dream of owning a business and begins to turn it into reality. There are no guarantees that your business will succeed, but a well-written and researched business plan plays an essential role in a business's success.

How do you write a business plan? Check your local library for books on business plan basics. Contact your local chamber of commerce or Small Business Development Center (SBDC) to help you draw up a plan. (See "Government Resources" in Part III.) You may also want to contact a professional business consultant to help you write a business plan. (See "Business Plan Consultant" in Part II).

The following are a few important questions to consider as you write your plan. This list is not all-inclusive. You may have additional questions to ask. Remember that the more questions you ask, the more complete your research will be. And the more complete your plan, the fewer surprises you'll have as you start out and the more successful you are likely to be!

1. **What is your business?**
First, write a broad definition, such as cleaning, entertainment, or child care. Then specify, for example, what type of cleaning you will be doing—homes? offices? both? Or what kind of child care—daytime? evening? drop-off? It is important to

keep both your broad and specific definitions in mind when your business starts. Your business may stay in the same broad category, such as cleaning, but may change directions as to the specific kind of cleaning you do, depending on what is most in demand in your area.

2. What are your objectives?

Be honest with yourself and list everything you hope to achieve, both businesswise and personally. Also, list both short-range and long-range objectives. Short-range objectives may include setting up your home office or applying for a loan to purchase basic equipment. Long-range objectives may include getting a certain number of customers in the first year or making a profit (for many small businesses, it may take two years before any profit is seen).

Review your objectives daily, weekly, monthly, and yearly to see if your business is headed in the right direction. You may need to add (or delete) some objectives as your business grows.

3. How do you research your market?

For your business to be successful, you have to know if (a) people have a need for your service; and (b) if they are willing to pay for it. Big businesses hire marketing research firms for thousands of dollars to find this out for them. You, however, can do your own smaller market survey. Here is a list of criteria that should be included:

❖ *Who will use my service?* Identify your potential customers so that you can target them for your business. Your local chamber of commerce can tell you the income level of your town's residents, the average number of people in a household, age levels, spending trends, and other economic details. Other service business owners in your area can also tell you about their customers.

Do not be discouraged if your preliminary research shows that the people in your area will probably not use your services. Check out nearby communities. Their residents, although they may be close in terms of distance, may have completely different profiles; for example, they may be college students or military personnel.

❖ *Do they need my service?* Ask people you know (and those you do not) if they would use your service and find out why or why not. If they use a similar service or have in the past, ask them what they would like to see improved.

❖ *What would they be willing to pay for my business services?* Survey similar businesses, both in your area and in other communities, to get an idea of what prices are charged. Then decide (based on your projected start-up costs and monthly expenses) how much you will need to charge in order to meet your financial objectives.

❖ *Is the market growing for my service business?* You need to know whether the sales potential for your business will be increasing. Contact your local chamber of commerce and nearest SBDC to find out how many service businesses are in your area. Also, find out how many other businesses like yours are in existence and if they are busy. Check with county offices dealing with small businesses, women's advisory councils, or the U.S. Department of Labor's *Occupational Outlook Handbook* to track down statistics on business growth in your area.

❖ *Examine competing businesses.* Interview customers from a competing business. Can you offer something unique and possibly better? Many businesses begin to lose customers when they grow, because they forget the adage "Satisfied customers are repeat customers." You may be able to attract customers by learning from your competitors' mistakes.

4. How will you get your customers?

Now that you have a pretty good idea who your customers are (be aware that your typical customer may change as you discover who really uses your business services), you will want to tell them (a) what services you provide; (b) what sets your business apart from the competition and how they will benefit from patronizing your business; and (c) how they can engage your business services.

Going back to your definition of your business will help when you want to list the services your business offers in your advertising and promotional materials or in answer to queries about your business. You may add to or subtract from these services, depending on what your customers want. Pam started her business by providing routine bookkeeping. She soon expanded her services to include billings, mailings, correspondence, and other business management matters as her customers asked her to do more. You may also want to make up a one-page, résumé-type business sheet or flyer to send out in response to inquiries about your business services.

Ask yourself, What can my business offer its customers that my competition cannot? Be specific. Can you offer a better price? better service? faster service? Will your business handle an aspect other businesses will not (odd hours, small jobs, etc.)? Emphasizing your business's unique features in your advertising will help draw customers to try your business services. Then, it is up to you to keep them!

Using the information from your preliminary research, you now have an idea of the customers you want to direct your business promotion toward. For example, if your research reveals that your best prospective customers are young married couples, you would choose different methods of promotion than if your customers are single professional businesswomen. You will want to decide on the most effective means of promoting your business, so that the target customers will be aware of you and how they can engage your services.

5. **Which promotional methods will you use?**

Promotion is essentially communication. The better you communicate to your prospective customers, the more business you will receive. Knowing which advertising will be the most effective may take a period of trial and error. Business promotion falls into two categories: *paid* and *free*.

Paid promotion or advertising comprises classified and display ads in newspapers, magazines, community booklets, and so forth; radio and television (network and cable) ads; promotional ads including signs, advertisements on vehicles, pencils, business cards, telephone directories, and so forth; direct mailings; and/or a business Web site.

Paid advertising, next to equipment, can be the biggest expense of your new business. Some business experts estimate that your advertising costs could be anywhere from 2 percent to 10 percent of your annual gross income, so you want every advertising dollar to count and to reach those who are likely to patronize your services.

Before you spend a single penny on advertising, list all of the local advertising sources and find out their rates. Ask whoever is in charge of advertising what types of people read or listen to (if it's radio) their advertising. Pay attention to the business ads that you come across, especially those offering business services. Notice how many are repeat ads from week to week. You might even call some of the businesses that advertise and ask them about the number of responses they get to their ads.

When you are ready to advertise, begin placing your ads where they will be read by prospective customers, based on your research. If you are not confident about writing a classified or display ad, ask the advertising representative for help. Most will offer free assistance in copywriting and layout.

Run your ad for as long as you can afford to and feel it will be effective. Keep track of the response to each ad, in terms of the number of responses and number of customers who actually hire your services. You can then gauge whether or not it is worth continuing to run that specific ad.

As your budget allows, try different types of media advertisements. Radio and television will reach several communities. With the growing popularity of cable television, it is worth trying their advertising. "Free" newspapers may also get good responses. Eventually, you'll know which method brings the best results for your business.

Free promotion or advertising includes public talks and appearances, press releases, feature articles in local newspapers, demonstrations, promotional events, or donations of your services to fundraising auctions, which will help people know your business exists.

Free publicity, especially for a service business, is one of the best ways to get business with a minimum amount of expense and a little effort and ingenuity. You can begin by sending out a press release to local newspapers announcing your business start-up. You can also use press releases later when your business is established to announce the sponsorship of a special event or the expansion of your business services.

Editors will be more likely to print your release—or follow up with a feature article—if you stick to the proper format (check sources in your library on how to write press releases). A press release must be neatly typed, doubled-spaced, concise, and written on your business stationery. You might also want to include a black and white photograph of yourself conducting business.

Do not forget to include the basics of news stories—who, what, why, when, where, and how. Make sure the answers to these questions appear in the first couple of paragraphs of your release. Do not forget to mention how people can reach you for more information about your services. Some other free methods of publicity include:

- ❖ *Word-of-mouth.* A good recommendation by a customer to a potential customer is one of the best ways to let people know your business is up and running. Begin by telling friends, relatives, and anyone you talk to that you have started your business. Always carry your business cards to hand out and give several to your friends and relatives to pass on. Network with other men and women in businesses (professional women's clubs, members of chambers of commerce, other home-based business owners, etc.). They may even give you tips to help your business grow—as long as your business does not compete with theirs. Then, *always* give the best possible service as you conduct your business. Word-of-mouth can keep your business going if you give that little extra to your customers. Remember, however, that word-of-mouth can also spread negative comments about your business, so never forget your customer, no matter how much your business grows!
- ❖ *Community bulletin boards.* You see these everywhere—in stores, banks, restaurants, and so forth. Ask permission to post your business cards or flyers (sometimes only non-profit organizations are permitted to post notices). Then

post your cards or flyers on the board, preferably at eye-level. Check back periodically to see if you need to replenish or rearrange your notices (sometimes accidentally or purposely, your materials may be covered up by other flyers). Make certain that your notices look professional and do not appear to be hastily scrawled and put together.

✤ *Offer a seminar or be a speaker.* Patricia Gallagher offers short courses for an adult education program on how to run a daycare center, based on her own former home-based business. She gets paid as an expert on this subject, plus she sells her book *So You Want to Open a Profitable Day Care Center.* She has also been a guest speaker for many community groups and has appeared on radio and television shows.

✤ *Have a "happening."* Hold a special occasion in connection with your business. You can announce it in a press release and either invite the newspapers to take photos or take your own. Elizabeth, who owns a garden consulting business, conducted a children's gardening workshop in the spring. The children learned planting basics, and Elizabeth had free publicity for her business.

✤ *Donate your services to a charitable event.* Auctions for non-profit organizations, raffles, and other fundraising events provide opportunities to publicize your business, not to mention being tax-deductible as well.

✤ *Advertise on the Internet.* Depending on your budget, you may want to consider having your own Web site. The potential to reach customers on the Internet is worldwide. In April 1998, the U. S. Commerce Department announced that the number of people connected to the Internet is doubling every 100 days—from 17 million last year to 62 million consumers in 1998.

You may want to join a local business association in your community; these businesses often advertise together on one site. Or you can have your own Web site designed, for a cost that can range from $1,500 to many thousands of dollars, depending on the number of pages, and the complexity of your site.

6. **What will you charge for your services?**

This depends on a number of factors: your expenses and your time; the quality of your service; your potential market; your competition's prices; how long you have been in business (you may charge more as you improve your business expertise and achieve a reputation for excellence); and what your customers are willing to pay.

A national and/or professional trade association connected with your business may offer current rate information and other sources that can provide help in establishing pricing and billing. Check with your library for business directories and the *Encyclopedia of Associations*.

With some service businesses, there may be price-charging guidelines, but if your business is unique or the only one in your community, you may have to set your own prices to make what you believe—and what your accountant or your bookkeeper tells you—to be a reasonable profit.

To find out if you are making a profit, you have to know your break-even point—when your projected income just covers your costs. At this point, you do not make or lose any money.

The SBA's pamphlet *Business Plan for Small Service Firms* gives this formula to find the break-even point:

$$\textit{Break-even point (in sales dollars)} = \cfrac{\textit{Total fixed costs}}{\cfrac{1-\textit{Total variable costs}}{\textit{Corresponding sales volume}}}$$

Once you know your break-even point, then you can begin to set a price for your services, knowing that you must at least charge a certain amount to reach this point. A service price for each job can be determined by using the following formula:

material/supply costs + labor (your time) + overhead
+ the percentage of profit you want to make = your price

Overhead costs include all costs other than materials used and your labor. If your business is your sole source of income, do not forget to include costs such as health insurance, Social

Security, taxes, loan payments, and so forth, in your overhead calculations.

Also, do not forget to charge for your labor. One of the biggest mistakes women business owners make is that they charge too little for their time. Women are the ones who traditionally have done volunteer work and thus may not be used to charging for their time. Some women who have not been in the business world do not put a value on their work the way their male counterparts do. Thankfully, these attitudes are changing as more women enter the work force, often being the sole supporters of themselves and their dependents. Pam says to her clients when they raise a question on her bookkeeping fees, "I tell them I have two children I am helping to support and this business is not just a hobby to me! That usually stops any complaints. My clients know I offer good service at competitive prices."

What percentage of profit do you include in your price? Some women use the service price equation mentioned earlier and double the total for their final price. Their price formula would be:

$$[material/supply\ costs\ +\ labor\ (per\ project\ or\ hour) \\ +\ overhead] \times 2\ +\ price$$

Once you've arrived at a price, compare your price to your competitors' prices and see whether potential customers would pay what you need to charge. It may take some time before you come up with the right price for both you and your customers. With a service business, prices often change based on a particular job or extenuating circumstances. Keep careful records of your time and expenses and, when in doubt, consult with your bookkeeper or accountant for help in determining what to charge.

The women profiled in this book each have their own methods of determining their prices, based on their experience with their businesses. For example, Donna Kramer, a wedding and party consultant, charges 10 percent to 15 percent of the gross cost of whatever part of the plans she handles, plus the cost of the supplies she uses.

Judi Wagner, who has a balloon decorating service, followed the price guidelines in a how-to video purchased through a balloon supply catalog. She also uses her own planning and estimation sheets to help determine the costs for each event.

For certain service businesses such as Kramer's and Wagner's, it is important to ask for a deposit when you are hired for a project. Wagner asks for a nonrefundable, $50 deposit, which will at least cover her costs in case her client backs out.

The pricing guidelines and formulas given in this book will not guarantee you a profit in your business. On average, a small business takes two years to show a profit. By carefully monitoring your records and seeking professional advice when you need it, your business can become self-supporting and profitable. The women who have successful businesses have done just that.

7. **How will you get repeat customers?**
"The best customers are satisfied customers." This adage applies to all businesses, especially small ones. You need your customers and cannot take any of them for granted, at any time. Following are some tips to keep your customers coming back:

+ *Be professional.* Treat your customers fairly, honestly, and with courtesy. Use business cards, stationery, forms, or brochures to help establish your business as official. Return phone calls and reply to letters and other inquiries promptly. Follow the ethics and etiquette of your business and avoid underhanded tactics.

+ *Be flexible.* Jackie Ruiz, who has a successful catering business, says, "Don't be afraid to go the extra mile for your customer [by] being competent in your business and complimentary in dealing with your customers."

  Going the extra mile might mean fulfilling a special request for a customer, or helping out in a way another business would not have time to do. As long as it does not interfere with the workings of your business or cause conflicts with your family or co-workers, you may find it advantageous to help out your customers in special ways. For example, Pam will sometimes see clients on

Saturday mornings or other unscheduled times, but she reciprocates by occasionally taking time off from her business to attend to family matters.

Small businesses can often be more flexible with clients' needs than can larger businesses, and every client likes to be treated with special attention. Clients will show their appreciation with repeat business and referrals to others.

❖ *Provide top quality service.* You may not be the biggest provider in your service area, but you can do your best for each client, and the word will spread to other prospective clients. Providing top quality service requires understanding what your client wants. You can better understand a client's expectations by asking the following questions:

> Have you ever used a similar service?
>
> If so, why are you considering changing?
>
> What do you expect (generally) from my service business?
>
> What do you need most from my service? (Please be specific.)
>
> Whom do I contact if I have questions or problems that might arise?
>
> What is your payment schedule?
>
> How long will you need my service? (year-round? seasonal?)
>
> Do you use the services of any other independent businesses? (You may want to contact others who have had business dealings with a new client to hear how they were treated by this company or individual.)
>
> What questions do you have about my service?

This list gives you an idea of what you might want to ask new clients. No doubt, you will develop your own list, based on your own experiences. Take careful notes of your clients' answers, and make a copy of them for future reference.

If you have questions when you begin working, do not assume you know what your client wants—ask more questions. It's better to clarify something in the beginning than to do work a client does not want or need.

❖ *Evaluate your business.* When you first start up your business, you will want as much feedback as possible from your customers. Ask them if they are satisfied with your service. Why or why not? Did they have any suggestions for improving your service? Are there any additional services they would like your business to provide? Would they use your business services again? Would they recommend your business services to another business or person?

You can ask these questions in person, over the phone, or in the form of a questionnaire. If your customer is extremely satisfied with your service, ask if they will write a letter stating the reasons they are satisfied. Then ask permission to use this testimonial to attract prospective customers.

When you have a number of testimonials, you can put them into a promotional notebook or packet, as Carol Manna has. Manna, owner/president of an organizational business, put together more than thirty articles and letters of satisfaction about her business into a portfolio that she gives to prospective customers. To each portfolio, Manna attaches plastic holders that contain her business cards and brochures. The result is a professional-looking and complete promotional package that both advertises and describes in detail Manna's business services.

Even if your business becomes successful to the point that your customers seek out your services, you should keep assessing your business services. By monitoring your customers' needs and satisfaction levels, you can keep your business up-to-date. If you lose touch with your customers, you may find them stolen away by competitors.

❖ *Know how to handle customer complaints.* No matter how many satisfied customers you have, someday you will probably have to handle a customer complaint. If you are the sole proprietor of your business (and actually do your business services), it is hard not to take complaints personally.

JoAnn Kaiser, who has her own wall decorating business, says, "When I had my first complaint, I was devastated! It really upset me that my customer was not satisfied. Fortunately, after I talked to my customer, I realized I had misunderstood what she really wanted. I changed what she wanted at no cost and my customer was happy again."

It's good business to adhere to the motto "The customer is always right" (even if they really aren't). If you are courteous, diplomatic, and really listen to the customer's complaint, you should be able to handle most of the problems that arise. Of course, some customers are easier to work for than others. If you get repetitive complaints from one person or business and you believe that you (or your employees) are doing the best possible job, you might suggest, politely, that you will help them find another service business similar to yours.

It is good, too, to have a service contract, especially for larger jobs. This protects both you and your customer should problems develop. If you are unsure how to word such an agreement, consult your lawyer.

8. How will you financially plan your business?

This is one of the most important parts of your business plan. A good financial plan includes information such as start-up costs, sources of financing, a balance sheet showing your assets and liabilities, a budget for each month of your first year of operation along with a profit and loss projection, break-even point determination, and a cash-flow prediction.

A business plan takes time to research and put together, but the better defined it is, the better you will be able to follow the right path toward success.

For More Information

1001 Ways to Market Yourself and Your Small Business, by Lisa Angowski Rogak Shaw. 1997, Perigee, New York.

One-Stop Marketing: What Every Smart Business Owner Needs to Know, by Johnathan Trivers. 1996, John Wiley & Sons, New York.

Books for Start-Up Businesses
Anatomy of a Business Plan, 3rd ed., by Linda Pinson and Jerry Jinnett. 1996, Upstart Publishing Company, Dover, NH.

How to Write a Successful Business Plan, by Jerre Lewis and Leslie Renn. 1997, Lewis & Renn Assocs., 10315 Harmony Dr., Interlochen, MI 49643. $14.95 + $3 postage and handling.

Growing Your Home-Based Business, by Kim T. Gordon. 1992, Prentice Hall, Upper Saddle River, NJ.

Surefire Strategies for Growing Your Home-Based Business, by David Schaefer. 1997, Dearborn Trade, Chicago, IL.

Your First Business: How to Really Start Your Own Business This Year, by Mainstay Company. 1997, 511 Avenue of the Americas, Suite 350, New York, NY 10011-8436. Send $19.95 (includes postage and handling) by check or money order.

Books for Financing Businesses
Launching Your Home-Based Business: How to Successfully Plan, Finance, and Grow Your New Venture, by David H. Bangs, Jr. 1997, Dearborn Trade, Chicago, IL.

Minding Her Own Business: The Self-Employed Woman's Guide to Taxes and Recordkeeping, by Jan Zobel. 1998, Easthill Press, Oakland, CA.

Small Business Financial Resource Guide (booklet). Write to: The National Federation of Independent Business (NFIB), 600 Maryland Ave., SW, #700, Washington, DC 20024. < http://www.nfibonline.com >

Books for Internet Sites
Cheapskate's Guide to Building a Web Site with Windows 95/NT, by Pete Palmer. 1998, Prentice Hall Professional, Upper Saddle River, NJ.

121 Internet Businesses You Can Start from Home: Plus a Beginner's Guide to Starting a Business Online, by Ron E. Gielgun. 1997, Actium, Brooklyn, NY.

Books on Legal Structure for Businesses

Choosing a Legal Structure for Your Business, by Stuart A. Handmaker. 1997, Prentice Hall Trade, Upper Saddle River, NJ.

Business Plan Guide

Entrepreneur's Business Guide, *Writing an Effective Business Plan.* (800) 421-2300. $69 + shipping and handling.

Business Plan Software

Palo Alto Software
144 East 14th Avenue
Eugene, OR 97401
(888) 752-6776   < http://www.palo-alto.com/ >

Jian
1975 El Camino Real
Mountain View, CA 94040
(800) 346-5426; < http://www.jian.com >

Microsoft Corporation
Redmond, WA 98052
(800) 426-9400; < http://www.microsoft.com >

American Institute for Financial Research
(800) 791-1000; < http://www.smartonline.com >

(Check for other software companies in trade and business publications.)

Marketing Sources

iMarket Inc.
460 Totten Pond Rd.
Waltham, MA 02154
< http://www.imarketinc.com >

Gives nationwide seminars on using desktop marketing to increase customers and sales.

Newsletters

The Art of Self-Promotion, Box 23, Hoboken, NJ 07030. $30 for 4 issues per year. A sample issue is available for $3.

Marketing Ink, Creative Ink Marketing Communications. 3024 S. Glencoe St., Denver, CO 80222. < http://www.marketing-ink. com >

Features low-cost, high-yield marketing strategies for small, home-based businesses. Check the archive or write for a listing of "the specific issues and topics you need to grow your business." 14 different issues available, $8 each.

Software

How to Choose the Right Accounting Software for Your Small Business, by Ellen DePasquale. $7.95. Order from

Small Office Success (S.O.S.)
Box 260226
Bellerose, NY 11426
< http://www.smallofficesuccess.com >

Marketing Plan Pro. A step-by-step guide to creating a marketing plan. Check in local computer software stores or call Palo Alto Software at (800) 229-7526.

MySoftware Company
1259 El Camino Real, Suite 167
Menlo Park, CA 94025-4227
< http://www.mysoftware.com >

Business cards, labels, mailing, business Web page.

Web-site Designer and Hosting Services
Information International
Box 579-PH
Great Falls, VA 22066
(703) 450-7049; < http://www.isquare.com >
Contact for rates.

ᘓ 4 ᘔ

Franchises and Distributorships

Franchises

Instead of starting a business independently, you may want to look into the options of franchises or distributorships.

What is a franchise? With a franchise, you pay someone else for the right to sell and distribute their products and use their trade name or trademark. A franchise fee is charged and, depending on the franchise, there may or may not be ongoing royalty fees, advertising costs, or the mandatory purchase of the company's supplies that are needed to run the franchise.

Franchises are now a popular way of being in business for oneself. According to the U.S. Department of Commerce, there are more than 3,000 franchises, with some 500,000 people who have invested in them. As of 1994, franchises accounted for 40 percent of all retail sales in this country and employed 7 million people.

The advantages to owning a franchise include the following:

✤ Risks and failures are fewer than in starting an independent business.
✤ Franchises can confer product-name recognition.

❖ Franchisors often provide a location and professional start-up advice.

❖ Franchisors will monitor franchises and help with any operating difficulties.

The disadvantages include the following:

❖ Franchises can be expensive to acquire.

❖ A franchise is not really your own business. What you actually have is a contract to operate the franchise, usually for ten years, which may or may not be renewed.

Although a franchise may be an attractive option for starting a home-based business, it is not something to rush into. For any of the business ideas given in this book, thoroughly research the business or franchise in which you may be planning to invest your time and money. This may take months or even years. Because a contract is mandatory in a franchise, it is wise to hire a lawyer who is familiar with franchise legalities to protect your investment.

Fortunately, the Women's Franchise Network (WFN), part of the International Franchise Association, is a good source of information for women interested in starting a franchise business (see later in this chapter for their address). The following information came from the summer 1994 *WFN News & Report*.

According to a 1992 report by Arthur Andersen & Company, 18.5 percent of all franchises were owned and operated by women. Substantially more women worked in franchise partnerships with their spouses or with male or female partners.

At the first regional WFN conference, Beth Pazienza, president of the Uniglobe Franchise Owners Association, suggested that women ask the following questions before buying a franchise:

Ask yourself:

❖ What are your personal strengths and how can you use them in each franchise?

❖ What hours do you want to work? Nine to five? Does working nights and weekends bother you?

* Do you like working directly with customers or would you rather work behind the scenes?
* How much capital do you have to invest? Or how can you obtain the capital you need?

Ask the franchisors:

* Based on my investment, what rate of return and break-even point can I expect?
* What costs should I expect to pay before I make a profit for myself: fees, rents, wages, and so forth?
* What is a typical day in the business really like?
* What regular support can I expect from the franchisor? Between regular visits, how accessible is the franchisor when I have a problem?
* What ongoing training for employees, managers, and owners does the franchisor provide?
* What is the length of the franchise contract and how easy is it to renew?
* What are the reasons for "disenfranchising," that is, reasons that I can leave the franchise and the reasons that the company can ask me to leave its systems?
* Does the home office compete with me for business?
* What is the company's regional and national five-year expansion plan and what role can I play in it?
* At what cost and under what criteria can I expand to additional locations or add more territories?
* What is the required advertising budget and how will it be used to benefit me directly?
* What is the franchisor's mission statement? And what does it say about its relations with franchises?

For More Information

Associations
Women's Franchise Network (WFN)
International Franchise Association (IFA)
1350 New York Avenue, NW Suite 900
Washington, DC 20005-4709
(202) 628-8000; (202) 628-0812 fax

Seeks to help women understand and take advantage of the diverse opportunities that franchising offers to women. Publishes *Franchise World*; send an LSASE for information. Their Internet site < http://www.franchise.org > has IFA's *Franchise Opportunities Guide Online®* as well as a listing of companies, code of principals and conduct, bookstores, and so forth.

American Association of Franchisees and Dealers
P.O. Box 81887
San Diego, CA 92138-1887
< http://www.aafd.org >

"A nonprofit trade association representing the rights and interests of franchisees and independent dealers throughout the United States." Also has publications on buying, financing, and other information concerning franchises. Send an LSASE for more information.

Books

A Woman's Guide to Her Own Franchise Business, by Anne Small. 1986, Pilot Books, 127 Sterling Ave., P.O. Box 2102, Greenport, NY 11944-2102. < http://www.pilotbooks.com > Pilot Books has been a leading U.S. publisher of franchising information since 1959. Their publications have been recommended by the U.S. Department of Commerce and the SBA. Send an SASE for a listing of additional franchise publications offered or call (800) 79-pilot for a catalog.

Franchise Fraud, by Robert L. Purvin, Jr. 1994, John Wiley & Sons, Inc., New York.

Franchise Bible: How to Buy a Franchise or Franchise Your Own Business, 3rd ed., by Erin J. Keup. 1995, Psi Research, Oasis Press, Grants Pass, OR.

Franchising 101: The Complete Guide to Evaluating, Buying, and Growing Your Franchised Business, by Ann Dugan (Ed.). 1998, Upstart Publishing Co., Dover, NH.

How to Open a Franchise Business (The 21st Century Entrepreneur), by Michael Powers. 1995, Avon Books, New York.

The 50 Best Low-Investment, High-Profit Franchises, 2nd ed., by Robert Perry. 1994, Prentice Hall, Englewood Cliffs, NJ.

The Complete Franchise Book, 2nd ed., by Dennis L. Foster. 1994, Prima Publishing, Rocklin, CA.

Government Sources

The Franchise Opportunities Handbook: A Complete Guide for People Who Want to Start Their Own Franchise, by Lavern Ludden (Ed.) and the U.S. Dept. of Commerce. 1995, Jist Works, Indianapolis, Indiana. Contains information on more than 1,500 franchisors.

The Federal Trade Commission (FTC)
Public Reference Branch
Washington, DC 20580
(202) 326-2222; < http://www.ftc.gov >

The FTC provides a free information package about the FTC Franchise and Business Opportunity Rules.

Magazines

Business Start-Ups, P.O. Box 0347, Boulder, CO 80323-0347. < http://www.entrepreneurmag.com >

One year /12 issues costs $14.97.

The Franchise Handbook, 1020 N. Broadway, Suite 111, Milwaukee, WI 53202. < http://www.franchise1.com > and < http://www.busop1.com >

One year/4 issues costs $22.95.

Successful Franchising Magazine, 16885 Dallas Parkway, Dallas, TX 75248. (972) 991-3333; (972) 960-9555; fax: (888) 545-9699. < http://www.successfulfranchising.com >

A monthly publication designed to help readers find exciting and profitable franchising opportunities and educate them to make wise franchise investment decisions.

Distributorships

In a distributorship, you distribute or sell another manufacturer's products. As a distributor, you are a wholesaler who has exclusive rights to market the goods of a manufacturer or company within a given territory.

A distributorship may also be a franchise held by a distributor. A distributorship is different from a franchise in that all you are doing is purchasing the rights to run the company; however, you can run it any way you wish. For example, each Hallmark store is run by the person who bought the rights. You buy the company name, but *you* pick and choose the products you wish to sell at that particular location.

For More Information
Opportunities for distributorships and franchises (as well as licensing) can be found in advertisements and articles in larger business newspapers such as the *Wall Street Journal* or in business magazines such as *Entrepreneur Magazine*'s annual business opportunity issue, *Business Start-Ups, Income Opportunities, Small Business Opportunities,* and others.

Other ways to sell another companies' products are through licensing and just general business opportunities (packages, wholesale buying, etc.).

Whichever way you sell another's products or services, be cautious and investigate the business thoroughly before you invest even one dollar.

Additional Resources About Business Opportunities, Direct Selling, and Multi-Level Marketing
American Business Opportunity Institute
c/o Andrew A. Caffey
3 Bethesda Metro Ctr., #700
Bethesda, MD 20814

A national information clearing house and seminar company specializing in business opportunity and franchise investment and regulation. Send an LSASE for more information on publications and programs.

Direct Selling Association (DSA)
1666 K St., NW, Suite 1010
Washington, DC 20006

Multi-Level Marketing International Association (MLMIA)
1101 Dove St., #170
Newport Beach, CA 92660

Membership comprises companies as well as distributors that are involved in the MLM aspect of direct selling.

Home Businesses You Can Buy: The Definitive Guide to Exploring Franchises, Multi-Level Marketing, and Business Opportunities. Plus: *How to Avoid Scams,* by Paul and Sarah Edwards and Walter Zooi. 1997, Putnam Publishing Group, New York.

Magazine—Network Marketing

Cutting Edge Opportunities Magazine, Cutting Edge Media, Inc., 29 S. Market St., Elizabethtown, PA 17022-2325.

Part II

101
BEST
BUSINESSES

Special Event Services

BALLOON DECORATING

This service business provides balloons to decorate clients' homes or offices for special occasions such as birthdays, theme parties, and company parties; or celebrations for newborns, anniversaries, graduations, retirements, and so forth. Other services may include creating special table centerpieces, balloon deliveries in clown or character outfits, and balloon "drops," in which balloons filled with ordinary air are suspended in large nets from the ceiling and are released in a colorful cascade.

As the business owner, you meet with clients in your home or theirs and fill out a planning sheet to agree on the kind and placement of balloons (sketches by clients are helpful). Then, you give a cost estimate with the aid of an order form you've had printed up and take a nonrefundable deposit that will at least cover your initial costs if the customer should cancel. Your telephone number (or a contact person's) should be listed on the customer's copy of the order form in case there are any questions.

Start-Up Costs and Financing Sources
❖ Approximately $500 to $1000 for basic supplies, rental fees, and brochures and flyers.
❖ Personal funds, loans from family or friends, credit cards.

Pricing Guidelines

❖ Fixed rates for certain events are recommended by the industry. For example, balloon wedding packages should cost $350 to $870.

Marketing and Advertising Methods and Tips

❖ Place advertisements on community bulletin boards, attach business cards to balloon arrangements, pass out flyers with your business description, sign up with local newspapers' business directories, post a signboard outside events, and encourage word-of-mouth referrals.

❖ Direct mailings to newly engaged couples, school districts that hold formal dances, and various organizations are effective in getting business.

❖ Put together a portfolio or photo album of your work to show to potential customers.

Essential Equipment

Balloons, mylars (foil-like balloons), curling iron to seal the mylars, netting, assorted marbles (to anchor balloons), helium tanks, air and gas fillers, miscellaneous supplies (scissors, string, ribbon, tape, balloon sticks, etc.).

Optional: forms for arches and trellises.

Recommended Training, Experience, or Needed Skills

❖ Have a flair for decorating.

❖ Study how-to videos.

❖ Attend balloon artists' conventions.

Income Potential

$250 to $400 per special event.

Type of Business

Out-of-the-home.

Best Customers
Engaged couples, families of retirees, companies and organizations that hold regular banquets, new parents, schools.

Helpful Tips
❖ Try different methods of advertising so that potential customers can hear about your service.
❖ The National Balloon Centers suggests the following: develop a game plan, keep good records, attend classes, study manuals and videos, and practice.

Franchises, Distributorships, and Licenses

Licensing Opportunities
National Balloon Centers
14108 E. Firestone Blvd.
Santa Fe Springs, CA 90670
(800) 927-9778
Contact: Matt McKinney

Offers balloons, toys, balloon wrapping, and other supplies for sale—many at wholesale prices. Also sells gifts-in-a-balloon machine.

Minimum capital needed is $599 for the basic trial package, which includes equipment, training materials, and start-up supplies. Eighty-five percent of those who buy this package are women. Wedding package materials cost $50 to $100. By charging $250 to $750 for the finished product, a business owner can make $50 to $100 per hour profit.

Balloon Wrap Inc.
18032 Lemon Dr., #C-144
Yorba Linda, CA 92886
(714) 993-2295
Contact: Less Wigger

Offers free consulting services and lifetime licenses. Dealerships range in price from $495 to $1,595. Video training, supplies, and inventory are all available from BWI. Everything is unbundled, but suggested orders can be used. "HOT product, lots of variety and creativity."

For More Information

Magazines

Balloons and Parties Magazine, Partilife Publications LLC, 40 Burlews Ct., Hackensack, NJ 07601

Balloon Journal, Amy Stewart's Balloon Journal, P.O. Box 6250, Beverly Hills, CA 90212. "For those who want to make a living balloon decorating." Send an LSASE for information.

Supplies

The Anderson Balloon Company, P.O. Box 723, Lakewood, OH 44107. < http://www.a-balloon.com >

Balloons Everywhere, 4658 Airport Blvd., Mobile, AL 36608.

Additional Business Ideas

❖ Balloon delivery service—Deliver bouquets of balloons. Order National Business Library's, *Balloon Delivery Service.* (800) 947-7724. $39.95 + shipping and handling.

❖ Balloon entertainment. Order *Balloon Magic—The Magazine,* Pioneer Balloon Co., P.O. Box 20061, Wichita, KS 67220. < http://www.balloonmagic.com >

ᑫᒪ 2 ᒪᑐ

GIFT BASKETS

According to a 1993 survey conducted by *Gift Basket Review,* the gift basket business had total annual sales worth about $700 million in 1992, up from $600 million in 1991. This includes earnings from commercial businesses such as florists, specialty shops, and small, home-based operations.

Giving gift baskets is a unique idea that has grown in popularity over the past few years. They can be filled with an assortment of specialty foods and gifts and can be tailored for almost any occasion, such as births, birthdays, house warmings, or ice cream sundae–making. You need an ample work and storage area, plus a method of delivery. In addition, an 800 telephone number and the ability to take credit card orders help increase business.

Start-Up Costs and Financing Sources
❖ From $3,000 to $5,000 for small operations to $12,000 and up, depending on the type of baskets offered, the availability of products (wholesale), type of customer, and so forth.
❖ Personal savings, small business loan.

Pricing Guidelines
Follow the industry guidelines (baskets usually range from $25 to $85 +).

Marketing and Advertising Methods and Tips
❖ Print up business cards and brochures (illustrated or with photos) describing baskets offered.
❖ Take out display ads in the local newspapers before major holidays.
❖ Donate some of your gift baskets to fundraising auctions.
❖ Conduct demonstrations for community groups on putting together gift baskets.
❖ Rent a table at local craft shows and let people make up their own baskets (say, for Mother's or Father's Day).
❖ Rent a booth at gift buyers' trade shows.
❖ Drop off complimentary jars filled with candies to local businesses and organizations along with your business cards and brochures.

Essential Equipment
Baskets (purchase them wholesale or at yard sales or from basketmakers), ribbons, straw filler, shrink-wrap machine (or shrink-wrap and hair dryer), basket items, table space for assembly, storage shelves for supplies and inventory, car or van for delivery.

Recommended Training, Experience, or Needed Skills
❖ Work at a gift basket shop.
❖ Subscribe to trade magazines and buy how-to videos.

+ Follow start-up guides, manuals.
+ Attend trade shows.
+ Have a talent for creating arrangements.

Income Potential
Depending on the volume of baskets you sell and your profit margin, annual income can range from $25,000 (average earnings of smaller businesses) to $50,000. A few gift basket business owners earn $100,000 to $200,000 per year!

Type of Business
Primarily an in-home business except for deliveries.

Best Customers
Companies that send gifts to valued customers and other company executives. This is a growing market, especially during the holiday season.

Helpful Tips
+ Offer free delivery within a certain mile radius, and then charge so many cents per mile beyond that.
+ Concentrate on your marketing and what makes your baskets special as compared to the competition's.

Franchises, Distributorships, and Licenses
Write to franchises listed in *The Franchise Handbook* magazine (see page 48).

For More Information
Association
    Gift Basket Professionals Network
    446 S. Anaheim Hills Rd., #167
    Anaheim Hills, CA 92807
    (714) 637-1455; (714) 282-8659 fax
    E-mail: < florabfine@aol.com >
    Contact: Flora M. Brown

    For information, send an LSASE with 55 cents postage.

Books

The Art of Creating Great Gift Baskets, by Sherry Frey. It's Write Here! Publications, 441 Hickory Ln., Chambersburg, PA 17201. Send an LSASE for listings.

The Directory of Wholesale Suppliers and Products, by Sherry Frey. See prior entry for ordering information.

How to Start a Home-Based Gift Basket Business, by Shirley George Frazier. 1998, Globe Pequot Press, Old Saybrook, CT.

Start-Up Guide

National Business Library's Start-Up Guide, *Gift Baskets.* (800) 947-7724. $39.95 + shipping and handling.

Publication

Gift Basket Review
Festivities Publication, Inc.
815 Haines St.
Jacksonville, FL 32206; < http://www.festivities-pub.com >

Monthly trade magazine covering issues of interest for owners of gift basket businesses. Also offers helpful trade books, videos, and trade show information.

Supplies

North American Floral and Packaging Supply, P.O. Box 342, Greenfield, NH 03047. (888) 249-9996. < http://www. nafps.com > Wholesale supplier for the gift basket enthusiast.

Additional Business Ideas

College student gift baskets—All students love to eat, especially while studying for mid-terms and finals. Put out cards and brochures on campus during homecoming and parents' weekends.

⳩ 3 ⳪
GIFT REMINDER SERVICE

In this business you get paid for reminding clients of important dates for special days—birthdays, anniversaries, graduations, and so forth, and shopping for appropriate gifts. If you are knowledgeable about fashion and trends, you could shop for the best buys for men and women executives who have little time to comparison shop.

Start-Up Costs and Financing Sources
* $3,000 minimum.
* Small business loans, personal savings, credit card purchases, friends or family loans.

Pricing Guidelines
You could charge a monthly fee averaging about $75 per client, depending on the amount of calls and services you would provide. If shopping, you would base your prices on mileage to and from stores and a percentage of the cost of the items you purchase.

A reminder service can charge $30 to $60 an hour, or a one-time setup fee with a monthly maintenance charge.

Marketing and Advertising Methods and Tips
* Encourage referrals by friends and satisfied customers.
* Send direct mail to company executives.
* Give "shopping tips" lectures to professional groups.
* Run display ads in business trade papers and local newspapers' annual business supplements.
* Leave brochures, business cards, or pamphlets at clothing and gift shops.

Essential Equipment
Answering machine, fax, separate telephone line, filing system (manual or computer system to keep dates and clients organized), typewriter or word processor or computer, record-keeping sheets or billing software, reliable vehicle.

Recommended Training, Experience, or Needed Skills
* Start small with one or two clients, or volunteer to do it for family or friends for a period of time to see if you can manage this business.

❖ Have a retail background in clothing or gift merchandise, as well as knowledge about fashion.

❖ Follow start-up guide recommendations.

Income Potential
Annual earnings range from $15,000 to $70,000, depending on the number and type of clients.

Type of Business
About one-third in-home for scheduling, planning, and calls, and two-thirds out-of-the-home for shopping.

Best Customers
For shopping—working couples, business executives. For reminder service—professional practices that schedule regular appointments (doctors, dentists, etc.); salespersons who send out regular thank-yous; auto service shops.

Helpful Tips
Other reminder services: medical appointments, wake-up calls at prearranged times.

For More Information

Software
Check your local computer store for scheduling and management software.

Start-Up Guide
Entrepreneur's Start-Up Guide, *Personal Shopping Service.* (800) 431-2300. $69 + shipping and handling.

ᦕ 4 ᦔ
PARTY AND EVENT PLANNER

A party and event planner hires caterers, florists, decorators; rents party supplies; reserves halls or banquet rooms; books entertainment; and helps with just about anything the client needs for a special occasion. Party planners might organize an entire event or just a part of it. Donna Duna of "Decorations to Dessert" says, "I tell my customers, 'Tell me what you want,' and then I start from there."

Start-Up Costs and Financing Sources
+ From $1,000 to $5,000.
+ Personal savings, small business loans, loans from family.

Pricing Guidelines
Hourly rates from $60 to $80; 15 percent to 20 percent of the cost of the arrangements the planner handles.

Marketing and Advertising Methods and Tips
+ Encourage word-of-mouth referrals.
+ Print up business cards, brochures, and flyers to post on community bulletin boards.
+ Take out an ad in the local newspaper's classified section.

Essential Equipment
Filing system (manual or computer), answering machine or service, fax machine, separate telephone line, printed promotional material.

Recommended Training, Experience, or Needed Skills
+ Volunteer (or charge a small fee to cover expenses) to help set up friends' or relatives parties.
+ Work in a catering business.
+ Have excellent organizational skills, work well under stress, and be able to handle people tactfully but assertively (especially with your suppliers).
+ Communicate well with your clients and understand their wants and needs.

Income Potential
Can charge an hourly rate, flat fee, or a percentage of an event's total budget—$100 to $1,500 per event ($75,000 annual net

profit). Experienced, full-time planners can earn annual incomes in the six figures.

Type of Business
Two-thirds in-home, coordinating and planning; one-third out-of-the-home, making sure everything runs as planned on the day before and day of the special event.

Best Customers
Parents of birthday-age (elementary) children; adult children of parents celebrating "milestone" wedding anniversaries; baby-boomers celebrating their fiftieth birthdays.

Helpful Tips
✤ According to Duna, "Only deal with and recommend the people (caterers, disc jockeys, etc.) who care about what they do, just as you do. Least expensive is not always the best! Follow up with calls to get your customers' reactions."
✤ Act as if this event were your affair!
✤ Pay attention to the smallest details and ask many questions—do not assume anything!
✤ Specialize and focus on the clients you serve best, focusing primarily on corporate or private social events.

For More Information

Association
International Special Events Society (ISES)
9202 N. Meridian St., Suite 200
Indianapolis, IN 46260
fax-on-demand: (888) 755-ISES (4737)
< http://www.ises.com >

ISES is the only nonprofit, professional, international organization dedicated to serving all the disciplines of the special events industry.

Book

Big Meetings Big Results: Strategic Event Planning for Productivity and Profit, by Tom McMahon. 1996, NTC Publishing Group, Lincolnwood, IL.

Publication

Special Events magazine, P.O. Box 16868, North Hollywood, CA 91615-6868. One year/12 issues costs $36.

Reports

How to Get Started in Party Planning and *Stress-Free Planning of Special Events.* Send $25 + $5 shipping and handling to Patty Sachs, 5827 Nicollet Ave., S., Minneapolis, MN 55419. < http://www.geocities.com/ ~ partyexpert >

Supplies

MeadowLark Party Shoppe, 2 Beistle Plaza, P.O. Box 10, Shippensburg, PA 17257. Send an LSASE for information.

Start-Up Guides

National Business Library's Start-Up Guide, *Party & Event Planning.* (800) 947-7724. $39.95 + shipping and handling.

Additional Business Ideas

❖ Plan company picnics.
❖ Meeting planner.

⤳ 5 ⤳

PARTY RENTALS

In this business you supply party items that people do not normally own, such as outdoor tents, extra folding chairs, large coffee makers, silverware, china, and so forth, and even sports equipment for volleyball or croquet, for example. Large party rental businesses have huge warehouses stocked with inventory. Your storage area may not be so large, but you could start small and use space in your garage or even rent a storage unit.

Consider specializing in certain types of parties or picnics to keep your business manageable.

Start-Up Costs and Financing Sources
* $1,000 to $5,000 minimum.
* Personal savings, small business loans, credit cards.

Pricing Guidelines
Follow the trade industry guidelines; call or visit party rental stores or showrooms and price their items.

Marketing and Advertising Methods and Tips
* Send out flyers to caterers.
* Place classified and display ads in local newspapers, especially before holidays, graduation times, and during the summer.
* Place an ad in the phone book's business pages under "Parties" and "Rentals."
* Purchase local radio and cable television ad time.

Essential Equipment
Phone, fax machine, inventory sheets, party equipment and supplies, a storage area, and a reliable truck or van.

Recommended Training, Experience, or Needed Skills
* Work in a party rental store or business.
* Volunteer to set up charities', friends', and relatives' parties.

Income Potential
$15,000 to $35,000 per year.

Type of Business
About three-fourths of your time is spent in-home, planning, organizing, and meeting with clients; about one-fourth of your time is spent delivering and picking up the rented items.

Best Customers
Caterers, event planners.

Helpful Tips

Decide if you want to rent party supplies for specific events (children's parties, company or family picnics, outdoor wedding receptions, etc.) or for formal or informal occasions. (You could sell paper products, too, if you specialize in informal events.) Then, target your customers accordingly.

For More Information

Association

American Rental Association
1900 19th St.
Moline, IL 61265
< http://www.arental.org >
Send an LSASE for information.

Publication

Special Events magazine, P.O. Box 16868 North Hollywood, CA 91615-6868. One year/12 issues costs $36.

Additional Business Ideas

Specialize in renting moving trucks, tools, formal wear, costumes, home improvement (wallpaper removal tools, paint sprayers, garden equipment).

⌒6⌒

REUNION PLANNING

Reunion planners arrange get-togethers for high schools, colleges, or other institutions, as well as for families and members of former military units. Reunions may be held annually or every five to ten years. One school alone could have as many as eight to ten reunions each year.

Because many people no longer have the time to plan these events themselves, professional reunion planning businesses have sprung up. The owner of a reunion planning business plans all the events leading up to the reunion day, including locating class members, mailing the invitations, hiring the entertainment, finding a location, and taking reservations.

Start-Up Costs and Financing Sources
* $5,000 to $15,000.
* Personal savings, small business loans.

Pricing Guidelines
The industry recommends charging a per-person fee based on the number that attend the reunion.

Marketing and Advertising Methods and Tips
* Send out direct mailings to schools and institutions.
* Ask your suppliers (caterers, photographers, banquet hall owners, florists, etc.) to recommend your service.

Essential Equipment
Computer with a modem as well as database and desktop publishing software, answering machine or service, fax machine, filing system.

Recommended Training, Experience, or Needed Skills
* Volunteer to help plan your own or your spouse's class reunion.
* Have excellent organizational skills.
* Use research skills to locate missing class members.
* Pay close attention to details and learn what was current for each group's graduation year or time period.

Income Potential
$2,000 average profit per event.

Type of Business
In-home, except when consulting with class members.

Best Customers
High school and college class members, large families, military units.

Helpful Tips

❖ Find as many classmates as possible to ensure good attendance.
❖ Send out attractive, attention-getting mailings. Make sure names and addresses on mailings are spelled correctly.
❖ Schedule appropriate entertainment.
❖ Make sure the space you rent is large enough to handle the number of attendees.
❖ Plan activities that will include everyone in the reunion.

For More Information

Books

The Reunion Planner: The Step-by-Step Guide Designed to Make Your Reunion a Social and Financial Success, by Linda Hoffman and Neal Barnett. 1992, Goodman Lauren Publishing, Los Angeles, CA.

Ten Steps to Planning a Magical Reunion, by Venice High School Alumni Association with Kimberly Stanséll. This 35 page booklet includes detailed instructions, surveys, and questionnaires, plus information on locating missing classmates. To order, send a check or money order for $10 payable to: Tom Anderson, 4180 Kenyon Ave., Los Angeles, CA 90066.

Additional Business Ideas

Set up a home-based research business to help locate missing persons for families, friends, or reunion planners.

✑ 7 ✑

VIDEOTAPING SERVICE

A videotaping service usually concentrates on weddings, parties, recitals, and other special events, but may also involve videotaping a person's or business's items for insurance purposes. In states permitting videotaping of some legal proceedings, lawyers may use your services as needed.

Start-Up Costs and Financing Sources

❖ Costs may range from $2,000 to $25,000, depending on whether you use rented equipment or purchase your own.

❖ Personal savings, small business loans, credit cards, loans from friends and family.

Pricing Guidelines

Follow industry standards; call other video services to get an idea of their fees.

Marketing and Advertising Tips and Methods

❖ Print up business cards and flyers; post them on community bulletin boards.

❖ Display magnetic signs on your vehicle.

❖ Purchase classified and display ads in your local newspapers.

❖ Ask party and wedding planners and suppliers to refer you to their customers.

❖ Send direct mailings to dance studios, schools and preschools, theater groups, local clubs, and organizations; lawyers and other professionals; home insurance companies; real estate companies.

❖ Purchase ads on your local cable television channel.

❖ Rent a booth at trade shows (home, bridal, sports, etc.).

❖ Take out an ad in the business telephone directory under "Video Production Services."

Essential Equipment

Video camera, player, color monitor, separate telephone line with fax machine, car or van to transport equipment.

Recommended Training, Experience, or Needed Skills

❖ Work in media department of schools or video businesses.

❖ Take courses at local schools and colleges for technical knowledge and advanced video skills.

❖ Volunteer to videotape family, club, or sports events.

❖ Have a working knowledge of videotaping techniques.

❖ Have good "people" skills and an artistic eye.

Income Potential
$10,000 to $40,000 and up, depending on your expertise and number of clients. Based on the number of tapings you do a week, Video Data Service (see under "Franchises") reports gross revenue earnings of $20,000 to $83,000 + per year.

Type of Business
Your time should be about equally divided between out-of-the-house taping and in-house paperwork and marketing.

Helpful Tips
+ Know the lighting conditions and environment in which you will be filming.
+ Ask the customer what they want highlighted during the event before you film.

Franchises, Distributorships, and Licenses

Franchise
Video Data Services
3136 Winton Rd. S., Suite 304
Rochester, NY 14623
(800) 836-9461

Their fee of $22,500 includes equipment (now lighter in weight) and provides training, monthly newsletters, and other services.

For More Information

Books
Basics of Video Production, by Des Lyver and Graham Swainson. 1995, Focal Press, Stoneham, MA.
Comprehensive Guide to Making Video, Videomaker. P.O. Box 4591, Chico, CA 95927. (800) 284-3226. $24.95 per year.
Making Money in Film and Video, by Raul Dasilva. 1992, Focal Press.

The Videomaker Handbook, by *Videomaker Magazine* Editors, 1996, Focal Press.

Internet Site
< http://videouniversity.com >
"Video University"—information for being a professional videographer.

Start-Up Guides
Entrepreneur's Start-Up Guide, *Video Production Service.* (800) 421-2300. $69 + shipping and handling.
National Business Library's Start-Up Guide, *Making Money with Your Camcorder.* (800) 947-7724. $39.95 + shipping and handling.
Videomaker magazine offers information for production businesses. $14.95 per year. Write to Videomaker, P.O. Box 4591, Chico, CA 95927.

⟡ **8** ⟡

WEDDING PLANNER AND CONSULTANT

The Association of Bridal Consultants estimates that brides and grooms spend $33 billion per year on their weddings. Bridal couples want their day to be special, but at the best price. A wedding consultant helps the couple establish a budget and finds the best suppliers to fit that budget.

Donna Duna also helps to plan weddings in her party and event planning business. She says, "If you are well organized and can remain calm while others are going crazy with the preparations and still love weddings, then this is the business for you."

Start-Up Costs and Financing Sources
✤ $5,000 to $11,000 average.
✤ Personal savings, small business loans, credit cards.

Pricing Guidelines
Industry standards suggest a flat fee or rate, 15 percent of anything booked.

Marketing and Advertising Methods and Tips
* Encourage referrals from clients and suppliers.
* Run classified ads in the local newspapers.
* Put together a portfolio of the weddings you have planned to show prospective clients.
* Print up business cards and brochures.
* Rent booths at bridal shows.
* Send direct mailings to engaged couples.

Essential Equipment
Answering machine or service, business telephone line, cellular phone, fax machine, filing system (computer), marketing materials (business cards, brochures, portfolio).

Recommended Training, Experience, or Needed Skills
* Volunteer to help plan friends' or relatives' weddings.
* Attend bridal trade shows.
* Join a professional association.
* Read trade and consumer magazines and newsletters to note the current trends.
* Attend seminars and workshops (see "For More Information.")
* Have excellent organizational skills and assertiveness to get your suppliers to deliver on time and to obtain high quality service.
* Have an ability to be tactful, even under trying circumstances! Be a good listener.

Income Potential
Rates vary in the different regions of the country. Consultants commonly charge 15 percent of the total wedding expenses. $25,000 to $150,000 a year; can average $1,500 to $2,000 a wedding.

Type of Business
Approximately two-thirds in-home, organizing the wedding; about one-third out-of-the-home, consulting with the bridal

couple and family, visiting the suppliers and places where the wedding and reception will be held.

Helpful Tips

❖ Having reliable and caring suppliers will make you a success.

❖ Project confidence so that your customers will trust you to handle their plans.

❖ Following each wedding, rate your performance. Have each person who worked at the wedding (including yourself) fill out an evaluation. It is also a nice touch to send flowers to the bride's mother (or whomever paid your consultant's fee) along with question sheets to get feedback about your services. Send the bride and groom a small, complimentary gift along with question sheets.

For More Information

Associations

Association of Bridal Consultants
200 Chestnutland Rd.
New Milford, CT 06776-2521
(860) 355-0464
E-mail: < bridalassn@aol.com >

An international trade organization with more than 1,300 members in 46 states and 12 foreign countries. Offers a professional development program, seminars, comprehensive home-study courses (*Weddings As a Business*—$80), a hotline, and a newsletter.

Association of Certified Professional Wedding Consultants (ACPWC)
Ann Nola, Director
7791 Prestwick Circle
San Jose, CA 95135
(408) 928-9000; fax (408) 928-9333
< http://www.acpwc.com >

Licensed by the State of California. Personalized and correspondence home study course. Call for a faxed copy of brochure.

Books

The Complete Idiot's Guide to the Perfect Wedding, rev. ed., by Teddy Lenderman, Master Bridal Consultant. 1997, Macmillan, New York.

The Everything Wedding Organizer: Checklists, Calendars, and Worksheets for Planning the Perfect Wedding, by Laura Morin. 1998, Adams Publishing, Holbrook, MA.

How to Have a Big Wedding on a Small Budget; The Big Wedding Planner, 3rd ed., by Diane Warner. 1997, Betterway Books, Cincinnati, OH.

Publication

Modern Bride magazine
P.O. Box 54370
Boulder, CO 80322

An excellent resource for brides and professionals in bridal services. One year/6 issues costs $17.97.

Start-Up Guide

National Business Library's Start-Up Guide, *Wedding Planning*. (800) 947-7724. $39.95 + $6.50 shipping and handling.

Additional Business Ideas

Expand into selling wedding supplies and accessories. Resources follow:

Bridal Accents Ltd.
38 Pond St., Suite 104
Franklin, MA 02038
(508) 528-2530; (800) 865-2228
< http://www.bridalaccents.com >

Offers in-home sales of bridal accessories through its Bridal Accents® Consultant Program.

Bridal Crafts
2400 Devon, Suite 375
Des Plaines, IL 60018-4618

A bimonthly magazine offering design projects for weddings.

Home Services

CLEANING: BLINDS

Residences, shops, offices, companies, and corporations will always need their blinds cleaned, so demand for this service is high. You can purchase a special blind-cleaning machine from the S. Morantz company (address listed later in this section) or find the best method and formula that works for you. You also may want to learn how to install and/or repair blinds as an extra service.

Start-Up Costs and Financing Sources
❖ $6,000 to $15,000 if you purchase a specialized machine. To keep initial costs down, rent cleaning equipment until you can purchase your own.
❖ Personal savings, small business loans.

Marketing and Advertising Methods and Tips
❖ Place classified ads in local newspapers.
❖ Post flyers on community bulletin boards.
❖ Send direct mailings to businesses that have blinds.
❖ Purchase a business telephone directory ad.

Essential Equipment
Buckets, drop cloths, small stepladder, cleaning cloths, hand-held vacuum cleaner, cleaning solution (one that demagnetizes the dirt so it is not just pushed around), tools for repair and installation, and a vehicle large enough to carry equipment.

Recommended Training, Experience, or Needed Skills
+ Work in a cleaning business to learn tricks of the trade.
+ Volunteer to clean relatives' and friends' blinds.
+ Contact blind manufacturers to see if they have cleaning booklets or offer seminars or workshops on cleaning blinds.
+ Need physical dexterity.

Income Potential
Average charge is $10 to $15 a blind. If you clean 60 blinds a day and charge $12 for each blind, you will make $720 per day.

Type of Business
One-fourth in-home for arranging appointments, record-keeping, marketing; three-fourths out-of-the-home.

Best Customers
Businesses.

Helpful Tips
Doing a "little extra" as well as being quick and efficient will result in referrals to other potential customers.

For More Information

Books and Publications
Cleaning Up for a Living, by Don Aslet. 1991, Betterway Books, Cincinnati, OH.
How to Sell and Price Contract Cleaning, 3rd ed. 1993, Cleaning Consultant Services, Seattle, WA.
(See also "Cleaning Consultant Services," page 81.)

Equipment
For information on the S. Morantz company's "Li'l Baby Blind Cleaning Machine," a portable, ultrasonic cleaning system, send an LSASE to S. Morantz, Inc., 9984 Gantry Rd., Philadelphia, PA 19115; or call (215) 969-0266, (215) 969-0566 fax.

Start-Up Guides
Entrepreneur's Start-Up Guide, Miniblind Cleaning/Installation. (800) 421-2300. $69 + shipping and handling.

Additional Business Ideas
Sell replacement blinds. For more information, contact Budget Blinds, Inc., 1570 Corporate Dr., Suite B, Costa Mesa, CA 92626. Send an LSASE for information.

～ 10 ～
CLEANING: CARPETS AND RUGS

Cleaning carpets and rugs is a competitive business. You have to aggressively market your service and be ready to tell potential customers why your service is better than another's.

Start-Up Costs and Financing Sources
✦ As low as $500 to $1,000 if you lease your equipment, as much as $10,000 to $20,000 if you buy equipment.
✦ Personal savings, credit card credit line, small business loans.

Pricing Guidelines
Usual charges range from 12 to 15 cents per square foot, up to 30 + cents per square foot if you have to move furniture. Some business owners charge a flat rate per room, which may vary with room size. Collect payment on completion of each job.

Marketing and Advertising Methods and Tips
✦ Send direct mail to businesses.
✦ Purchase ads (with coupons for discounts) in co-op mailing services to homes.
✦ Take out an ad in the business telephone directory.

Essential Equipment
Business phone with answering machine, service, or voice mail; carpet and drapery cleaning machine (can be leased), vehicle.

Recommended Training, Experience, or Needed Skills

✤ Work in a carpet cleaning business, or rent a machine and clean your and your friends' carpets to get on-the-job training.
✤ Become knowledgeable on how to clean different kinds of carpets.

Income Potential

Once your business is established, you can earn as much as $50,000 + a year. Some business owners who have cleaning crews earn into the six figures.

Type of Business

One-fourth in-home; three-fourths out-of-the-home doing the cleaning or supervising.

Best Customers

Apartment dwellers, homeowners, hotels, motels, offices.

Helpful Tips

✤ Pick a unique name for your business and buy uniforms for a recognized look.
✤ Establish a regular cleaning schedule with your customers—in a signed contract—to ensure a predictable and regular income.

Franchises, Distributorships, and Licenses

Franchise

Chem-Dry® Carpet Cleaning (Harris Research, Inc.)
1530 North 1000 West
Logan, UT 84321

Specializes in the care of carpets, draperies, upholstery, and most fabrics. Sells a patented, nontoxic cleaner and specializes in the removal of red dyes, pet stains, and odors. This franchise can be run out of an office or your home, part-time or full-time. Send an LSASE for more information.

For More Information

Books and Publications
Carpet cleaning books. Cleaning Consultant Services, Inc., P.O. Box 1273, Seattle, WA 98111. < http://www.cleaning consultants.com > Write for catalog.
Cleaning Business, P.O. Box 1273, Seattle, WA 98111. Quarterly magazine covering cleaning and self-employment issues. $20 for a one-year subscription.
The Cleaning Encyclopedia, by Don Aslett. 1993, Dell Books, New York.

Start-Up Guides
Entrepreneur's Small Business Start-Up Guide, *Carpet-Cleaning Service*. (800) 421-2300. $69 + shipping and handling.
National Business Library's Start-Up Guide, *Carpet Cleaning*. (800) 947-7724. $39.95 + shipping and handling.

Additional Business Ideas
Specialize or also offer drapery cleaning, upholstery cleaning, carpet dyeing, or hardwood and non-carpeted floor cleaning.

ᘓᘖ 11 ᘗᘚ
CLEANING: HOMES AND APARTMENTS

With so many women working out-of-the-home today, the need for a high quality cleaning service has grown. Many home and apartment cleaners are sole proprietors, but some hire a staff and then manage the business. Cleaning is a physically demanding job, which is why an owner who does everything herself is somewhat limited in her income potential.

Arrange cleaning visits on a regular basis according to your customers' needs. It may be a good idea to have yourself or your workers bonded. Be aware that these businesses traditionally have a high turnover of employees.

Start-Up Costs and Financing Sources
+ $1,000 to $12,000.
+ Personal savings, credit card line of credit.

Pricing Guidelines
$15 to $20+ per hour for cleaning and organizing; extra charges for ironing, mending, and so forth.

Marketing and Advertising Methods and Tips
+ Encourage word-of-mouth referrals from satisfied customers.
+ Post flyers on community bulletin boards.
+ Place ads in weekly classified newspapers.
+ Place magnetic signs on your vehicles.
+ Print up brochures describing your cleaning services.
+ Research the locations of white-collar neighborhoods through your chamber of commerce. Concentrate your advertising on reaching those residents.

Essential Equipment
Various kinds of cleaning equipment, telephone answering machine or service, filing and billing systems.

Recommended Training, Experience, or Needed Skills
+ Work in a cleaning business to learn professional tips on how to clean quickly and efficiently.
+ Be well-organized; pay attention to detail.

Income Potential
In a sole proprietorship, you can average $15,000 annually, part-time to $35,000+, full-time. Count on twice that amount if you hire a staff. Some cleaning business owners report personal earnings of $500 to $700 per week.

Type of Business
One-fourth in-home for billing, scheduling, and organizational matters; three-fourths out-of-the-home for cleaning visits.

Best Customers
Single professionals, married working couples with families, households earning $45,000 or more per year.

Helpful Tips

✤ Use a checklist to know customer needs.

✤ Purchase liability insurance.

✤ Offer "extras" or specialties with your service such as carpet cleaning, cleaning out garages, organizing closets, and so forth, and bill accordingly.

Franchises, Distributorships, and Licenses

Franchise
Maid Brigade Systems
4 Concourse Parkway, Suite 200
Atlanta, GA 30329
< http://www.maidbrigade.com >

Write for information.

Consultant Service
Cleaning Consultant Services, Inc.
P.O. Box 1273
Seattle, WA 98111
(206) 682-9748; (206) 622-6876 fax
< http://www.cleaningconsultants.com >
E-mail: < wgriffin@cleaning consultants.com >

Offers cleaning industry training and educational materials (books, magazines, software, and videos), seminars, and a product index. Provides information for custodial managers.

For More Information

Association
Cleaning Management Institute
13 Century Dr.
Latham, NY 12110-2197
< http://www.facility-maintenance.com >

Offers monthly magazine, newsletter, many publications, and training programs.

Books and Publications
Cleaning business books. Order from Cleaning Consultant Services, Inc. See address under "Consultant Service."
Start & Run a Profitable Home Cleaning Business, by Susan Bewsey. 1995, Self-Counsel Press, Bellingham, WA.

Start-Up Guides
Entrepreneur's Start-Up Guide, *Maid Service*. (800) 421-2300. $69 + shipping and handling.
National Business Library's Start-Up Guide, *Maid Service*. (800) 947-7724. $39.95 + shipping and handling.

Additional Business Ideas
Specialize in window washing, garage or attic cleaning, one-time cleaning (before and after) for parties, holidays, or special occasions. See *More 101 Best Home-Based Businesses for Women*, by Priscilla Y. Huff. 1998, Prima Publishing, Rocklin, CA.

✑ 12 ✑
ESTATE SALES

This business involves organizing and selling the entire contents of a house or property. Profits are made on a set percentage of the sales. Some estate sale specialists focus on types of properties or specify a minimum amount of money for the properties they will liquidate.

Start-Up Costs and Financing Sources
✦ $4,000 to $7,000.
✦ Personal savings, credit line on credit cards, small business loans.

Pricing Guidelines
A contract should designate the percentage of profits or commission you expect. An average fee is 30 percent of total sales.

Marketing and Advertising Methods and Tips
✦ Encourage word-of-mouth referrals.
✦ Place ads in the local newspapers.

❖ Print up business cards.

❖ Charge clients for advertising their estate sale: send out flyers to antique merchants; place announcements in newspapers, local cable television and radio stations; post flyers on community bulletin boards.

Essential Equipment
Computer and software for keeping a database of current values for antiques and collectibles; business telephone line and fax; tables and linens to display items; tags, receipt books, or portable cash register; assorted bags and boxes for items sold.

Recommended Training, Experience, or Needed Skills
❖ Work for an auctioneer of estates, at an auction house specializing in the sale of antiques, or at an antique shop.

❖ Read antique trade publications and price guides to familiarize yourself with the current prices of objects.

❖ Attend estate sales to see how they are conducted.

❖ Volunteer to help at a relative's or friend's estate sale.

❖ Be well-organized.

Income Potential
$3,000+ gross per sale.

Type of Business
One-eighth in-home for organizing and marketing the business; seven-eighths out-of-the-home for conducting sales.

Best Customers
People who are moving into nursing homes or smaller homes.

Helpful Tips
❖ If you are not sure of an object's value, hire appraisers.

❖ If possible, do not have the customer present during the sale.

❖ Clean, polish, and display the items to look their best.

❖ Hire helpers to keep things running smoothly and to help prevent theft.

❖ Build your business to have a reputation of being honest and professional.

For More Information

Books and Business System
The Estate Master System: includes book, *How to Establish and Operate a Successful Estate/Tag Sale Business,* by August R. Fetcko. Includes sample forms, marketing ideas, and so forth. Make a check or money order payable to Past Glories Publishing, 29 Gibson St., Suite 432-PYH, North East, PA 16428. (814) 725-4092. $45 plus $3 for shipping and handling (PA residents add $2.70 sales tax). Allow two weeks for delivery.

Kovel's Antiques and Collectibles Price List, 30th ed. 1998, Crown Publishers, New York.

The Where-to-Sell-It Directory; order from Pilot Books, 127 Sterling Ave., P.O. Box 2102, Greenport, NY. (800) 79-pilot.

Publication
Antiques & Auction News, P.O. Box 500 West, Mount Joy, PA 17552.

Seminars
Certified Estate Liquidator and Appraiser seminars are sponsored by Edinboro University of Pennsylvania, Continuing Education, 139 Meadville St., Edinboro, PA 16444. Send an LSASE for more information.

Additional Business Ideas
Antiques sales and restoration.

ᘓ 13 ᘏ
GARAGE SALES

In this business you sell the household goods and clothing of people who are too busy or do not want to go through the process of holding their own garage sale.

A garage sale—also called a yard, patio, basement, porch, or moving sale—may run one, two, or more days. They may be held by a single family, several families, an entire neighborhood block, or organizations and clubs.

A garage sale business, like all businesses, benefits from a well-thought-out business plan that lists start-up costs along with your pricing, advertising, and marketing strategies.

Start-Up Costs

$500 to $1,000, depending on the size and length of the sale, or if you or the customers pay for advertising. Costs are more if you have to carry liability insurance, or have a lawyer draw up a standard contract.

Pricing Guidelines

Offer a free or a small-fee consultation. Draw up a contract stating your terms and services. Average commissions run from 15 percent to 30 percent of sales.

Marketing and Advertising Methods and Tips

For Your Business

- ✤ Run classified ads in the local newspapers.
- ✤ Place flyers on community bulletin boards; pass out flyers to residents in new developments.
- ✤ Send out direct mailings to real estate agents.
- ✤ Print up business cards to hand out at garage sales.
- ✤ Encourage referrals from customers.
- ✤ Send out a press release every spring to your local newspaper, giving tips on organizing a garage sale.

For the Sale

- ✤ Place ads in local daily and/or weekly newspapers.
- ✤ Put up posters where permissible.
- ✤ Post flyers on community bulletin boards.
- ✤ Purchase ads on local cable television stations.

Essential Equipment

Tags, receipt books, bags for purchases, signs for advertising, and, at the sale itself, portable cash register; telephone line with answering machine or service; record-keeping forms.

Recommended Training, Experience, or Needed Skills

❖ Visit other garage sales to familiarize yourself with the re-sale prices of most items. Used items are usually sold for 20 percent to 30 percent of their original price; clothing, 10 percent. Special baby items and new or slightly used products can be priced higher.

❖ Hold a garage sale yourself or for your friends.

❖ Be well-organized and people-friendly.

❖ Take courses in antiques and collectibles (often offered at adult evening schools), read books on current prices of collectibles in case you run across items that may be valuable. Urge your customers to consult with a professional appraiser if in doubt.

Income Potential

$50 to $200 per sale. You may want to limit yourself to only large or multiple family sales to make it worth your time.

Type of Business

Primarily an out-of-the-home business.

Best Customers

Busy families or couples, working couples who have just moved into a new home.

Helpful Tips

❖ Be honest about pricing and market value with your customers and with the people attending the sale.

❖ Decide on policies for people making offers on items—some items may have firm prices; others may be sold "as is," and so forth.

❖ Start planning early. Have an alternative or rain date in case of unforeseen circumstances.

For More Information

Books

The Backyard Money Machine, by L. R. Schmeltz. 1993, Silver Streak Publications, Bettendorf, IA.

The Complete Garage Sale Kit: Everything You Need to Make Money at Your Next Garage Sale! by Monica Rix Paxson and Diana Rix. 1994, Sourcebooks, Naperville, IL.

The Fabulous Money-Making Garage Sale Kit, by Diana Rix and Monica Rix Paxson. 1993, Sourcebooks, Naperville, IL 60566. Includes tips, templates for tags, signs, and so forth.

Garage Sale and Flea Market: Cashing In on Today's Lucrative Collectibles Market (annual), by Sharon and Bob Huxford. 1997, Collector Books, Paducah, KY.

The Garage Sale Handbook, by Peggy Hitchcock. 1993, Pilot Books, 127 Sterling Ave., P.O. Box 2102, Greenport, NY. (800) 79-pilot.

Garage Sale Business (booklet), by Priscilla Huff. Send $4 to P. Huff, Box 286, Sellersville, PA 18960.

Additional Business Ideas

✤ Specialize in tag sales for people who are moving. Items to be sold are tagged and customers can walk through several rooms of the house to see what there is to buy.

✤ Specialize in cleaning garages.

◄◊ 14 ◊►
HOUSESITTING

This service business involves staying at or checking up on a customer's house or apartment while they are away on vacation or business. Your service may include taking care of pets, watering plants, mowing the lawn, checking that appliances and heaters are running properly, collecting and holding or forwarding mail, and making sure the home is secure.

You can charge by the day, or have a flat rate and charge extra for each chore that you do. Check with your insurance agent to see if you should be bonded.

Start-Up and Financing Sources

✤ $1,000 to $5,000. You will need to spend money on advertising, lawyer fees (for contracts), insurance payments, a computer for billing, and business records. You may also

need supplies for the extra services your business may offer such as cleaning, mowing the lawn, or making minor household repairs.
❖ Personal savings, line of credit on your credit card, small business loans.

Pricing Guidelines
Go by the recommendations of experts in the industry (see "For More Information," later in this section); check other housesitters' fees.

Marketing and Advertising Methods and Tips
❖ Place classified ads in newspapers and real estate papers.
❖ Post flyers on community bulletin boards.
❖ Ask for referrals from satisfied customers.
❖ Send out press releases.

Essential Equipment
Bookkeeping supplies; separate telephone line with answering machine or an answering service; contracts, worksheets, and other business forms.

Recommended Training, Experience, or Needed Skills
❖ Volunteer to watch a friend's or relative's house while they are away.
❖ Work for a housesitting business.
❖ Need to be honest, trustworthy, and dependable.
❖ Know exactly what the customer wants.

Income Potential
$20,000 to $40,000+ annually, full-time. Earnings depend on the population density and ages of those who live in your area (older persons may travel more).

Type of Business
One-eighth in-home for running the business; seven-eighths out-of-the-home.

Best Customers
Professional individuals or couples who are frequent business travelers, vacationing families or individuals, retirees.

Helpful Tips
✤ Understand customer needs.

✤ Have the ability to handle emergencies, such as power outages, appliance failures, and so forth, and know whom to contact to handle them (and, of course, how to contact the customer in case of an emergency!).

Franchises, Distributorships, and Licenses

Franchises
Homewatch International, Inc.
2865 S. Colorado Blvd.
Denver, CO 80222
(800) 777-9770; (303) 758-7290

Friend of the Family
880 Holcomb Bridge Rd., Suite 160
Rosewell, GA 30075-2215
(770) 643-3000; (770) 643-3020 fax
< http//www.afriend.com >

In-home care referral service for child care, elder care, pet care, house watching, shopping, errands, home secretarial services.

For More Information

Book
How to Run a Housesitting Business (mail order only). Make check or money order payable to Jane Poston, 1708 E. 9th St., Tucson, AZ 85719-5535. $40. Contains reproducible forms, contracts, and more.

Additional Business Ideas
Watch vacation homes—if you live in an area where there are numerous summer or winter vacation homes, you might offer your housesitting services to these homeowners.

༜ 15 ༝
INTERIOR DESIGN

Home decorating and remodeling have grown in the past few years due to the rising real estate prices. People are more likely to change the look of their interiors rather than go deeper into debt by buying a new house.

An interior decorator or designer has to have the knowledge, training, and/or on-the-job experience to be competitive in this market. Interior designers plan the layouts for interior decorators and are required to be licensed by some states. Interior decorators concentrate more on the material aspects of rooms and spaces.

Interior designers and decorators appraise, plan, and design interiors of homes, businesses, and institutions. They coordinate colors and materials in the spaces to be used, all within the clients' budgets. Many specialize according to their own training and preferences.

Start-Up Costs and Financing Sources
* $8,000 to $19,000.
* Personal savings, small business loans.

Pricing Guidelines
Your fee will vary according to your expertise and experience—whether you are certified or have completed a degree program.

Pricing options include the following:

* Flat fee.
* Hourly rate, which can range from $40 to $150 per hour.
* A service charge that is added on to the price of any items purchased for your client.
* Per-room charge, for example $75 to $195 for an average sized room, $300 for a large room.

Marketing and Advertising Methods and Tips
* Take out an ad in the business telephone directory.
* Encourage referrals from customers, home furnishing retailers, painting and wallpapering businesses, home decorating

centers, builders, real estate agents, fabric centers, and floor covering retailers.
* Place classified ads in local and regional newspapers and magazines.
* Send out direct mailings to home furnishing retailers.
* Rent a booth at home furnishing trade shows.

Essential Equipment

Drafting equipment, computer and graphic design software, copier, telephone with fax, answering machine or service, samples, swatches.

Recommended Training, Experience, or Needed Skills

* Work for an interior decorator.
* Become familiar with industry standards—join a professional association, read trade publications.
* Work as a sales clerk in stores selling interior finishings.
* Work as a decorator's apprentice.
* Attend classes at professional schools that offer two- or three-year certificates or diplomas in interior design. (See "For More Information," later in this section.) Many architectural firms, design firms, stores, and so forth, hire only designers with formal training.
* Have a sense of color, balance, and proportion; keep abreast of current fashion trends.
* Communicate well with clients and understand their preferences.
* Need to be able to coordinate and work with suppliers of your decorating services, furnishings, and so forth.

Income Potential

$35,000 to $100,000+ per year, depending on your clientele and education, certification, and reputation as a designer.

Type of Business

About one-half in-home, coordinating and planning; one-half out-of-the-home, consulting with suppliers, customers, and overseeing the work done.

Best Customers

New homeowners, single or married professionals, clients in wealthy neighborhoods.

Helpful Tips

✤ Pay attention to detail.
✤ Check zoning and licensing requirements for your state.
✤ Draw up a contract that leaves no room for doubt as to what you will do and what the customer wants.

Franchises, Distributorships, and Licenses

Franchise

Decorating Den Interiors
19100 Montgomery Village Ave., #200
Montgomery Village, MD 20886
(800) DEC-DENS; (301) 272-1500
< http://www.decoratingden.com >

For More Information

Association

The American Society of Interior Designers
608 Massachusetts Ave., NE
Washington, DC 20002-6006
(202) 546-3480

Membership requires six years of education and experience. Qualify for professional membership by passing the NCIDQ exam (National Council for Interior Design Qualification).

Books and Publications

How to Start a Home-Based Interior Design Business, by Suzanne DeWalt. 1997, Globe Pequot Press, Old Saybrook, CT.

Marketing and Selling Design Services: The Designer-Client Relationship, by Mary V. Knackstedt. 1997, John Wiley & Sons, New York.

Start Your Own Interior Design Business and Keep It Growing! Your Guide to Business Success, by Linda M. Ramsay. 1997, Touch of Design®, 475 College Blvd., Suite 6290, Oceanside, CA 92057. < http://www.touchofdesign.com >

Send an LSASE for information.

Computer Software
Interior Design Software: Pulsar USA, Inc., P.O. Box 1712, Mishawaka, IN 46546-1712. Send an LSASE for prices and information.

Home Study Courses
International Correspondence Schools, Interior Decorating diploma. (See "Home Study" in Part III.)

Professional Career Development Institute
3597 Parkway Ln., Suite 1001
Norcross, GA 30092

Send an LSASE for course listings.

Magazine
Interior Design, Interior Design, P.O. Box 52331, Boulder, CO 80323-2331. (800) 542-8138. Trade publication that includes an annual buyers' guide and bonus issues of *Market,* a large-format publication issued twice a year that features popular products for the trade. Send an LSASE or call for subscription information.

Additional Business Ideas
+ Holiday decorating service—for homeowners and stores.
+ Design interiors for persons with physical or mental disabilities.
+ Design home offices
+ Design interiors using furnishings that people already have—help them rearrange and add different accents, and so forth. This is a much more affordable service for clients, and thus is a popular alternative to complete redecoration. Potential income could reach $100,000 or more per year.

ᦒ16ᦒ
LAMPSHADES

Before the invention of the light bulb, most shades for gas lamps were made of glass or pierced metal to prevent them from catching fire. After Thomas Edison invented the first commercial incandescent light bulb in 1879, lampshades were made from various fabrics to cut down on the glare.

Early on, most shades were purely functional, but as the interest in interior design flourished, lampshade makers began to create them to match a room's decor or to complement a uniquely designed lamp.

Many women are finding that making lampshades is a lucrative and creatively satisfying home-based business.

Start-Up Costs
$500 minimum for supplies, books, course fees, advertising, and so forth.

Pricing Guidelines
$50 for a simple shade to $550+ for a more elaborate one; extra charges for fringes, handpainted scenes, expensive material. Some lampshade makers charge by the inch, measuring the bottom circumference of the shade.

Marketing and Advertising Methods and Tips
+ Encourage word-of-mouth referrals.
+ Take out an ad in the business telephone directory and local newspapers.
+ Print up business cards and flyers to post on community bulletin boards, or leave them at lamp shops, antique shops, and decorating centers.
+ Send out direct mailings to interior decorators.
+ Take time to build up a solid reputation for quality and beautiful work.
+ Take samples of your work to antique shops, home furnishings stores, and Victorian specialty shops. They may not

only buy your products and services outright, but also refer customers to you.

Essential Equipment

Sewing machine and notions, paint supplies, assorted fabrics and art paper for cut-out or painted shades, craft knife and tracing paper, unusual frames (look for these at garage sales and flea markets), printed business cards and flyers.

Recommended Training, Experience, or Needed Skills

* Study how-to books and videos, and practice on your own shades or on those bought at flea markets or garage sales.
* Enroll in lampshade-making courses at craft centers or adult evening schools.
* Have artistic talent.

Income Potential

$500 to $600 a week. Some lampshade makers earn $18,000 to $30,000 per year.

Type of Business

Primarily an in-home business. Your customers can come to you for consultation and estimates.

Helpful Tips

* Dorothy Gillis, a lampshade maker for years says, "You should be able to make both hard and cloth shades as well as do basic repairs as an added service."
* Gillis gives estimates to her customers at the consultation and tells them to give her a call if they want her to make the shades. This gives them time to consider spending money on a custom shade, which is more costly than a manufactured one.
* Keep a portfolio of your designs and photos of your custom shades to show to clients.
* Keep a file card for reference on each shade you make with the time it took to make it, the fabric and supplies used, and the price charged.

For More Information

Books

The Lamp Shade Book: 80 Traditional and Innovative Projects, by Dawn Cusick. 1996, Sterling Publications, Inc., New York.

Lamps & Shades: Beautiful Ideas to Make and Decorate, by Juliet Bawden. 1997, Sterling Publications.

Shade Parade, by Donna Babylon. Includes 25 designs. Available from Clotilde Inc., B3000, Louisana, MO 63353-3000. (800) 772-2891. Call for a catalog.

Other manuals: *Lampshades; Lampshade Construction;* and others from The Lamp Shop (see address under "Supplies").

Supplies

The Lamp Shop
P.O. Box 3606
Concord, NH 03302-3606
(603) 224-1603-phone; (603) 224-6677 fax
E-mail: < lampshop@juno.com >
< http://www.lampshop.com >

Catalog available, a book on making lampshades along with a price guide, supplies, lamp parts, and so forth. Call or write for price of catalog and price guide.

Videos

Basic Lampshade Making and Advanced Lampshade Making. Order from Faye Murray, Heirloom Shades, 12490 Celestial Way, Auburn, CA 95603. $49.94 each.

How to Make Victorian Style Lamp Shades—$48; *How to Restore Traditional Style Lamp Shades*—$45; *How to Make Victorian Sugar Shades and Advanced Techniques*—$49.50. VISA or MasterCard (800) 398-4981 or (916) 783-4802. Shipping is $3.95 on any video and if two or three videos are bought together price is $40, any combination. Order from Heart Enterprise, Custom Designs by Mary Maxwell, 101 Sharon Way, Roseville, CA 95678. Artist/Designer Mary Maxwell is available for coaching over the telephone.

Additional Business Ideas
Offer to repair and make lamps as an added service. Look in your local library for books on making and repairing lamps. Order parts from The Lamp Shop (see address under "Supplies").

ꙥ 17 ꙥ
REFERRAL SERVICE

This service refers potential customers to businesses that offer various products or services to consumers. Clients might include small home remodeling contractors, hairdressers, special event and wedding planners, house- and pet-sitting services, and professional services offered by dentists, doctors, day care services, nannies, home healthcare experts, and tutors.

The owners of a referral service are paid by the business or sometimes by both the business and the customer. Fees can be charged at regular intervals or on commission, based on the number of customers a business receives through your referrals. Constant evaluating of the businesses you refer and searching for new ones to add are important elements in the success of this business.

Start-Up Costs
$6,000 to $15,000 per year.

Pricing Guidelines
15 percent to 20 percent of what the businesses you recommend charge their customers.

Marketing and Advertising Methods and Tips
+ Put up flyers.
+ Send out direct mailings to the businesses in which your referral business will specialize.
+ Make appointments to interview prospective businesses.
+ Get names of businesses recommended by people you know. Ask prospective clients for references from satisfied customers.

❖ Send out press releases to business section editors of the local newspapers or the business supplements of regional newspapers.
❖ Rent a booth at a local home show.
❖ Make sure your local chamber of commerce knows your referral service is in business.

Essential Equipment
Filing system (computer is best) and business and database software; business telephone line with fax, an answering service, or voice mail; a modem if you offer on-line computer referrals; promotional materials (business cards, brochures, etc., for a professional look); a standard contract (consult with your lawyer).

Recommended Training, Experience, or Needed Skills
❖ Work in the business or businesses in which your service specializes so you are knowledgeable about the industry.
❖ Make customer service your number one priority.
❖ Be confident and handle business matters and any problems with a professional and confident manner.
❖ Enjoy working with people.

Income Potential
$50,000 to $100,000+ per year, depending on whether you work by yourself or have assistants.

Type of Business
About one-half in-home for general business matters, making new contacts, and calling customers who use your service; the other one-half is spent out-of-the-home interviewing new businesses.

Best Customers
Newcomers to your community, new businesses in your community, busy working couples.

Helpful Tips
* ❖ Your goal is to make people happy with the businesses in your referral service and to help good quality businesses get the customers they need.
* ❖ Evaluate the businesses through interviews with customers—only keep those that are the best!

For More Information

Books

The End Result: How to Run a Home Referral Service, by Teddi Kessie. Order from The End Result, 13061 Hartsook St., Sherman Oaks, CA 91423. $49.95 + $6 shipping and handling.

How to Start & Manage a Referral Services Business, by Jerre G. Lewis & Leslie Renn. 1996, Lewis & Renn Associates, 10315 Harmony Dr., Interlochen, MI 49643. $14.95 + $3 shipping and handling.

Additional Business Ideas

Call your county's consumer bureau and ask what types of service businesses consumers file complaints against most often. Then start a referral business specializing in that occupation or business.

⋙ 18 ⋘
WALLPAPERING AND PAINTING

Women of all ages and former occupations are finding painting and wallpapering to be a creative and lucrative home-based business and one that will be in demand as long as people want to remodel or redecorate their homes. JoAnn Kaiser, a home decorating store clerk, started "Wall Works" after a customer there asked if Kaiser would paper her walls after she had bought some wallpaper. Kaiser did the job and the customer, the dean of a woman's college, urged JoAnn to go into wallpapering and painting as a business.

After enrolling in a series of small business start-up seminars, Kaiser began to look for wallpapering jobs part-time while she held another job in home health care. She says, "I gained confidence and perfected my skills when I did papering part-time and had the opportunity to figure out a pricing guide." When it became too much to do both jobs, Kaiser decided to go full-time into wallpapering and has been doing it ever since.

Start-Up Costs and Financing Sources
❖ About $7,000 for basic supplies and office equipment.
❖ Personal savings, line of credit on credit cards, loans from friends or family, small business loans.

Pricing Guidelines
❖ Wallpaper hangers and painters charge by the roll, by the hour, and according to the difficulty of the job. Find out what other paperhangers in your area charge.
❖ Painting is priced according to the square foot and the kind of paint used.
❖ Stenciling is priced from $6 to $8+ a linear foot with extra charges for multicolor stenciling.

Marketing and Advertising Methods and Tips
❖ Encourage word-of-mouth referrals from satisfied customers.
❖ Hand out flyers and business cards.
❖ Place classified ads in local newspapers.
❖ Buy ad time on local cable television channels.
❖ Offer a wallpapering workshop at a local decorator's shop.
❖ Send out direct mailings to retirement homes, schools, businesses, and interior decorators.

Essential Equipment
Ladders, assorted paintbrushes and rollers, papering brushes and rollers, knives, razor blades for cutting paper, drop cloths, a vehicle for carrying your supplies.

Your home office would require a telephone line with an answering machine, answering service, or voice mail; a filing system (manual or computer for billing, customer and supplier database, etc.).

Recommended Training, Experience, or Needed Skills

✤ Work with a professional paperhanger. JoAnn Kaiser says, "I would have learned the tips and methods faster if I had worked for a paperhanger before I started doing it on my own."

✤ Volunteer with friends and family to help them wallpaper or paint, or try it in your own home.

✤ Take a course at a school or local decorating, hardware, or paint center. (See "For More Information," later in this section.)

✤ Need physical dexterity, a working knowledge of math, familiarity with color, and an ability to communicate well with your customers.

Income Potential

$18,000 to $100,000+ average annual earnings; $600 to $1,000 per week.

Type of Business

Primarily an out-of-the-home business—for consultations and for doing the work.

Helpful Tips

✤ Kaiser says that after you and your customer agree on the estimated cost, "Always get a signed contract to ensure payment."

✤ Pay attention to detail, protect the furniture and belongings of your customers, and do quality work, which will lead to referrals to other potential customers.

For More Information

Association

National Guild of Professional Paperhangers (NGPP)
910 Charles St.
Fredericksburg, VA 22401

Provides a directory, certified program, educational videotapes, bimonthly publication, annual convention, NGPP Wallcovering Installer. Send an LSASE for more information.

Books

The Complete Book of Paint: A Comprehensive Guide to Paint Techniques for Walls, Floors, Furniture, Fabrics and Metalwork, by David Carter and Charles Hemming. 1996, Clarkson Potter, New York.

The Complete Guide to Wallpapering, by David M. Groff. 1993, Creative Homeowners Press, Upper Saddle River, NJ.

Stencil Source Book (1994); *Stencil Source Book 2* (1995), by Patricia Meehan. North Light Books, Cincinnati, OH.

Magazine

PWC, Painting & Wallcovering Contractor, Finan Publishing, 8730 Big Bend Blvd., St. Louis, MO 63119-3776. A one-year subscription costs $19.95; foreign addresses should send $45 in U.S. funds.

Additional Business Ideas

Paint store windows for holidays.

∽ 19 ∾
WELCOMING SERVICE

In this service, you welcome new homeowners to your community by introducing them to banks, stores, medical services, day care facilities, private schools, recreational facilities, and other community businesses. You are paid by these establishments to promote their products and services.

Start-Up Costs and Financing Sources

✤ $5,000 to $10,000 per year.
✤ Personal savings, credit lines on credit cards, sponsorship by businesses you promote.

Pricing Guidelines

Businesses may pay you monthly or based on the number of responses they receive from the people you visit. Track this through the coupons or inquiries the business receives as a result of your visits.

Marketing and Advertising Methods and Tips
- ❖ Place ads in free real estate booklets and classified newspapers.
- ❖ Send out direct mailings to real estate agencies who can refer you to new people who have just moved into the community.
- ❖ Advertise on your local radio or cable television.
- ❖ Schedule appointments with prospective sponsors and your local chamber of commerce. Give them a brochure describing how your service works and how it can help increase their business and sales.

Essential Equipment
Standard home office supplies, including a copier, computer with billing software, business telephone line with answering machine or service, professional wardrobe, a dependable and attractive vehicle, a pager.

Recomended Training, Experience, or Needed Skills
- ❖ Work part-time for a welcoming service in a nearby (but not competing) community.
- ❖ Make a good impression: have poise, be well-spoken, congenial, enthusiastic, and knowledgeable about your community.

Income Potential
$75 or more with each household you visit. This is more of a part-time business than a full-time one.

Type of Business
One-third in-home for general business matters and to schedule appointments with businesses and newcomers; one-third out-of-the-home, introducing yourself to businesses who will be paying you to sell their services; and one-third out-of-the-home visiting newcomers.

Best Customers
New and established businesses, newcomers.

Helpful Tips
✤ Entice newcomers to use your clients' services with gifts or welcome baskets filled with free samples or coupons.
✤ Be professional in dealing with the businesses and show them that you can increase their sales.
✤ Do follow-up evaluations with your newcomers: How did they like the businesses and services you recommended? You can pass this information on to the businesses to help them improve.
✤ Try different methods of advertising to see which type gets you the best response.

Franchises, Distributorships, and Licenses
Check in franchise opportunities books. Also check with your local chamber of commerce and/or home business association.

Additional Business Ideas
Start an unpacking service that helps new homeowners or apartment dwellers unpack and organize their household goods and personal belongings in their new residence. Either unpack alone (with a detailed diagram from the customer) or work alongside your customer.

Customers most likely to use this service would be working couples, the elderly, or persons with disabilities. Check with your insurance agent to find out if you need liability insurance or whether you should be bonded. Consult with a lawyer to draw up contracts.

You could charge an hourly rate, a per-job rate, or a fee according to the square footage of the residence. Special services like washing windows or general cleaning could be charged extra. Income potential averages $50,000 per year.

Personal Services

⤳ 20 ⤶
CHILD CARE

With millions of preschool children in need of day care and a shortage of spaces in day care centers and preschools, the need for in-home day care businesses is great and will continue to be so for some time to come. Most home-based day care businesses care for four to six children, who may come full-time, part-time, or as drop-ins. Some businesses specify the age range of the children they feel most comfortable with and can handle.

Before starting a home-based child care service, check your state's regulations and licensing requirements. Many states require a background check for those who teach or work with children.

Start-Up Costs and Financing Sources
* Can be as low as $500 or as high as $15,000, depending on the equipment you buy and use. If you need to remodel a room or play area, the upper estimate applies.
* Personal savings, SBA loan, line of credit on your credit card, government funding (in some states, government funds are available to sponsor children of low-income families who attend your day care).

Pricing Guidelines
$125 to $250 a week per child; $35 to $45 per day for infant care; $30 for a half-day and $40 for a full day. (Prices vary for different parts of the country.)

Marketing and Advertising Methods and Tips
+ Encourage word-of-mouth referrals.
+ Place a listing with a child care referral service.

Essential Equipment
Good furniture (it can be bought used), learning toys (checked for safety), cribs, high chairs, playpens, first aid supplies, craft supplies, business telephone line.

Recommended Training, Experience, or Needed Skills
+ Work in a day care center and see if you would like to do this kind of work every day.
+ Take courses in child care at local community colleges.
+ Use your experience with children from infancy to six years old as a mother (if you were one) or a caretaker.
+ Have a love of children and enjoy teaching and working with them!
+ Have patience, be well-organized, and think like a child in the way you plan activities for them.

Income Potential
$125 to $250 per child; $25,000 to $45,000 a year.

Type of Business
An in-home business.

Best Customers
Parents who work, parents who want to go shopping or to an appointment.

Helpful Tips
+ Have a lawyer draw up a contract so both you and the parents are sure about the terms of the day care arrangement (especially payment and when parents should pick up their children).
+ Have a trial period for newcomers.

✦ Have a back-up worker ready in the event you should become ill.
✦ Know emergency and first aid procedures.
✦ Be sure you can handle five days a week, ten hours a day.

Franchises, Distributorships, and Licenses

Franchises

Wee Watch America Inc.
Douglas MacKay, President
7400 North Oracle Rd., Suite 323
Tucson, AZ 85704
(520) 219-8872

Refers and monitors at-home child care providers

Wee Watch America Inc. (in Canada)
Terry Fullerton, President
105 Main St.
Unionville, Ontario Canada L3R 2Gl
(905) 479-4274

Sitters Unlimited
23015 Del Lago, #D2-105
Laguna Hills, CA 92653

In-home child-sitting service. Territory limited to California and Hawaii. Send an LSASE for information.

License

A Friend of the Family
880 Holcomb Bridge Rd., Suite 160-B
Roswell, GA 30076-1999
(770) 643-3000; (770) 643-3020 fax
< http://www.afriend.com >

Provides in-home care referral services of child care, companion care, home secretarial, shopping, and errands.

For More Information

Associations

Send an LSASE for information on membership, accreditation, etc.

National Association for Family Child Care
206 Sixth Ave., #900
Des Moines, IA 50309

National Association for the Education of Young Children
1509 16th St., NW
Washington, DC 20036-1426
< http://www.naeyc.org >

Child Care Action Campaign
330 Seventh Ave., 17th Floor
New York, NY 10001

Child care advocacy organization.

Books
Start Your Own At-Home Child Care Business, rev. ed., by Patricia Gallagher. 1994, Mosby-Year Book, St. Louis, MO.
Tips About Organizing Day Care Programs and *Common Day Care Problems*, $2 each. Order from P. Gallagher, Young Sparrow Press, P.O. Box 265, Worcester, PA 19490.

Home Study Course
International Correspondence Schools
925 Oak St.
Scranton, PA 18515

Offers diploma in child day care.

Start-Up Guides
Entrepreneur's Start-Up Guide, *Child-Care Services*. (800) 421-2300. $69 + shipping and handling.
National Business Library's Start-Up Guide, *Child Care*. (800) 947-7724. $39.95 + shipping and handling.

Additional Business Ideas
✤ Nanny, child care referral service. Find baby-sitters, then check their qualifications and references and refer them to people needing reliable child care services. You are paid by the persons looking for baby-sitters. Earnings range from $15,000 to $60,000 + per year.

Also, contact A Friend of the Family, 10825 Stroup Rd., Roswell, GA 30075-2215. (770) 643-3000. They provide personnel referrals for child care. Other resources follow:

The International Nanny Association, Station House #438, 900 Haddon Ave., Collingswood, NY 08108. Send an LSASE for information.

Mother's Helpmates Franchising, Inc., 3814 Polumbo Dr., Valrico, FL 33594. (813) 681-5183. < http://www. mothershelpmates.com > In-home placement service for child care or elderly care.

✤ Child care consulting service. Help businesses start a day care center for their employees' children. Charge $5,000 to $15,000 for a consulting fee.
✤ Child transportation service. Order Entrepreneur's Start-Up Guide, *Transportation Service.* (800) 421-2300. $69 + shipping and handling.
✤ Child care for sick children.
✤ Play group. Order *Starting and Operating a Play Group for Profit,* by Susan Chidakel. Pilot Books, 127 Sterling Ave., P.O. Box 2102, Greeenport, NY 11944-2102. (800) 79-pilot. < http://www.pilotbooks.com >

◈21◈
CREDIT CONSULTING

In this service, you offer credit counseling and take steps to restore the credit of your customers. Requirements for credit repair agencies fall under the Credit Organization Act. Not all states have this law, however, and legislation differs state by state.

Deborah McNaughton offers two programs: the Credit Consulting Business ($599), which shows individuals how to set up a credit consulting business, and a distributorship, the Credit and Financial Strategies seminars ($500 to $1,500+), which includes books, manuals, and audio and video tapes.

Start-Up Costs
$2,000 to $11,000.

Pricing Guidelines
Flat fee of $400 to $700; $175 per credit report from one of the three credit-reporting bureaus. Married couples may receive a discount.

Marketing and Advertising Methods and Tips
+ Place ads in newspapers and classified ads, community publications, or other inexpensive weeklies.
+ Send flyers to individual businesses that qualify individuals for lines of credit.
+ Arrange referrals from mortgage companies, car dealers, and real estate companies.

Essential Equipment
Business phone line with voice mail or answering machine, typewriter, computer and modem, insurance, cellular phone, pager, stationery, copier.

Recommended Training, Experience, or Needed Skills
+ Study manuals, take seminars.
+ Gain experience by working in credit offices. This is helpful but not necessary.
+ Degree in related field.
+ Knowledge of banking industry and online research tools.

Income Potential
$30,000 to $65,000 and more a year, depending on the number of clients you have.

Type of Business
Can be in-home or out-of-the-home in an office.

Best Customers
Any individual who needs guidance or assistance with credit issues: establishing credit, dealing with credit problems, credit repair.

Franchises, Distributorships, and Licenses

Distributorship
> Deborah McNaughton
> 1100 Irvine Blvd. #541
> Tustin, CA 92780
> (714) 541-2637

Offers Credit and Financial Strategies seminars and "Yes, You Can" distributorships.

For More Information

Books and Publications
Credit Card Debt Management, by Scott Bilker. 1996, Press One Publications, Barnegat, NJ. < http://www.debtsmart.com >

The Insider's Guide to Managing Your Credit, by Deborah McNaughton. 1998, Dearborn Financial Publishing, Chicago, IL.

The Ultimage Credit Handbook, New ed., by Gerri Detweiler. 1997, Plume, New York.

Solving Credit Problems and Your Credit: A Complete Guide. Booklets from the Consumer Information Catalog, P.O. Box 100, Pueblo, CO 81002.

༺22༻
SPECIAL DATING SERVICE

Because one out of every two marriages ends in divorce, and over 60 million single adults live in our country, legitimate and reliable dating services are in high demand, with over 1,200 of these introduction services in existence (according to the International Society of Introduction Services). You have to determine if there is a large enough population of singles in your area. Check with the Census Bureau or local county seat for population statistics.

Some of the most popular dating services cater to specialized populations: the physically challenged; ethnic groups; religious affiliations; or people with similar hobbies, education, and interests. Survey single people in your area to find out if they have ever used a dating service. If so, what did they like or not like about it? Maybe you will come up with a dating service unique to your area.

You must have a reliable way to verify the identification of each client and suggest a public place for the first meeting of your matched couples. One dating service in Philadelphia has the matched couple meet at a city restaurant for lunch. Each person pays for his or her lunch. It is a fun and safe way to meet new people.

You should also urge your clients to think of blind dating as a way to meet other persons with related likes and dislikes—not as a potential marital partner. Matchmaking experts say this helps to promote realistic expectations in your clients and less anxiety in using a matchmaking service.

You can match your clients using a computer, videos, questionnaires, or all three methods. Follow-up calls and evaluations are important to improve and update your service.

Start-Up Costs and Financing Sources

+ $15,000 to $30,000 for equipment and a home office to receive clients. Most money will be spent on advertising in the beginning.
+ Personal savings, small business loan, investors.

Pricing Guidelines

Charge a monthly or retainer fee or annual fee (call other dating services in your area to see what the going rates are and charge accordingly). You want to charge enough to make sure your clients are serious about finding suitable dates. Arrange for a bonus fee if the client marries.

Marketing and Advertising Methods and Tips

✤ Market and advertise constantly. Turnover of clients is high—some (happily) get married, others move, and some may try other services.

✤ Target your advertising, if you are specializing your service, to the proper magazines and newspapers.

✤ Send out press releases to newspapers, magazines, and local television and radio stations, which may result in articles or stories that will help increase your service's visibility.

✤ Encourage word-of-mouth referrals from satisfied clients.

Essential Equipment

A business telephone line with an answering service or voice mail; computer with software for matching clients, billing, and database capabilities; video equipment if you tape your clients; business cards; stationery; brochures.

Recommended Training, Experience, or Needed Skills

✤ Work in a dating service as an interviewer or investigate other services in non-competing geographical regions or areas of interest. See what appeals (or does not) to you about them.

✤ Make people feel at ease if you interview them personally.

Income Potential

From $40,000 to $100,000 or more a year, depending on the number of clients and your initial registration and ongoing fees.

Type of Business

An in-house business. You should have a home office with a conference area or room for interviewing or taping clients. Be sure zoning laws permit such an office along with parking space.

Best Customers

Singles who are interested in meeting new people.

Helpful Tips

❖ Have a public meeting place for the first date that is interesting and impressive (a prestigious restaurant, a lecture, a musical event) and arrange occasional private gatherings of your clients so they can see and meet more than one person at a time.

❖ Have all clients screened for their protection. Make sure they are single and have no criminal history.

❖ Have the finances to advertise and sustain your business. Dating service owners say it takes a couple of years to get established.

❖ Check with your lawyer and insurance agents concerning privacy laws and liability insurance.

Franchises, Distributorships, and Licenses

Calculated Couples
4829 E. Greenway Rd., #183
Scottsdale, AZ 85254
(602) 230-4172; (800) 44-MATCH

"Singles Matchmaking Party service. All cash singles business, part-time okay, no office space required; 51 cities since 1983. Full turn-key package $4,995. New 'partner' starter packages available."

For More Information

Association

International Society of Introduction Services &
    The National Association of Ethical Matchmakers
P.O. Box 4876
West Hills, CA 91308
< http://www.match.com >

Send an LSASE for information.

Books

Dating for Dummies, by J. Browne. 1997, IDG Books, Foster City, CA.

The Dating Service Maze: The Experts' Guide to Dating Services, by Lynda M. Johncock. 1994, Queen of Hearts Publishing, Phoenix, AZ.

Start-Up Guide
Entrepreneur's Start-Up Guide, *Dating Service.* (800) 421-2300. $69 + shipping and handling.

Additional Business Ideas
Start a member newspaper or newsletter profiling registered clients in your service.

∾23∾
ELDER CARE SERVICES

The U.S. Census Bureau estimates that by the year 2030, more than 70 million people will be elderly. With the costs of nursing homes and private care escalating every year, every month, the demand for high quality, affordable in-home or day care services for the elderly is also growing. Many adults cannot take care of their elderly parents: They may have moved out of the area or maybe both the husband and wife work and have demanding schedules because of their children.

Elder care services can encompass a range of needs to include transportation to stores and medical appointments; running errands and shopping; daily monitoring of those who live at home; handling Social Security checks; arranging visits by nurses and other professionals; and providing respite care workers when families go on vacation.

A free consultation is offered to evaluate and assess what services are needed. Each service is priced accordingly. Contacts are made with referral agencies if home professional care is needed. You coordinate the services and supply the needs of each of your clients.

Start-Up Costs
$5,000 to $11,000 minimum for office equipment, advertising, and publicity materials for marketing and advertising.

Pricing Guidelines

Charge weekly, monthly, and per service. You may also be paid a fee by any referral agencies that get business through you.

Marketing and Advertising Methods and Tips

❖ Contact social service and home health care agencies with direct mail and then schedule an appointment with them for a presentation.

❖ Encourage word-of-mouth referrals from adult children.

❖ Purchase radio and local cable television ads.

❖ Put together professional-looking promotional materials describing your services.

Essential Equipment

Home office equipment: computer; record-keeping and billing software; business telephone line and answering machine, service, or voice mail; fax machine and copier; cellular phone; insurance; suitable furniture if you have clients and workers come to your office to be interviewed or for consultations; a dependable vehicle.

Recommended Training, Experience, or Needed Skills

❖ Work in your county's home services agency to familiarize yourself with seniors' needs.

❖ Enroll in courses in geriatrics.

❖ Work as a nursing assistant in a nursing or group home.

❖ You need to be patient, yet persistent, in finding persons who will provide the best quality services your clients need.

❖ Be well-organized.

Income Potential

$25,000 to $60,000+ a year, depending on the number of clients you have and whether you hire employees.

Type of Business

Primarily an in-home business, except to interview referrals and clients.

Best Customers

Seniors who are relatively independent but need some at-home support and monitoring.

Helpful Tips

❖ Treat every client as an individual and provide the best services possible for each one's needs.
❖ Check with your insurance agent and lawyer as to what insurance or contracts you should have to protect yourself and your business.
❖ Check with state and local officials to see if you need permits or licenses.

Franchises, Distributorships, and Licenses

Franchise

Basic Needs Home Companion Services
CMP, Inc.
P.O. Box 12672
Lexington, KY 40583-2672
(606) 269-7611

Specialized non-medical, home care service for the elderly or homebound. Provides support services for daily activities to enable the elderly to remain independent.

Home Instead Senior Care
11104 S. 76th Ave.
Omaha, NE 68124
(402) 391-2555

Homewatch
Homewatch International, Inc.
2865 S. Colorado Blvd.
Denver, CO 80222
(800) 777-9770; (303) 758-7290

Specializes in pet and home sitting as well as elderly care.

Licenses
A Friend of the Family
10825 Stroup Rd.
Roswell, GA 30075-2215
(770) 643-3000; (770) 643-3020 fax
< http://www.afriend.com >

Provides in-home care referral service for child and elder care, as well as for house sitting, pet care, shopping, and errand services.

For More Information

Association
National Association for Home Care
228 Seventh St., SE
Washington, DC 20003

Send an LSASE for information.

Books
The Complete Eldercare Planner: Where to Start, Questions to Ask, and How to Help, Rev. ed., by Joy Loverde. 1997, Hyperion, New York.
LeBoeuf's Home Health Care Handbook, by Gene LeBoeuf. 1996, Noel Press, Inc., Great Falls, VA.

Additional Business Ideas
Monitoring service. For more information, send a long SASE with your phone number included to Robert and Anna Major, Home Alone Monitoring Services, 11122 Walnut St., Redlands, CA 92374-7692. They offer a computerized telephone service that calls and checks on seniors, elderly shut-ins, adults who are convalescing, and latchkey children.

ཡྃ 24 ལྃ
ERRAND SERVICE

This business is as varied as the many errands individuals or businesses need to run almost every day. Trips to and from day care centers, pharmacies, grocery stores, post offices and mailing centers, bill payment centers, and libraries are just a few of the errand-running possibilities.

You can specialize in picking up and delivering forms and documents for businesses, or go food shopping for individuals (see "Shopping Service," page 141). Or you can diversify and perform any number of tasks for people who cannot get away from their jobs or homes to run errands themselves. Conduct market research surveys in your community to see which errands are most in demand. Once you start, you may find other errands that need to be run, which you did not know existed until you receive requests for them.

Start-Up Costs and Financing Sources
✤ From $550 for basic ads and the printing and copying of flyers and business cards to $7,000 for a computer and cellular phone and/or pager.
✤ Personal savings, small business loan, personal line of credit on credit cards.

Pricing Guidelines
$15 to $60 per hour ($100+ per hour in large metropolitan areas or for some corporate clients). You can charge weekly or monthly fees for an agreed number of errands within a certain mile radius (charge more for mileage if outside that radius).

Marketing and Advertising Methods and Tips
✤ Place classified ads in the local newspapers.
✤ Post flyers on community bulletin boards and leave them at individual residences and businesses.
✤ Send a press release to your local paper to prompt a follow-up article on your business.
✤ Purchase local radio and cable television ads.
✤ Offer free hours of errand running at a community benefit auction.

Essential Equipment
A reliable vehicle that gets good gas mileage, for use in all kinds of weather; record-keeping and billing files or software;

a business telephone line with an answering machine, answering service, or voice mail; a cellular phone and/or pager; an organizer.

Recommended Training, Experience, or Needed Skills

* Work for a messenger or errand service.
* Volunteer to do your relatives' errands for a time to see if it will be profitable.
* Know your area and the location of services, businesses, and stores.
* Be well-organized, prompt, and use your time as efficiently as possible.

Income Potential

$10,000, part-time; $50,000, full-time. Earnings can be more if you hire others to run the errands.

Type of Business

One-fourth in-home running the business and scheduling runs; three-fourths out-of-the home, running the errands.

Best Customers

New mothers, persons recuperating from illnesses or injuries, shut-ins, persons with certain disabilities or serious illnesses, people on business trips or vacations, seasonal customers who do not have time to shop for gifts or fill out and send tax forms, working couples.

Helpful Tips

* Check licensing requirements and tax laws.
* Check with your insurance agent for liability coverage. See if you need to be bonded.
* Consult with your lawyer on contracts you should have.
* Have the option to turn down a job if the distance is too far (unless the client is willing to pay for your extra time and mileage) or if the job is not one you want to do.

Franchises, Distributorships, and Licenses

Licenses

A Friend of the Family
880 Holcomb Bridge Rd., Suite 160B
Roswell, GA 30076-1999
(770) 643-3000; (770) 643-3020 fax
< http://www.afriend.com >

Provides in-home care referral services for child care, elder care, pet care, house-watching, shopping and errand services.

For More Information

Book

How to Start and Operate an Errand Service, 1996, by Rob Spina. Call (888) 725-2639 or send a check or money order for $29.95 to Rob Spina, Legacy Marketing, 403 Hobart Dr., Laurel Springs, NJ 08021.

⋘ 25 ⋙
FINANCIAL CONSULTANT

A financial consulting service helps people manage their money, borrow money for college or business, and plan for a financially sound future through wise investments, a well-constructed budget, and money-management strategies.

Start-Up Costs and Financing Sources

✤ $10,000 to $20,000. You will need to have a fully equipped, professional in-home office that is suitable to receive clients. This start-up estimate also includes advertising and promotional costs.

✤ Personal savings, small business loan.

Pricing Guidelines

✤ By the hour—from $50 to $200.

✤ A one-time fee for a basic search and for financial aid and scholarship searches.

❖ $250 plus per financial plan.
❖ A one-time fee and a monthly retainer.

Marketing and Advertising Methods and Tips
❖ Take out an ad in the business telephone directory.
❖ Give talks, workshops, or seminars on financial planning.
❖ Produce a quarterly newsletter and send it out to prospective clients.

Essential Equipment
Home office equipment, including a computer, fax, and financial management software and report-writing software to put all your information into organized reports for your clients. For financial aid consulting, you will at least need a computer with the capability to download information from databases.

Recommended Training, Experience, or Needed Skills
❖ Have formal training or education—a bachelor's degree and more, if you are planning to be a certified public accountant (CPA) or certified financial planner (CFP). Licenses and certifications are needed to sell stocks, insurance, or real estate.
❖ With financial aid services, you need to be familiar with the forms and procedures involved in getting loans and scholarships and have access to computerized databases on colleges and private schools. You are paid by the college student or his or her family for the information you find.

Income Potential
For a financial planner: $18,000 and more (part-time) to six-figure incomes if assisting wealthier clients. For a financial aid adviser: $7,000 to $80,000 a year, depending on the number of students you assist.

Type of Business
One-third out-of-the-home meeting with clients; two-thirds in-home meeting with clients, plus researching and planning.

Best Customers
People who have money to spend and invest, professional working couples, college-bound students (any age, these days).

Helpful Tips
✤ Understand what the client wants and hopes to achieve financially.
✤ Keep current with financial information and trends that deal directly with your clients' needs.
✤ With financial aid services, use computer databases to keep current on what money is available as well as changing regulations.

Franchises, Distributorships, and Licenses
(Look in the franchise publications listed in the "Franchise and Distributorships" chapter.)

National Association of Student Financial Aid Administrators
920 L St., NW #200
Washington, DC 20036-5020
< http://www.nasfaa.org >

For More Information

Books
America's Best College Scholarships (annual), published by John Culler & Sons, Camden, SC.
College Financial Aid Made Easy for the 1998-99 Academic Year, by Patrick L. Bellantoni. Ten Speed Press, Berkeley, CA.
Financial Services Direct Marketing, by James R. Rosenfield. 1991, Sourcebooks, P.O. Box 372, Naperville, IL 60566.
How to Become a Successful Financial Consultant, by Jim H. Ainsworth. 1997, John Wiley & Sons, New York.

Magazine
Family Money Magazine, P.O. Box 242227, Charlotte, NC 28254-0188. Offers good information for planning family finances. $14 subscription.

Start-Up Guide
Entrepreneur's Start-Up Guide, *Financial Aid Service.* (800) 421-2300. $69 + shipping and handling.

Additional Business Ideas

✤ Financial services for seniors. Help take care of seniors' personal financial matters. Contact the following resources:

Home Financial Services for Seniors
1219 Cumberland Ave.
Syracuse, NY 13210
Send a long SASE for information about their program.

International Association for Financial Planning (IAFP)
5775 Glenridge Dr., NE, Suite B-300
Atlanta, GA 30328-5364
< http://www.iafp.org >

Nonprofit organization that represents over 17,000 financial professionals who help clients (of all ages) manage and invest their money to reach their financial goals and objectives. Holds conferences and publishes a trade newspaper and a compliance, liability handbook. Send an LSASE for information.

✤ Tax preparation for individuals and small and home-based businesses. (See "Tax Preparation Service," page 358.)

~❧26❧~

IMAGE CONSULTING SERVICE

In this business you assist individuals—men and women—and corporate employees in improving their overall appearance, speech, and manners, thereby enabling them to project the image they need to achieve their personal or professional goals. Some of the reasons professional image consultants are hired include the following: job promotions, interviews for jobs or admittance to programs, appearances on television, public speaking, competitions (such as beauty pageants), adult rehabilitation programs, companies wanting to upgrade their employees' images, entertainers wanting to improve their public image.

In this business, an image consultant can specialize in make-up or wardrobe, for example, or advise clients about several areas in which they wish to improve.

Start-Up Costs
From $6,000 to $8,000 for a home office equipped to receive customers for consultation.

Pricing Guidelines
$40 to $80 an hour (up to $300 an hour for corporate clients). You might also charge a flat fee per day or session—$200 to $1,000 and up.

Marketing and Advertising Methods and Tips
* Research your target market well to know what type of advertising will attract customers.
* Network with professionals and let them know of your service.
* Have professional-looking, well-designed promotional materials ready to hand out or present at meetings, conventions, seminars, and business trade shows.
* Give talks or hold workshops for companies.
* Contact the chamber of commerce and other local and civic groups for individual clients.

Essential Equipment
A good personal wardrobe and accessories; business telephone line with an answering machine, answering service, or voice mail; copier; fax machine; comfortable chairs and a small conference table for talking with clients; audio and visual aids if you are giving talks or conducting workshops; a portfolio of before and after photos of clients; a camera.

Recommended Training, Experience, or Needed Skills
* Talk with personal image consultants for tips.
* Decide if you will specialize or generalize.

✤ You need expertise in your area or areas. Many image consultants have had training or experience in fashion design,
cosmetology, clothing merchandising, make-up techniques,
public relations, and speech and grammar education.
✤ You need to be positive and self-assured, which will help instill confidence in your advice to your clients.

Income Potential
From $10,000 (part-time) to $20,000 to $100,000+ and up.

Type of Business
One-fourth in-home for initial consultations, running the business, gathering information, and planning; three-fourths out-
of-the-home for making presentations, giving instructions,
shopping with the client for wardrobe, and so forth.

Best Customers
Professionals or executives who want to enhance their images
to help them in their careers, new college graduates, women
who are returning to the work force, people who want to prepare for job interviews.

Helpful Tips
✤ According to the Academy of Fashion and Image, you can be
a successful image consultant if you have at least two of the
following:

1. A natural sense of style or color.
2. Background in the retail, fashion, or cosmetic industry.
3. An ability to structure your time and set your own hours.
4. A genuine desire to help others look and be their best.

✤ Encourage word-of-mouth referrals from satisfied clients.
✤ Develop different sidelines to your business, such as conducting workshops or seminars; helping people who are
physically or mentally challenged to find professional-
looking clothes for their jobs; and writing articles or columns
on how to put together a wardrobe when on a budget.

For More Information

Association
Association of Image Consultants, International
1000 Connecticut Ave., NW, #9
Washington, DC 20036

Send an LSASE for information.

Books and Publications
The Image Networker, P.O. Box 494, Haverford, PA 19041. (610) 896-0330. E-mail: < Image4UNow@aol.com >

"The information source for image professionals. A tri-annual trade publication with references, resources, and articles about events, products, services, and new developments in the image industry."

Looking Good: A Comprehensive Guide to Wardrobe Planning, Color & Personal Style Development, by Nancy Nix-Rice. 1996, Palmer Pletsch Publishing, Portland, OR.

Home Study Courses and Schools
The Academy of Fashion and Image
9503 West Menadota Dr.
Peoria, AZ 85382
(602) 572-8719; (602) 572-2954 fax.

This is the oldest and most comprehensive training center in the United States and was founded by image consultant expert Brenda York (McDaniel). "Trains prospective image consultants, provides continuing education for experienced consultants." Offers five-day sessions, home study programs, and certification. Publishes *How to Start Your Own Fashion and Image Consulting Business.*

Additional Business Ideas
❖ Hold self-improvement seminars. See *How to Make It Big in Seminars*, by Paul Kuraski. 1995, McGraw-Hill, New York.
❖ Sell cosmetics and fashion accessories.

༤27༈
INVENTORY SERVICE

This service business involves taking a one-time or periodic inventory of an individual's possessions or a business's stock of merchandise. Inventories are important for insurance purposes and help businesses know what products they have on hand. You can run this business by yourself or hire others part-time to work with on large projects.

Start-Up Costs and Financing Sources
✤ $1,000 to $5,000 and up.
✤ Personal savings, line of credit on credit cards, small business loan for home office equipment and/or vehicle.

Pricing Guidelines
$75 to $100 + an hour. $750 for average-size single home.

Marketing and Advertising Methods and Tips
✤ Send out direct mailings to stores, institutions, and warehouse clubs.
✤ Make presentations on the value of inventories in crime prevention to neighborhood watch groups, local law enforcement officials, and insurance agents for business referrals.
✤ Rent a booth at home trade shows.
✤ Print brochures, business cards. Collect letters from satisfied customers.
✤ Advertise on radio and local cable television.
✤ Give talks to local chamber of commerce groups.

Essential Equipment
Home office supplies: computer with inventory (with report capabilities, billing software), video recorder, instant photo camera, engraving tool, business line and answering devices or service, a dependable vehicle.

Recommended Training, Experience, or Needed Skills

* Work in a department store doing their annual inventories.
* Work in an insurance company and take courses about protecting home valuables and assets.
* Be familiar with insurance and law enforcement rules and procedures.
* Be efficient, well-organized, and professional.

Income Potential

$30,000 to $60,000 and up, depending on your clients and the number of inventories you do per year.

Type of Business

One-fourth in-home for running the business and preparing reports; three-fourths out-of-the-home for the inventories.

Best Customers

Homeowners or apartment dwellers who own valuables; institutions; general merchandise department stores; businesses that want their equipment and inventory protected; schools, hospitals, or other institutions that need inventory reports to write their annual budgets.

Helpful Tips

* Consult with your insurance agent about liability coverage and being bonded.
* Check with your lawyer about drawing up contracts and assessing your liability needs.
* Know how insurance agents and law enforcement officers want items to be inventoried in the event of theft.
* Give detailed reports and inventories to your clients and keep their records confidential.

For More Information

Kit

Home Inventory Kit, Partners in Residence—The Home Inventory Specialists. 901 Carrick St., High Point, NC 27262.

(336) 882-7941. < http://members.aol.com/WILTel3/index.html >
Kit includes VHS tapes, disposable flash 35mm cameras, two
view binders, inventory blanks, and directions for conducting a
complete home inventory. Custom kits available. Contact Wil
and Sharrie Thames.

Additional Business Ideas

Offer your inventory services to estate sale holders, auction
houses, nonprofit organizations, and businesses.

❦28❦
PERSONAL SALON SERVICES

One of the earliest types of home-based businesses run by
women were home beauty salons. Today, home salons offer
varied beauty treatments such as facials, cosmetic consulting,
pedicures, and nail treatments, in addition to offering haircuts
for the entire family.

Sue Marx has run her home salon for twenty years. After
discovering she would no longer receive a commission for part-
time work at the beauty shop where she was employed, she
promptly quit and began to do hairdressing in her apartment.
She and her husband saved to build their house, which includes
a salon they designed.

Marx went from just cutting women's hair to cutting the hair
of entire families. "It makes it more convenient for families to all
come together for their haircuts these days," says Marx, "because families' lifestyles are so hectic with work, school sports,
and other activities."

Marx has to renew her cosmetologist license each year and
her salon is inspected every year by a state inspector. She has
never had to advertise—all of her customers come from word-
of-mouth referrals. She has steady work and prefers to work
only from Wednesday afternoons to Saturdays at noon, leaving
time for her two sons and husband. Her salon has its own business telephone line and electrical line, separate from her house.

Marx was able to start with good used equipment and has had her chairs reupholstered when she wanted to remodel her shop. Her husband has built cabinets, installed shelves, and finished the decor to Marx's specifications. "It's been a good business for my family. The customers have been great in scheduling appointments whenever I have wanted to take a scheduled or impromptu day or week off."

Start-Up Costs and Financing Sources
* $3,000 to $30,000 or more for equipment and furnishings. Costs vary for the services you offer, the new or good used equipment you buy, the costs of your products, and so forth. This does not include the cost of your training and licenses or permits to operate from your home.
* Personal savings, small business loan.

Pricing Guidelines
Check with the going rate for hair, skin, and nail care services and make your prices competitive. If you have a home salon, you can offer lower prices because you will not have to pay rent, but you still have to figure in your overhead and expenses to run your business.

If you do not have the training to offer additional services, you can have specialists offer their services on certain days of the week at your salon. They pay you a percentage of their take, or pay rent for the space used, or pay a commission for each customer you schedule for them.

Marketing and Advertising Methods and Tips
* Encourage word-of-mouth referrals from satisfied customers.
* Offer special deals for the entire family.
* Offer coupons in advertising mail services for a free facial or nail treatment.

Essential Equipment
Home office business supplies; standard equipment and supplies; business line and answering machine, service, or voice mail. Also, commercial supplies such as hair dryers, chemicals, linen, and fixtures.

Recommended Training, Experience, or Needed Skills

✤ Attend cosmetology or beautician schools.
✤ Work in a commercial salon for the experience and to develop a following.
✤ Enjoy working with people.

Income Potential

From $20,000 to $50,000 and up, depending on your clients, the kinds of personal care services you offer, commissions from other beauty specialists, sale of related beauty products, and so forth.

Type of Business

In-home.

Best Customers

You can cater to entire families or certain age groups.

Helpful Tips

✤ Listen to what your customers want and try to make those services available.
✤ Keep up-to-date on the latest trends and products through trade shows and publications.
✤ Know what licensing and training requirements you need.
✤ Check the local and state government regulations regarding home salons.

Franchises, Distributorships, and Licenses

There are a number of commercial hair, skin, and nail franchise opportunities. Order the *Franchise Handbook*, 1020 N. Broadway, Suite 111, Milwaukee, WI 53202.

For More Information

Associations

Association of Cosmetologists and Hairdressers (ACH)
1811 Monroe
Dearborn, MI 48124

Send an LSASE for membership information.

National Cosmetologists Association
3510 Olive St.
St. Louis, MO 63103
< http://www.nca-naw.com >

Send an LSASE for membership information and availability of publications. Publishes brochures such as *How to Open a Salon*.

Nails Industry Association (NIA)
2512 Artesia Blvd.
Redondo Beach, CA 90278
(800) 84-NAILS (846-2457)

Offers support and education materials and represents the nail care industry.

World International Nail & Beauty Association
1221 N. Lake View
Anaheim, CA 92807

"Professionals in nail and skin care industries."

Books
500 Beauty Solutions: Expert Advice on Hair and Nail Care—What to Buy and How to Use It! by Beth Barrick-Hickey. 1993 Sourcebooks, P.O. Box 372, Naperville, IL 60566.
Andre Talks Hair, by Andre Walker. 1997, Simon & Schuster, New York.
Milady's Art & Science of Nail Technology, 2nd ed. 1997, Milady Publishing Corporation, Albany, NY.

Internet Site
< http://www.beautytech.com >

Comprehensive site for hair dressers, nail technicians, cosmetologists, and salon owners. Many sources—links, suppliers, books, tapes, videos, and so forth.

Publications
Contact industry associations that provide their members with related publications.

Software

Harms Software, *Salon Solutions for Windows.* 113 Main St., Hackettstown, NJ 07840. < http://www.salon-solutions. com >

Start-Up Guides

Entrepreneur's Start-Up Guide, *Family Hair Salon.* (800) 421- 2300. $69 + shipping and handling.

National Business Library's Start-Up Guide, *Nail Salon.* (800) 947-7724. $39.95 + shipping and handling.

Additional Business Ideas

❖ Home-based nail salon. To keep up with the latest nail care methods, trends, products, and licensing, nail technicians recommend attending trade shows and seminars. See notices in *NAILS* magazine and information from the Nails Industry Association. Check state regulations regarding licenses for a nail salon.

❖ Facialist or cosmetician. You need a state license.

❖ Traveling hair dresser. Do hair for recovering hospital patients, nursing home residents, shut-ins, special needs persons residing in group homes; go to brides' homes or churches to do their hair on their wedding days; do special hair braiding in customers' homes.

❧29❧
PROFESSIONAL ORGANIZER

Carole J. Manna of Skokie, Illinois, has always been an organized person. Even when she was three years old, she would arrange her toys in order. She quit her teaching job and went to work in broadcasting in California. While there, she realized she had a talent for organizing, which she applied while working on different assignments and projects in her company's office.

Manna decided to go out on her own and for the past fourteen years, her business, Organization Unlimited, has served both residential and corporate clients in setting up library and filing systems in addition to general time and space management. She also produced a video on organizational tips that was sponsored by Stanley Hardware and Rubbermaid.

Manna says, "Eighty percent of clutter is not due to insufficient space but disorganization. I help people regain control of their surroundings once again, which gives them peace of mind in their otherwise hectic schedules."

Start-Up Costs and Financing Sources
+ $5,000 to $7,000.
+ Personal savings, small business loans, credit line on credit cards.

Pricing Guidelines
$25 to $125 an hour, depending on your clients (individuals, corporations); have at least a four-hour per day minimum. Options include setting up a one-time service or a regular, periodic service. More can usually be charged in urban areas than rural. Charge more according to your experience and expertise.

Marketing and Advertising Methods and Tips
+ Develop a marketing program and modify it to fit the customers you are targeting. You need different marketing methods for corporate clients and residential clients.
+ Send out press releases with follow-up phone calls when you are ready for business.
+ Volunteer to give speeches on organizing.
+ Offer one free hour of consultation to benefit auctions.
+ Advertise on local radio and cable television.
+ Put together a portfolio to give to prospective clients. Manna's portfolio includes copies of letters from satisfied customers, copies of articles written about her in newspapers and magazines, and a business card and brochure of her services. Also include before and after pictures.
+ Advertise in the business telephone directory.
+ Leave promotional materials at closet organizing stores.

Essential Equipment

Filing system (manual or computerized); business telephone line with answering machine, answering service, or voice mail; a dependable vehicle; space containers; organizing supplies based on customer needs.

Recommended Training, Experience, or Needed Skills

✤ Volunteer to organize others' residential rooms or offices to see if you like this business and if you have a talent for it.
✤ Read books on organizing.
✤ Have a talent for organizing and be able to visualize (almost like an artist) what needs to be done to a room or space, according to Manna.
✤ Have good people skills and be able to deal with individual styles and tastes.

Income Potential

$30,000 to $57,000.

Type of Business

One-fourth in-home for running the business and planning; three-fourths of the time out-of-the-home for organizing and giving talks.

Best Customers

Professionals with business or home offices; people who work full-time and are involved in community projects at the same time; people with extensive, private libraries; people who work from their homes, such as writers, researchers, college students, professional practitioners.

Helpful Tips

✤ Teach your clients how to stay organized through effective and easy-to-follow methods.
✤ Customize your knowledge to your customer's needs.
✤ Always put your customer's needs first. Be flexible.
✤ Market your business continually to keep the customers coming.

For More Information

Association
National Association of Professional Organizers
1033 La Pasada Dr. #220
Austin, TX 78752-3880
Send an LSASE for membership information.

Books
Clutter's Last Stand, by Don Aslett. 1994, Betterway Books, 1507
Dana Ave., Cincinnati, OH 45207. (800) 289-0963.
Conquering the Paper Pile-up: How to Conquer Clutter, by Stephanie
Culp. 1990, Betterway Books.
Don Aslett's Clutter-Free: Finally and Forever. 1995, Betterway
Books.
The Office Clutter: How to Get Out from Under It All, by Don Aslett.
1995, Betterway Books, Cincinnati, OH.

Start-Up Guide
Entrepreneur's Start-Up Guide, *Professional Organizer.* (800) 421-
2300. $69 + shipping and handling.

Additional Business Ideas
❖ Conduct research studies for specific businesses on how to
make the most efficient use of their space and time.
❖ Specialize in organizing closets.

❧ 30 ☙
RÉSUMÉ WRITING SERVICE

No matter what shape the economy is in, résumés are always
needed by job seekers. A well-written and presented résumé is
an important asset in helping a person land a job: It creates
a first impression that can make a difference between a person getting hired or not, especially if there are many applicants.

The goal of a résumé writing service is to promote your client's abilities, training, and work experience in concise language that emphasizes the strengths of your client and targets what an employer is looking for.

Résumé writers can offer to type a résumé, edit those written by clients, or interview a client and write it. The standard formats are chronological, functional, and a combination of both. Résumés run from one page to several depending on the employer who will be doing the screening. Styles and formats change somewhat, so it is important to keep up with the latest industry standards through trade publications and associations.

Start-Up Costs and Financing Sources
❖ $5,000 to $10,000 for a home office set up to receive customers.
❖ Personal savings, line of credit on credit cards. Start with only typing résumés and put the money you earn toward purchasing the furnishings and equipment you need.

Pricing Guidelines
$100 to $300+ for résumé packages: $95 for student, first-time job search; $140 to $200 for customers with several years of job history; for executives, up to $350+. Also check with industry standards (See Professional Association of Résumé Writers entry, later in this section).

Marketing and Advertising Methods and Tips
❖ Advertise in the business telephone directory.
❖ Encourage word-of-mouth referrals.
❖ Post flyers on college bulletin boards.
❖ Place classified ads in newspapers and on local cable television stations.
❖ Give résumé writing tips seminars or talks to companies or government agencies that are downsizing or laying off employees. Leave your brochures and business cards on completion of your talk.

Essential Equipment

Computer and word processing software (store your client's résumé on a computer disk and sell them the disk as part of the package); office and résumé software; laser printer for professional quality print-out; copier and inexpensive copy paper for rough drafts; standard (8 1/2" × 11") white bond paper (20 or 25 lb. weight) for final version; envelopes for mailing.

Recommended Training, Experience, or Needed Skills

+ Volunteer to write the résumés of friends, co-workers, and relatives.
+ Take courses and seminars, study examples of the different types of résumés.
+ Work for a résumé writing service.
+ Research the trade language for a particular position.
+ Write concisely, accurately, factually, creatively, fast, and in an easy-to-read style that accentuates your clients' attributes and strengths.

Income Potential

$35,000 to $150,000+.

Type of Business

An in-home business, unless you interview your clients in some other location.

Helpful Tips

+ Produce professional-looking (no spelling or grammatical errors or typos), creative résumés in a relatively short time, which will produce referrals from satisfied customers.
+ Do your market research to find out who are the best customers in your area.
+ Learn the professional standards in this business and practice them before you open for business.
+ Translate former military positions into civilian jobs and skills so that prospective employers can understand what duties or functions the client did in military service.
+ Know English grammar.

For More Information

Association

Professional Association of Résumé Writers
3637 Fourth St., N., Suite 330
St. Petersburg, FL 33704-1336
Offers courses and holds seminars.

Books and Publications

Cover Letters That Knock 'Em Dead, 3rd ed., by Martin Yate. 1997, Bob Adams, Inc., Holbrook, MA.

How to Start a Home-Based Résumé Business, 2nd ed., by Jan Melnick. 1997, Globe Pequot Press, Old Saybrook, CT.

Résumé Pro: The Professional's Guide, by Yana Parker. 1993, Ten Speed Press, P.O. Box 7123, Berkeley, CA 94707. This is a good manual on setting up and running a résumé writing business.

Résumés, Application Forms, Cover Letters, and Interviews. Consumer Information Catalog, Consumer Information Center, P.O. Box 100, Pueblo, CO 81002. $1.

Start Your Own Résumé Writing Business, by Jo Ann Padgett. 1996, Prentice-Hall Trade, Englewood Cliffs, NJ.

The Upstart Guide to Owning and Managing a Résumé Service, by Dan Ramsey. 1994, Upstart Publishing Co., Dover, NH.

Software

Ready-To-Go Résumés, by Yana Parker (Book & Disk). 1995, Ten Speed Press, Berkeley, CA.

Start-Up Guides

National Business Library's Start-Up Guide, *Résumé Writing*. (800) 947-7724. $39.95 + shipping and handling.

Additional Business Ideas

✤ Offer additional writing services: cover letters, brochures, reports, editing, proofreading, and so forth.

✤ Offer job counseling, referrals.

७७31 ᴼᴼᵌᵌ
SHOPPING SERVICE

You can either generalize or specialize your services to shop for items such as gifts (see "Gift Reminder Service," page 59), clothes, groceries, or other everyday goods that busy people do not have the time to get for themselves. Of course, you must like to shop, know the best stores (or the stores your customers prefer), recognize a good's quality, and know current prices.

Along with individual consumers, business executives are good potential customers. They need someone to shop for gifts for clients, to find caterers, and to contract or engage other services for them that they do not have time to search out.

Start-Up Costs and Financing Sources
❖ $3,000 to $4,000 average for advertising and home office supplies and equipment (not including a dependable vehicle).
❖ Personal savings, credit line on credit cards.

Pricing Guidelines
Average charges include 15 percent to 30 percent of the purchase price of the item(s). Factor in your time, expertise, overhead, and wear and tear on your vehicle: You might include a minimum charge, then, so many cents per mile and an additional charge per stop of $3 to $5+. Or you can simply charge by the hour.

Marketing and Advertising Methods and Tips
❖ Send out direct mailings and make presentations to the stores you know best. If you plan to shop regularly in certain stores, have them help advertise your business, refer you to their best customers, and even offer you discounts.
❖ Post flyers on community bulletin boards.
❖ Print up business cards.
❖ Offer seminars and talks to groups you know are your target customers.

✤ Place ads in publications and newspapers that your target customers read.

Essential Equipment
Publicity and marketing materials; business telephone line with answering machine, answering service, or voice mail; computer database of your customers, stores and their layouts, contact persons (retailers and wholesalers), and so forth; car phone and pager.

Recommended Training, Experience, or Needed Skills
✤ Have experience, knowledge, and expertise either from personal or work experience, or training and study in the area of shopping in which you plan to specialize.
✤ Be efficient, dependable, honest, and know what kind of purchases best please each of your customers.

Income Potential
Depending on your clientele, you can earn anywhere from $20,000 per year to a six-figure income if you have higher income and corporate clients.

Type of Business
One-fourth in-home, marketing and running the business; three-fourths out-of-the-home shopping, making presentations, and meeting with clients.

Best Customers
Professional working couples, business executives.

Helpful Tips
✤ Prove to your customers that they can trust you to get the best quality items for their money and that you are dependable.
✤ Know the clients you want to target, their tastes, and the stores they like best.
✤ Consult regularly with contact people at the stores you visit for the latest tips on sales, trends, and so forth.

❖ Be able to shop for more than one customer at once.

❖ Print up a checklist of each regular store's merchandise for your customer to fill in and give or fax to you or call in.

For More Information

Start-Up Guide
Entrepreneur's Start-Up Guide, *Personal Shopping Service*. (800) 421-2300. $69 + shipping and handling.

Additional Business Ideas

❖ Food delivery service. You contract with local sandwich, specialty restaurants, and so forth, to deliver food to customers. Resources follow:

Entrepreneur's Start-Up Guide, *Food Delivery Service*. (800) 421-2300. $69 + shipping and handling.

(See also "Food-Related Businesses" chapter, page 333.)

❖ Mystery shopping service (you evaluate employees' customer service for employers). Contact National Shopping Service Network LLC, 3190 E. Evans Ave., Denver, CO 80210. Write for investment costs.

❧ 32 ❧
TUTORING SERVICE

With cutbacks in funding for education, crowded classrooms, and rising numbers of students dropping out of school every year, tutoring and remedial education services are needed in almost every area of the country. People who need help with their educational skills include the following: college-bound students, adults wanting to brush up on their basic skills or to prepare to go or return to college, people in physical or drug rehabilitation programs, and new citizens wanting to get a better grasp of the English language.

Deborah Schadler and a friend, both former teachers who had stopped teaching to have children, decided to start their own tutoring business after receiving many requests to tutor their friends' children. Schadler and her friend consulted with a lawyer about starting their own tutoring business and then registered with local and state authorities. Next, they established accounts with educational publishers so they could get next-day delivery of materials when needed.

Schadler even had an addition built onto her home to accommodate her home business, and business grew with referrals from parents and schools. Schadler and her friend contacted local school teachers and invited them to come to Schadler's home to review their materials and credentials. "We work closely with a student's teacher and have a checklist for the teacher to fill out and then give periodic reports to keep the communication going between teacher, student, the parents, and us."

Today, Schadler's friend has returned to teaching, and Schadler has gone on to expand her business, called Teach Me Tutoring, to include preparing for the SATs, helping honor students apply for scholarships, consulting for home schooling lessons, and teaching homebound students who are recuperating from illnesses. Schadler also tutors youths at a drug rehabilitation center and goes to a local hospital every week to help head trauma victims with their cognitive skills.

Companies also ask her to review English and grammar skills with executives and to help Hispanic employees learn English. Often parents of students will request tutoring for themselves in subjects they feel they never really grasped while in school.

In order to accommodate her growing business, Schadler purchased a nearby older, three-story home, which she says involved adhering to a number of state and local regulations. She has had to hire teachers to tutor her growing list of students. "I hire teachers who really care about my students, and it gives us all the satisfaction of having the time to help those who really need it."

Start-Up Costs
$5,000 to $10,000 for home office supplies and equipment, educational materials, tables, desks, and lamps.

Pricing Guidelines
$35 to $50+ an hour; $600 to $900 for an SAT preparation course. If you hire tutors to work for you, you can take 30 percent of their pay.

Marketing and Advertising Methods and Tips
+ Encourage word-of-mouth referrals from parents of students.
+ Arrange for referrals from local schools.
+ Place classified ads in local newspapers about special summer reading camps, an SAT test preparation course (class and independent study with a computer and software program), and special study groups.
+ Call to offer your service to social service agencies that help prepare and train low-income adults for a job or career.

Essential Equipment
Educational materials and supplies for ages K–adult, computer(s) and educational software, copier, study areas, desks, tables, business line with answering machine or service, brochures, business cards.

Recommended Training, Experience, or Needed Skills
+ Have a background in education or counseling.
+ Work at a tutoring center or volunteer in local programs that teach adults to read to see if you like this type of business.
+ Check with your state's department of education for regulations and licensing requirements.
+ Enjoy helping others to learn. Have patience and a good sense of humor.

Income Potential
$20 to $25,000, part-time; $30,000 to $50,000, full-time; more if you have other tutors working for you.

Type of Business
At first, it may be both in-home and out-of-the-home because you (or your tutors) may tutor at the students' homes. Schadler added an addition to her home to serve many students at once.

Helpful Tips

❖ Work with the child's teacher and parents to establish good communication.

❖ Check licensing regulations.

❖ Expand your tutorial service to include all ages, in addition to community businesses and programs.

❖ Care about your students and accentuate the positive.

❖ Teach your students good study habits and good organizational skills to prevent them from falling behind in their subjects, Schadler advises.

Franchises, Distributorships, and Licenses

HOPE Career Centers (Helping Others Pursue Education Career Goals)

2735 S. Newton St.

Denver, CO 80236

Minimum capital investment is $699. Provides educational information and financial aid services for high school graduates, workers who have lost their jobs, people wishing to change careers, and businesses that offer partial reimbursement programs for their employees.

For More Information

Association

National Association of Tutoring

Jacksonville State University

Ramona Wood Bldg. #105

700 Pelham Rd. N.

Jacksonville, AL 36265-1402

Send an LSASE for membership information.

Books

Becoming an Effective Tutor, by Lynda Myers. 1990, Crisp Publications, Menlo Park, CA.

Educational Games, Books, Supplies. Send $2 for the catalog of *The Education Connection,* P.O. Box 1417, Tehachapi, CA 93581.

The Master Tutor: A Guidebook for More Effective Tutoring, by Ross
B. MacDonald. 1994, Cambridge Stratford, Ltd., England.
Tutoring for Pay: Earn While You Help Others Learn, by Betty O.
Carpenter. 1991, Charles C. Thomas Publisher, S. First St.,
Springfield, IL 62794-9265.

Additional Business Ideas

❖ Home schooling consultant. See *A Field Guide to Home
Schooling,* by Christine Moriarty Field. 1998, Fleming H.
Revell Co., Old Tappan, NJ. Or order *Home Education Press,*
P.O. Box 1587, Palmer, AR 99645. < http://hom-ed-press.
com > Send an LSASE for subscription information.

❖ Classes (not tutoring). Teach your expertise to others at adult
evening school classes, colleges, in seminars, and so forth.

Health Services

HOME HEALTH CARE

The National Association for Home Care reported that a total of 14,000 home health-care agencies were in existence in 1993. With the rising cost of medical care and lack of facilities to handle our health needs, home health-care businesses are in demand. This service coordinates and provides caring health services to people at home for a fraction of the price of hospitalization or institutional care, while enabling persons to stay in the comfort and familiarity of their own homes.

Some health-care agencies specialize in medical and follow-up care, others add other services in their businesses. At present, it is difficult and time consuming to get funding from government agencies for any of your services. Many home health-care agencies bypass the government altogether and are paid by the clients, their families, or their private insurance carriers.

This is a good business for those who enjoy helping people and their families and are skilled at coordinating and organizing services.

Start-Up Costs
* $7,000 to $200,000, depending on whether you want to start small and build up your client base and services later, or start large right away.

Pricing Guidelines

Check with trade associations for industry standards. Interview a number of agencies to see what services they offer and how much they charge, what contracts they have, how often they make visits, and so forth.

Marketing and Advertising Methods and Tips

* ✤ Place an ad in the business telephone directory.
* ✤ Send out direct mailings to developments or homes where older adults live.
* ✤ Make presentations to health-care professionals, networking groups, institutions, senior citizen centers, adult day care centers, child care centers (for sick-children care), social service agencies, nonprofit associations and groups serving mentally and physically challenged persons, hospice programs.
* ✤ Advertise on radio and local cable television stations.

Essential Equipment

Home office supplies and equipment: computer with billing, mailing, and management software; business telephone line with answering machine or service and fax; pagers for employees; comfortable furniture if you receive clients in your office for consultation; copier. Promotional materials: brochures, videos (if you can afford to send tapes to prospective clients).

Recommended Training, Experience, or Needed Skills

* ✤ Work for a home health-care agency or have experience and/or health-care training with older adults or nonambulatory persons.
* ✤ Be able to hire workers who care and are knowledgeable in their job.
* ✤ Have a caring and positive attitude.

Income Potential

$100,000 and up, depending on the number of clients and employees you have.

Type of Business
About one-half in-home, and one-half out-of-the-home when you start the business. Full-time in-home for running the business, scheduling, and so forth, if you hire employees to be the caregivers.

Best Customers
Older adults, families with special needs children or relatives, anyone who needs some assistance in his or her home.

Helpful Tips
+ Check on licensing requirements for your area and get approval to operate.
+ Find caring and capable employees to provide services as soon as you begin operating.
+ Research thoroughly all the aspects of this business before you open. Take the time to learn all you can.
+ Look for your "niche" or specialty—for example, providing respiratory medications, equipment, and related services to patients in their homes on a physician-referral basis.

For More Information

Associations
National Association for Home Care
228 7th St., SE
Washington, DC 20003

American Federation of Home Health Agencies, Inc.
1320 Fenwick Ln., Suite 100
Silver Spring, MD 20910

Publications
HomeCare, 23815 Stuart Ranch Rd., P.O. Box 8987, Malibu, CA 90265-8987. (310) 317-4522 or (800) 543-4116. One-year subscription costs $65 (U.S.), $75 (Canada). < http://www. homecaremag.com >

Start-Up Guide
How to Start and Manage a Nursing Home Care Business, by Jerre G.
Lewis and Leslie D. Renn. 1995, Lewis & Renn Associates,
10315 Harmony Dr., Interlochen, MI 49643. $14.95 + $3
postage and handling.

Additional Business Ideas
* Services other than health care: cleaning, shopping, running
  errands, preparing meals, assisting with personal needs,
  providing transportation, day companions, respite care
  while caregivers are away.
* Mentor Program. Contact the Mentor Program Corporate Offices, 313 Congress St., Boston, MA 02210. (617) 790-4800.
  Mentors are independently contracted service providers
  who offer twenty-four hour a day supervised care within a
  natural family environment. Populations served include children and adolescents with behavioral or medical needs, individuals with mental retardation/developmental disabilities,
  individuals with neurological impairment, and the elderly.
  Twenty-four hour per day back-up and support is available.
  This is not a franchise.
* Nursing. Order the Nurse's Guide to Starting a Small Business,
  by Betty Hafner from Pilot Books (see "Books Through the
  Mail" in Part III). $7.95. Also see the National Nurses in
  Business Association, in 101 Best Small Businesses for Women,
  by Priscilla Huff. 1997, Prima Publishing, Rocklin, CA.

∽34∾
MEDICAL CLAIMS PROCESSING

Entrepreneur's Small Business Development catalog listed this
service business as one of their Top 25 Businesses for 1994. The
health insurance industry is an ever-growing and bureaucratic
segment of the economy. Many people—or their health care
professionals—have to file medical claims accurately and
quickly. The owner of a medical claims processing business as-
sists clients in completing and filing claims or disputing those
claims rejected by Medicare or private insurance companies.

A knowledge of regulations and procedures for filing claims along with fast and accurate service will increase referrals from health-care professionals, institutions, and patients themselves.

Start-Up Costs and Financing Sources
* $7,000 to $15,000.
* Personal savings, loans from family or friends, small business loans, lines of credit on credit cards.

Pricing Guidelines
Average is $35 to $80 per hour.

Marketing and Advertising Methods and Tips
* Send direct mail to physicians' offices and medical insurance companies.
* Place ads in local newspapers.
* Attend hospital seminars.
* Encourage word-of-mouth referrals.
* Place an ad in the business telephone directory.
* Print business cards and brochures.

Essential Equipment
Updated computer and a tape back-up system to handle claims processing, billing, and spreadsheet software; fast modem for transmitting and receiving claims; photocopier; fax and separate telephone line with answering machine or answering service.

Recommended Training, Experience, or Needed Skills
* Take courses offered by medical insurance companies and local business schools.
* Work in a medical or insurance claims office.
* Be familiar with sending and receiving information over a modem.
* Be familiar with insurance and Medicare policies and procedures.
* Know medical terminology.

Income Potential
$30,000 to $80,000+ .

Type of Business
Primarily an in-home business.

Best Customers
Doctors and other medical professionals who need to file claims to insurance companies or Medicare; individuals who need to file claims or dispute rejections of claims.

Franchises, Distributorships, and Licenses

Licenses
National Claims Service
5000 Windplay Dr., Suite 1
El Dorado Hills, CA 95762
(800) 697-1569 ext. 512

"Home- or office-based electronic medical/dental claims processing. Complete electronic medical billing center package available. Fee includes 3-day training seminar, hotel, software, industry materials, complete marketing kit including printed and tested direct-mail pieces, telephone and direct-contact training/manuals. Call for more information."

For More Information

Books
Processing Medical Documents Using WordPerfect, by Robert P. Poland. 1995, Glencoe, Westerville, OH.
Start Health Service Businesses on Your PC and Make a Bundle, by Rick Benzel. 1997, McGraw-Hill, New York.

Software
The Automated Office, Inc., *Electronic Medical Claims Submissions Software*. 29 Bala Ave., Bala Cynwyd, PA 19004-3206.

Start-Up Guide
Entrepreneur's Start-Up Guide, *Medical Claims Processing* #1345.
(800) 421-2300. $59 plus shipping and handling.

∼35∼
PERSONAL FITNESS TRAINER

As each decade passes, more technological advances are taking over physical chores for us, and more Americans—both adults and children—lack physical fitness. Statistics show that even though we spend billions of dollars on fitness equipment and exercise tapes, the majority of us remain unfit. Many start an exercise routine or regimen, but few maintain it over time. Family and job demands make it difficult to find even a few minutes to exercise. Lack of motivation and boredom with a fitness plan also diminish the desire to exercise.

Being physically fit is more than just a fad. It increases both mental and physical health and helps prevent a myriad of health problems, including heart disease. A personal fitness trainer designs custom fitness plans for individuals in such a way to keep clients motivated to stay fit. By guiding clients through their workouts on a regular basis, the probability of their getting bored and abandoning exercise is reduced.

If you have the experience and expertise necessary, you can train athletes for the sports in which they compete. You can go to clients' homes, gyms, recreation facilities, or to businesses that have workout areas and equipment for their employees. You can plan individual training sessions or hold classes for groups, or go to schools and day care centers on a contract basis to give exercise classes. Market research will show you what age groups or people would be most likely to use your services.

Start-Up Costs
About $2,000 to $5,000.

Pricing Guidelines

Some trainers charge from $45 to $130 per session. Others charge $20 to $35 an hour for classes. One option is to charge $250 for a six-week, twice a week, program that teaches basic exercise principles and techniques (stretching, cross training, prevention of athletic injuries) plus instructs on the proper way to use fitness equipment.

Marketing and Advertising Methods and Tips

* Encourage personal referrals. Arrange for referrals from the gym you belong to. (You may even hold classes or training for members at the gym.)
* Give talks, presentations, and demonstrations to community groups, hospital wellness fairs, workers at businesses that promote employee fitness.
* Advertise on local cable television. See if you can have a daily or weekly exercise program.
* Give workshops for coaches.
* Write a weekly column on fitness for your local newspapers.
* Be fit yourself!
* Put together a portfolio of before and after photos of clients.
* Send direct mail to nursery schools, day care centers, and senior citizen centers for fun fitness sessions.

Essential Equipment

A video player, portable tape player, portable fitness equipment (small weights, jump ropes, etc.). Balls, hoops, and so forth, if teaching children. Exercise outfits; audio and video tapes; reference books on physical fitness, weight training, nutrition, games, and exercises; separate telephone line and answering machine or service; business cards; brochures; liability insurance, computer, skinfold calipers; memberships to professional organizations.

Recommended Training, Experience, or Needed Skills

* Know fitness and exercise basics and sensible nutrition either through your own sports experiences, training, and/or

education or from taking community college courses on exercise, nutrition, sports psychology, and athletic training.

✤ Have a basic knowledge of human or child psychology, which helps you understand what motivates people.

✤ Enjoy working and teaching the age group(s) with which you are working.

✤ Become certified by the American Council on Exercise or the American College of Sports Medicine (see addresses later in this section).

Income Potential
$20,000 to $80,000 a year, depending on your credentials, your clients, and what other classes or groups you teach or give talks to.

Type of Business
Most of your time is spent out-of-the-home for training and teaching. Some time is spent in-home, managing your business and planning workouts.

Best Customers
Professionals who do not have the time or motivation to exercise by themselves, schools or centers that do not have the funds to hire a full-time exercise specialist, athletes who want specialized training for a competition, individuals who just want to look and feel better or who are told by their physicians to get into shape.

Helpful Tips
✤ Be able to design fitness programs that your clients will continue to do on their own. Educate them on the correct way to exercise and how to plan their own exercise programs that are both challenging and fun.

✤ Have your clients' doctors' permission to start an exercise program if they have not been exercising previously.

✤ Check with your lawyer and insurance agent about liability coverage.

Franchises, Distributorships, and Licenses

Franchise
Fitness On Wheels
1185 S. Milwaukee
Denver, CO 80210
(303) 693-3626

For More Information

Associations
American College of Sports Medicine
Certification Dept.
P.O. Box 1440
Indianapolis, IN 46206-1440
(317) 637-9200; < http://www.acsm.org >
Offers certification programs.

American Council On Exercise (ACE)
5820 Oberlin Dr., Suite 102
San Diego, CA 92121-3787
(800) 825-3636; < http://www.acefitness.org >
Provides information on certification exams and study materials. Publishes a personal trainer manual.

Books and Publications
Exercise and Weight Control. Consumer Information Catalog Consumer Information Center, P.O. Box 100, Pueblo, CO 81002. < http://www.pueblogsa.gov > $.50.
Getting Fit Your Way, a twelve-week personal program. Consumer Information Catalog.
Walking for Exercise and Pleasure. Consumer Information Catalog. $1.
Personal Trainer Manual: The Resource for Fitness Instructors, 2nd ed., edited by Richard T. Cotton. 1996, American Council on Exercise, Reebok University Press, Boston, MA. Write for price.

Home Study Courses

Exercise Etc., Inc.
2101 N. Andrews Ave. #201
Fort Lauderdale, FL 33311
(800) 244-1344

Approved certification programs for fitness professionals and dieticians. Call or write for current listing of courses.

Internet Sites

< http://www.netsweat.com >
Fitness sources.

< http://www.afpafitness.com >
American Fitness Professionals & Associates.

Magazine

American Fitness. Aerobics and Fitness Association of America (address in the following paragraph). One year/6 issues costs $27.

Additional Business Ideas

Aerobics Instructor. Contact Aerobics and Fitness Association of America, 15250 Ventura Blvd., Suite 200, Sherman Oaks, CA 91403-3297. (800) 446-2322. < http://www.aerobics.com > They offer certification and home study courses.

See also Exercise, Etc. (address listed under "Home Study Courses").

໔໖36໔໖
PERSONAL WEIGHT MANAGEMENT CONSULTANT

Medical reports published in recent years have stated that an increasing number of adults—and children—are becoming overweight to the point of being dangerously unhealthy. In June 1998, the American Heart Association stated that obesity was not just "a contributing risk factor" for heart disease but a "major" risk factor, equating it with smoking, high cholesterol, high blood pressure, and a sedentary lifestyle.

The diet industry is making millions of dollars on people who are desperate to lose weight. People's obsessions about weight have led to anorexia, bulimia, and other eating disorders. Diet and health professionals advise that people follow sensible, individualized weight-loss plans that use a combination of exercise, nutritional education, and behavior modification methods. These plans encourage clients to change their bad habits, by creating a diet and exercise plan tailored to their needs that they can follow the rest of their lives.

As a personal weight management consultant, you can help overweight people shed those unwanted pounds. You may start small, using an extra room in your home to meet clients as individuals or in small groups, or you can visit your clients at their homes or work to guide and advise them on methods to lose weight.

Start-Up Costs and Financing Sources
* ❖ $3,000 to $18,000 for advertising and home office supplies. Costs will be more if you purchase a franchise.
* ❖ Personal savings, loan from family or friends.

Pricing Guidelines
Charge per session (call local weight-loss centers for the going rates). Some consultants charge $500 to $1,000 for a twelve-week program of periodic weigh-ins and counseling.

Marketing and Advertising Methods and Tips
* ❖ Attend health fair shows.
* ❖ Send direct mailings to hospitals, health-care professionals, and businesses that promote health and exercise programs for their employees.
* ❖ Give talks or write a column in the local newspaper on personal weight management, fitness, or nutrition.
* ❖ Advertise in the business telephone directory and on local radio and cable television stations.

❖ Print promotional materials: business cards, a portfolio of before and after pictures, and testimonials.

Essential Equipment
Business telephone line and answering machine or service; computer and diet software; contracts; home library of nutrition and fitness books; accurate weight scale; comfortable, attractive furniture if you meet clients in your home office.

Recommended Training, Experience, or Needed Skills
❖ Have an educational background or experience in the health, nutrition, or fitness professions.
❖ Work as a weight-loss counselor in a franchise program.
❖ Try one of the popular weight-loss programs if you need to lose weight to see what you liked or disliked about their methods.
❖ Take nutrition and fitness courses at local colleges.
❖ Take home study courses on weight loss and fitness.
❖ Check with state regulations about licensing requirements.
❖ Be an encouraging, positive person with good communication skills.

Income Potential
$15,000 to $75,000 and up, depending on your location and number of clients.

Type of Business
This depends on whether you meet your clients in-home or out-of-the-home.

Helpful Tips
❖ Rent a community room in a church or library to have your meetings if you don't have adequate space in your home.
❖ Check with your local and state regulatory agencies on certification and licensing requirements.
❖ Concentrate on advertising and promotions to get your first clients. If they successfully lose weight, their referrals will be your best source of new customers.

✤ Try to help each client achieve some success. Concentrate on personal attention to each client, giving more than they would get at the larger franchise operations.

✤ Be honest and set realistic and achievable goals for your client.

✤ Require that all clients have approval from a physician before they enroll in a diet or exercise program.

Franchises, Distributorships, and Licenses

See sources in "Franchises and Distributorships," page 44, in Part I.

For More Information

Association

American Dietetic Association
216 West Jackson Blvd., Suite 800
Chicago, IL 60606
(312) 899-1979; < http://www.eatright.org >

Books and Publications

Dietary Guidelines for Americans. Consumer Information Catalog, P.O. Box 100, Pueblo, CO 81002. 50 cents.

Exercise and Weight Control. Consumer Information Catalog (address above). < http://www.pueblo.gsa.gov > 50 cents.

Home Study Course

International Correspondence Schools
925 Oak St.
Scranton, PA 18515

Offers diploma in fitness and nutrition.

See also Exercise, Etc. in the previous section, "Personal Fitness Trainer."

Internet Site

< http://www.bodywise.net >
"Information to heighten your awareness of health information." Sponsored by Global Publishing, Inc., North Kingstown,

RI. Check with health care providers for professional diagnosis and treatment.

Other
American Council on Exercise (ACE) Consumer Fitness Hotline (800) 529-8227. Provides free health and fitness information. Distributes literature on health and fitness topics.

Software
Parsons Technology, *Diet Analyst*. (800) 223-6925.
Weight Commander™ *(for Windows)*, 220 E. Walton, Suite 4W, Chicago, IL 60611. < http://www.interaccess.com/weightcmdr/index.html/ >

Additional Business Ideas
+ Nutritional and exercise counseling for children and teenagers. Studies show that obesity rates are rising in children, just as they are in adults. Cooperate with physicians to find out what is appropriate for a certain age group and body type. Help instill good eating and exercise habits to improve self-esteem and overall health.
+ Sell nutritional products as an independent distributor: Herbalife®—for more information, write Kay LaRocca, 4003 Forest Dr., Aliquippa, PA 15001.

◅◈ 37 ◈▻

REFLEXOLOGIST

Reflexology works on the principle that reflexes in the feet, hands, head, and other parts of the body are related to each and every organ and part of the body. Foot and hand reflexology is the type most often practiced. Reflexology should not be confused with massage, although some reflexologists may add massages to their services.

According to the International Institute of Reflexology, the Original Ingham Method of Reflexology is used primarily for releasing tension. It helps normalize body functions but is not intended to replace conventional medical treatment.

Claudette Price, a single mother of two, studied a year with a certified reflexologist and then went on to receive her certification. She has been a reflexologist for twenty-four years. Today, she works 25 to 40 hours a week, offering appointments of 30 minutes for reflexology alone or 45 minutes of reflexology and massage, in which she is also certified. Price started her business in her home but moved to a former machine shed that she remodeled, which is only a short walk from her house. Working close to home gives Price the flexibility to adjust her schedule around her children's needs. She also likes having a separate area to meet clients.

Start-Up Costs and Financing Sources
+ $400 to $5,000. Costs are at the higher end if you plan to remodel a room into your office. Training by a reflexologist or enrolling in courses costs $1,000 to $3,000.
+ Personal finances. Buy more equipment as your client list grows.

Pricing Guidelines
$30 per 30 minute reflexology session; $45 for 45 minutes of reflexology and massage (charge as recommended by the profession).

Marketing and Advertising Methods and Tips
+ Advertise in the business telephone directory.
+ Place a sign in a place visible to drivers.
+ Encourage word-of-mouth referrals.

Essential Equipment
Lounge chair, business telephone line and answering machine or service, scheduling book, record-keeping system, books on reflexology.

Recommended Training, Experience, or Needed Skills
+ Generally, you do not have to be licensed. Claudette Price took weekly instructions from both a reflexologist and a masseuse for a year.

* It helps to get certified by a reflexology institute or through a seminar.
* You can take reflexology courses at some community colleges.

Income Potential
$700 and more a week. Price has clients she sees weekly, every other week, monthly, or schedules sessions as needed. If a client is sick or in the hospital, Price will go to them for a session.

Type of Business
Primarily an in-home business, except if you go to the client's home or to a hospital.

Best Customers
Men and women of all ages who need to reduce their stress and tension.

Helpful Tips
* Treat each client, each day, as if he or she were your first client. Do not get complacent or bored with your work.
* Treat your profession as a business and keep accurate records and report your earnings honestly.
* Charge enough for your services, but reasonably.
* Study, study, study! Keep up-to-date on the information and issues concerning reflexology.
* Offer off-hours appointments. Many clients can only come to you in the evening, after work.

For More Information
Association
   International Institute of Reflexology
   Ingham Publishing, Inc.
   5650 1st Ave., N.
   P.O. Box 12642
   St. Petersburg, FL 33733

   Send a long LSASE for information on seminars and how to contact a certified reflexologist near you.

Books

Body Reflexology: Healing at Your Fingertips, Rev. ed., by Mildred Carter and Tammy Weber. 1994, Parker Publishing, West Nyack, NY.

The Practitioner's Guide to Reflexology, by Barbara and Kevin Kunz. 1985, Prentice Hall, Englewood Cliffs, NJ.

Reflexology, by Anya Gore. 1993, Charles E. Tuttle, Inc., Boston, MA.

Reflexology: The Definitive Practicioner's Manual, by Beryl Crane. 1998, Element Publishing, Rockport, MA.

Stories the Feet Can Tell Through Relexology: Stories the Feet Have Told Through Reflexology—both by Eunice D. Ingham. 1984, Ingham Publishing, St. Petersburg, FL.

Additional Business Ideas

Massage therapy. Read about it in *More 101 Best Home-Based Businesses for Women,* by Priscilla Y. Huff. 1998, Prima Publishing, Rocklin CA.

Sewing Services

Sewing Resources

Sewing at home is a popular leisure-time activity. The American Home Sewing and Craft Association estimates that more than 21 million people sew from their homes. Many sew designer clothes from patterns at a fraction of the cost of buying them ready-made, as well as decorations, quilts, crafts, and countless other items.

Some have turned their sewing skills from hobbies into profitable businesses. In this chapter are presented a few of the many ways women are making money by sewing. These examples may give you the impetus to start your own business.

Here are some helpful resources to start you on your way:

Associations

American Home Sewing and Craft Association (HSA)
1350 Broadway, Suite 160
New York, NY 10018
(212) 302-2150; < http://www.sewing.org >

A must for all home sewers! Offers a sewing guild network, educational materials, a quarterly publication, and show directories. Holds a semi-annual convention.

Professional Association of Custom Clothiers (PACC)
P.O. Box 8071
Medford, OR 97504-0071
(541) 772-4119; < http://www.paccprofessionals.org >

An association for individuals who operate sewing-related, home-based businesses.

Sewing and Fine Needlework Guild
P.O. Box 1606
Knoxville, TN 37901

Publishes a quarterly magazine, *Sewing and Fine Needlework.* Offers a design competition, teacher accreditation and master's programs, and in-depth study courses. Holds an annual national convention.

The Embroiderer's Guild of America, Inc.
335 W. Broadway, Suite 100
Louisville, KY 40202
(502) 589-6956

Books and Publications

The Business of Sewing, by Barbara Wright Sykes. 1992, Collins Publications, 3233 Grand Ave., Chino Hills, CA 91709-1318.

The Crafts Supply Sourcebook, 5th ed., edited by Margaret Boyd. 1996, Betterway Books, 1507 Dana Ave., Cincinnati, OH 45207.

Creative Cash: How to Profit from Your Special Artistry, Creativity, Hand Skills, and Related Know-How, by Barbara Brabec. 1998, Prima Publishing, Rocklin, CA.

Creative Machine Arts series and the *Know Your Machine* series. Chilton Book Co., 1 Chilton Way, Radnor, PA 19089.

Sew to Success: How to Make Money in a Home-Based Sewing Business, by Kathleen Spike. 1995, Palmer Pletsch, Portland, OR.

How to Start Making Money with Your Sewing, by Karen L. Maslowski. 1997, Betterway Books, Cincinnati, OH.

Directory

Designer Source Listing, by Maryanne Burgess. 1998, Carikean Publishing, 846 W. Ainslie St., Suite R1, Chicago, IL 60640-0771. (773) 728-6118. Comprehensive listing of sources—beads, blanks, books, buttons, fabrics, millinery supplies, notions, patterns, videos, and more!

Internet Sites
< http://www.Kayewood.com >
Quilting, sewing, and craft links.

< http://www.palmerpletsch.com >
Palmer Pletsch sewing books.

< http://www.sewingconnection.com >
Shirley Adams, Sewing Connection, 786 Cheltenham Way, P.O. Box 688, Plainfield, IN 46168.

Magazines and Catalogs
Nancy's Notions, 333 Beichl Ave., P.O. Box 683, Beaver Dam, WI 53916-0683; (800) 833-0690. < http://www.nancysnotions. com >

Notions Catalogs, Clotilde, Inc., B3000, Louisiana, MO 63353-3000. (800) 772-2891. < http://www.clotilde.com > Also includes sewing books, videos, and patterns.

Publishers of Sewing Books & Publications, Chilton Books, 1 Chilton Way, Radnor, PA 19809.

Sew News, 1 Fashion Center, P.O. Box 56907, Boulder, CO 80322. < http://www.sewnews.com > $19.97 for 12 issues.

SewWHAT?, 180 Buckeye Access Rd., Swannanoa, NC 28778. (704) 686-3185. < http://www.professionaldrapery.com > Draperies and window coverings. Call or write for subscription information.

Threads Magazine, Taunton Press, 63 S. Main St., P.O. Box 5506, Newtown, CT 06470. (203) 426-8171.

Palmer Pletsch, P.O. Box 12046, Portland, OR 97212. < http:// www.palmerpletsch.com > Send an LSASE for a listing of books, videos, products, etc.

Success Publications, 3419 Dunham, Box 263, Warsaw, NY 14569. Write for a catalog of latest books, guides, and reports for the small business person.

Sewing Machines and Parts
Hayes Sewing Machine Co., Inc., 9 E. Baltimore Pike, Clifton Heights, PA 19018. (610) 259-5959; (800) 437-5959. < http: //www.trevhayes.com > Parts for old sewing machines:

Bernina, Singer, serger dealer; also out-of-print books. Call or write for information.

Correspondence Course
Just Sew Tuition Services, Woodstock Rd., London NW11 8ER, United Kingdom. < http://www.mistrko.uk/justsew/ >

Additional Business Ideas

❖ Children's cloth books. *How to Make Cloth Books for Children*, by Anne Pellowski. 1992, Chilton Books, Radnor, PA.

❖ Doll clothes. *The Doll's Dressmaker: The Complete Pattern Book*, by Venus A. Dodge. 1991, David & Charles, United Kingdom.

❖ Hats. Contact the *Wonderful World of Hats*, 897 Wade Rd., Siletz, OR 97380. They provide videos and hatmaking home study courses and publish the *Hat Lover's Dictionary*. See also *The Hat Book* by Juliet Bawden. 1994, Lark Books, Asheville, NC.

❖ Sewing classes. *Start a Sewing School*. Order from Success Publishing, 3419 Dunham, Box 263, Warsaw, NY 14569. Also see *The Business of Teaching Sewing*, by Marcy Miller and Pati Palmer. 1996, Palmer Pletsch, Portland, OR.

❖ Windsocks. *Let's Make Windsocks* and *Let's Make Seasonal Windsocks*, by Valerie J. Lund. 1992, Central Coast Creations, San Luis Obispo, CA; *Soft Kites & Windsocks*, by Jim Rowlands. 1993, St. Martin's Press, NY. (Also windsocks books in Clotilde catalog.)

❖ Banners. A Banner Year, 1125 Swiss Alpine Valley, Elizabeth, PA 1503. Send $1 for their catalog of how-to books and selection of banner patterns and banner-making supplies. (See also "Flags" entry next.)

❖ Flags. Contact Bob's Flags, 10726 Pineville Rd., Pineville, NC 28134. Catalog costs $1. Bob's Flags is one of the largest retailers of banners, flags, and windsocks. President Bob Burke also buys banners to carry in his catalog. Designs must be original and copyrighted to be considered. Send an LSASE for details.

❖ Window Shades. *The Shade Book*, by Judy Lindahl. 1996, Palmer Pletsch, Portland, OR.

⋘38⋙
ALTERATIONS

Today, many people don't have the time to make alterations to their favorite or used clothing. Tracy Reichman, a young mother, opened a consignment shop in the bottom of her home and soon found customers asking if she would make alterations to the used clothing they bought.

Reichman started out replacing zippers and sewing hems, but as news of her alterations spread, customers began requesting other kinds of modifications. To find out how much she should charge for various alterations, Reichman called cleaners and tailors and then came up with her own prices. With her alterations and home consignment shop, Reichman's business is steadily growing due to word-of-mouth referrals and her convenient location.

Start-Up Costs
$500 to $3,000, depending on whether you own a sewing machine.

Pricing Guidelines
$6 to $15 per garment, depending on the complexity of the job. You can add a 20 percent to 30 percent charge for a rush job.

Marketing and Advertising Methods and Tips
❖ Encourage word-of-mouth referrals.
❖ Place seasonal sales ads in newspapers.
❖ Put up flyers on community bulletin boards.
❖ Place classified ads in weekly shopper papers.
❖ Send direct mailings to cleaners and clothing stores that do not offer alterations.

Essential Equipment
Heavy-duty sewing machine (contact sewing machine repairmen for used commercial machines for sale), sewing notions and threads, iron and ironing board, sewing reference books.

Recommended Training, Experience, or Needed Skills

❖ Take sewing courses on tailoring and alterations (contact your local sewing center or fabric outlet).

❖ Work in a clothing alteration or tailor shop.

❖ Volunteer to do alterations or mending for your family, friends, or a thrift shop.

❖ Have professional-quality alteration skills.

Income Potential

$9,000 to $30,000 and more a year, depending on your location and number of customers.

Type of Business

An in-home business.

Best Customers

Single men, working women with expensive wardrobes.

Helpful Tips

❖ Be confident when you talk with your customers so that they, in turn, will have the confidence in you to do their alterations. Be honest if you feel you do not have the expertise to do the modification they ask.

❖ Do fast and expert work.

❖ Have a home-based location convenient to other shopping areas, so customers can drop off their clothing to be altered.

For More Information

(See also "Sewing Resources," pages 166–169.)

Association

Professional Association of Custom Clothiers (PACC)
P.O. Box 8071
Medford, OR 97504-001
(541) 772-4119; < http://www.paccprofessionals.org >

A professional organization for individuals who operate sewing-related home-based businesses.

Books
Easy, Easier, Easiest Tailoring, by Pati Palmer and Susan Pletsch. 1983, Palmer Pletsch, Porland, OR.
Fabulous Fit, by Judith Rasbard. 1998, Fairchild Books, New York.

Videos
The Best of Tailoring. Order from Nancy's Notions (800) 833-0690.
Tailoring Videos by Mary A. Roehr. Custom Tailoring, 500 Saddlerock Circle, Sedona, AZ 86336. Send LSASE for prices and video information.

Additional Business Ideas
Start a clothing (and used toy) consignment shop in your home. Order *The Consignment Workbook*, by Sue Harris. Scandia International, 133 Olney Rd., Petersburgh, NY 12138. < http:// www. consignment.org> Prepayment of $23.00 is respectfully requested. Other resources follow.

Start-Up Guides
Entrepreneur's Start-Up Guide, *Consignment/Resale Clothing Store*. (800) 421-2300. $69 + shipping and handling.
National Business Library's Start-Up Guide, *Consignment Shop*. (800) 947-7724. $39.95 + shipping and handling.

◦◦39◦◦
COSTUMES

Costumes are worn at dances, ceremonies, parades, and to celebrate holidays and special events. Many school, community, and college theater groups need costumes for their plays and musicals, but do not have the funds to purchase costumes outright.

If you are skilled in sewing and talented in design, you may want to open your own costume sales, consulting, and rental business. You may start out of your garage or basement (with a separate outside entrance and zoning approval) and have customers come to you, or you can go to them.

Start-Up Costs and Financing Sources
+ $5,000 to $27,000.
+ Personal savings, credit at fabric stores, lines of credit on credit cards, small business loans.

Pricing Guidelines
$20 to $85+ a day for rental. Period costumes can sell for $1,500 or more, depending on the complexity of design, fabric used, sewing details, and so forth. A consultant for a large cosmopolitan theater group may charge $75 to $150 per hour.

Marketing and Advertising Methods and Tips
+ Send direct mailings to schools, theater and musical groups, and churches.
+ Advertise in the business telephone directory.
+ Participate in community parades.
+ Encourage word-of-mouth referral from satisfied customers.
+ Write a special seasonal column in your local newspaper on costume-making tips for mothers.
+ Print promotional materials: business cards, brochures.
+ Purchase ads on local radio and cable television stations.
+ Hold community workshops or courses (at schools or fabric centers) on how to make children's costumes.

Essential Equipment
Heavy-duty sewing machine, assorted fabrics, costume boxes, storage space, changing space, sewing forms and notions, business telephone line and answering machine or service, record and billing system (manual or software), computer with design capabilities if you design costumes, personal library of period and present-day costume books.

Recommended Training, Experience, or Needed Skills
+ Take sewing classes. Gain work experience in garment sewing.
+ Work or volunteer in creating and constructing costumes for local theater groups or plays.
+ Have a talent for designing and enjoy creative challenges.

❖ Know the history of different eras of period clothing.
❖ Having background, experience, or training in theater is a plus.

Income Potential
$35,000 to $50,000 for a small business; up to $250,000 for a large costume rental business in an urban area.

Type of Business
An in-home business except for fittings or consulting.

Best Customers
Theater groups, schools or college drama clubs or societies, film makers, individuals who need costumes for a holiday or special event, civic groups sponsoring special events, parades, historical groups, museums, entertainers (clowns, magicians, mascots, etc.), large church groups who hold religious pageants.

Helpful Tips
❖ Learn how to be creative in your marketing; appear at special community functions—fairs, parades, and holiday celebrations.
❖ Be willing to design and create a costume to the customer's specifications even if you have never made one before.
❖ Be able to bring in business during slow periods and keep up with business in hectic periods.

For More Information

Association
The United States Institute for Theater Technology, Inc.
American Association of Design and Production
Professionals in the Performing Arts
443 Ridings Rd.
Syracuse, NY 13206
(315) 463-6463

Twenty percent of the members are costumers. Offers projects and resources. Holds conventions and conferences.

Books

Child's Play: Quick and Easy Costumes, by Leslie Hamilton. 1995, Crown Publishing Group, New York.

The Fantastic Costume Book: 40 Complete Patterns to Amaze and Amuse, by Michelle Lipson and Friends. 1993, Sterling Publishing, Inc., New York.

The Fantastic Costume Book, by Michelle Lipson and Friends. 1992, Sterling Publishing.

The Illustrated Encyclopedia of Costume and Fashion, by J. Cassin-Scott and Run Greene, 1994, Sterling Publishing.

Magazine

Costume!, published by Festivities Publications, Inc., 815 Haines St., Jacksonville, FL 32206-6050.

Supplies and Patterns

Amazon Drygoods
2218 East 11th St.
Davenport, IA 52803

Catalog contains more than 1,000 patterns for men, women, and children. Medieval through 1950s clothing, with an emphasis on the Victorian era. $5.

Alter Years
3749 E. Colorado Blvd.
Pasadena, CA 91107
(626) 585-2994

Patterns covering the years 1100 through 1949. $5 for catalog; $8 priority mail.

Additional Business Ideas

❖ Specialize in costumes for theater, television, or film.
❖ Specialize in making mascots for high schools, colleges, professional sports teams, stores, and other businesses.
❖ Specialize in costumes for children for holidays, dance recitals, children's theater groups, and church pageants.
❖ Specialize in different countries' costumes for celebrations of their cultural-awareness days, museums, and so forth.

❖ Make costumes for pets and sell wholesale to pet stores and distributors.
❖ Make costumes for historic dolls.
❖ Make costumes and/or puppets for puppet theaters.

❧ 40 ❧
CURTAINS, DRAPERIES, AND SHADES

Sewing custom curtains, draperies, and shades is a profitable home-based business for many women. Some began by using their sewing skills to decorate their own homes and then expanded to friends, relatives, and eventually customers' window treatments. Others have worked in curtain and drapery workrooms and discovered they could make more money in their own businesses.

If you think a window treatment business is one you would like, try sewing for yourself, your family, or friends. Check with your local sewing center to see if they offer special classes on making curtains, draperies, and shades. Start off your business part-time, before you invest in expensive equipment.

Start-Up Costs
$2,000 if you own a sewing machine.

Pricing Guidelines
$300 to $1,000+ per window treatment, depending on the style, size, and material chosen. Consult trade publications for pricing guidelines.

Marketing and Advertising Methods and Tips
❖ Place classified ads in local publications.
❖ Encourage word-of-mouth referrals.
❖ Contact local interior decorators for referrals.
❖ Put together a portfolio of windows you have done.
❖ Leave business cards and flyers at sewing centers, on community bulletin boards, and in drapery hardware stores.
❖ Send direct mailings to owners in new housing developments.

Essential Equipment

Professional sewing machine(s), workspace and table, sewing notions and supplies, samples of materials.

Recommended Training, Experience, or Needed Skills

+ Take sewing courses, workshops, attend seminars.
+ Sew your own curtains, draperies, and shades.
+ Work for a drapery company.

Income Potential

$25,000 to $45,000 a year.

Type of Business

In-home for sewing; out-of-the-home to meet with customers.

Best Customers

Owners of newly built homes, people remodeling their homes, middle- to-upper-income couples.

Helpful Tips

+ Charge a fee to give an in-home estimate, which is refundable and can be used toward the purchase of curtains, draperies, or shades.
+ Keep up-to-date with others in the industry.

For More Information

Books

Complete Book of Window Treatments and Curtains, by Carol Parks. 1993, Sterling Publishing Co., Inc., New York.

Complete Step-by-Step Guide to Home Sewing, by Jeanne Argent. 1990, Chilton Books, Radnor, PA.

Curtains, Draperies, and Shades, 2nd ed., by *Sunset and Southern Living* Editors. 1993, Menlo Park, CA.

Curtains and Shades, by Melanie Paine. 1997, Reader's Digest Assn., Inc., Pleasantville, NY.

Make It with Style! Draperies & Swags, by Donna Lang. 1997, Clarkson-Potter, New York.

The Shade Book, by Judy Lindahl. 1996, Palmer Pletsch, Portland, OR.

Publication
International Newsletter for Professional Drapery Workrooms. Order from *SewWHAT?,* 180 Buckeye Access Rd., Swannanoa, NC 28778. (704) 686-3185. < http://www.professionaldrapery. com > Draperies and window coverings. Call or write for subscription information.

～41～
CUSTOM APPAREL

If you are talented with a needle and thread, then consider the three examples of custom apparel businesses that follow: wedding gowns, accessories, and headpieces; christening gowns and prom gowns; and clothing for people with special needs.

Start-Up Costs and Financing Sources
❖ Wedding gowns and accessories: $5,000 to $10,000.
❖ Christening gowns and prom gowns: $3,000.
❖ Clothing for those with special needs: $4,000 to $6,000, which includes advertising and protecting designs.
❖ Financing sources for all three: personal loans, lines of credit on cards, credit at fabric stores, small business loans.

Pricing Guidelines

Wedding Gowns
Charge according to the complexity and detail of the job and the fabrics used. You can charge more for an original design as opposed to one with a pattern. Accessories: Compare prices at bridal shows and see how your work and designs compare. (Make sure the designs are your originals and not a copyrighted design.) Bridal veils and headpieces: $40+ and more.

Christening Gowns
$65 to $90 for a gown from a pattern, $175+ for an original design.

Prom Gowns
$110 and up.

Special Needs Clothing
Clients include nursing mothers, people in wheelchairs, women with mastectomies.

Per hour price = cost of materials + time + overhead percentage

See "Sewing Resources" for sewing business books that give recommendations on pricing for custom sewing. Network with other clothing professionals in your area about pricing.

Marketing and Advertising Methods and Tips

Wedding Gowns, Accessories, Headpieces
✤ Encourage word-of-mouth referrals.
✤ Place ads in local newspapers' bridal sections or supplements.
✤ Attend bridals shows and craft shows at malls (for accessories).
✤ Leave your business cards and brochures at fabric shops.

Christening Gowns, Prom Gowns
✤ Encourage word-of-mouth referrals.
✤ Place ads in local newspapers.
✤ Post flyers or business cards on community and hospital bulletin boards.
✤ Place ads in school programs.
✤ Attend teen fashion shows.

Special Needs Clothing
✤ Send direct mailing to rehabilitation centers and support groups.
✤ Rent a booth at health fairs.
✤ Advertise in seniors' publications and nonprofit group newsletters.
✤ Send out press releases to newspapers and magazines.
✤ Attend fashion shows.

Essential Equipment (for All Three)

Industrial sewing machine, overlock machine to finish seams, serger, cutting table, sewing notions, a mannequin, storage for patterns, fabric, source of fine fabrics, design and reference sewing books.

Recommended Training, Experience, or Needed Skills

Wedding Gowns
- ✤ Apprentice at a bridal shop.
- ✤ Work in a fabric shop that has a wedding department to learn about fabrics and laces.
- ✤ Take workshops and courses.

Christening and Prom Gowns
- ✤ Read books on sewing for infants and children, take courses at fabric centers.
- ✤ Take dressmaking courses.

Special Needs Clothing
- ✤ Take courses on design and sewing at community colleges, vo-tech schools, or other schools of design.

Income Potential

Wedding Gowns
Hundreds to thousands of dollars—network with other dressmakers and members of the Professional Association of Custom Clothiers (address listed later in this section).

Christening and Prom Gowns
$80 to $100+ per christening gown. For prom gowns, check with retailers for average prices and network with other dressmakers.

Special Needs Clothing
$50 to $75 per garment, depending on time spent and materials used.

Type of Business
An in-home business except if you go to a person's home for fittings.

Best Customers
Newly engaged women; new parents and grandparents; high school and college students; people with permanent or temporary physical disabilities in nursing homes, group homes, or institutions.

Helpful Tips
❖ For sewing wedding gowns, be able to work under pressure and to understand what the bride and/or mother-of-the-bride wants.

❖ With prom gowns, you have to be able to please both the young woman and the person who is buying it as far as taste, expense, and so forth. Keep up-to-date on the latest fashions.

❖ With christening gowns, embroider your name and date on the gown.

❖ With special needs clothing, talk with people who have disabilities to find out what kind of modifications to clothing would best suit them. Make the clothing comfortable, washable, and easy to put on and take off.

For More Information
Send an LSASE for information and industry price guidelines.

Associations
Professional Association of Custom Clothiers (PACC)
P.O. Box 8071
Medford, OR 97504-001
(541) 772-4119; < http://www.paccprofessionals.org >

An association for individuals who operate sewing-related, home-based businesses.

American Cancer Society Information Center
(800) ACS-2345

Provides special patterns for mastectomy patients.

Books

Bridal Couture: Fine Sewing Techniques for Wedding Gowns and Evening Wear, by Susan Khalye. 1997, Krause Publications, Iola, WI.

Bridal, Prom, and Evening Dresses, by Cowles Creative Publishers, 1994, Minnetonka, MN.

Designer Techniques: Couture Tips for Home Sewing, by Kenneth D. King. 1998, Sterling Publications, New York.

Sew a Beautiful Wedding, by Gail Brown and Karen Dillon. 1995, Palmer Pletsch, Portland, OR.

Wedding Bells: A Guide to Designing Your Own Wedding Gown. Order from the American Home Sewing and Craft Association (see "Associations" in "Sewing Resources," page 166).

Home Study Courses and Schools

Couture Sewing School
4600 Breidenbaugh Lane
Glenarm, MD 21057
(410) 592-5711

Offers week-long instruction in the fine art of couture bridal sewing, which is taught by Susan Khalje (nationally known teacher, author, and custom dressmaker).

Lifetime Career Schools
101 Harrison St.
Archbald, PA 18403

Offers dressmaking courses.

Supplies

Bridals International
45 Albany St.
Cazenovia, NY 13035

Bridal fabrics and laces; $9.50 for catalog.

Brides 'n Babes
P.O. Box 2189
Manassas, VA 22110

Publishes a directory of bridal suppliers, bridal gown accessories, and patterns, as well as the book *Learn the Bridal Business.*

Additional Business Ideas

✤ Children's custom clothing. Design your own line. Or specialize in baby clothes. See "Patterns" in the *Designer Source Listing* (listed in Sewing Resources). Also *Singer Children's Clothes, Toys, & Gifts, Step-by-Step,* by Singer Sewing Co. 1995, Cowles Creative Publishing, Minnetonka, MN.

✤ Sportswear. Design and sew your own styles to sell at craft shows and sports fairs.

✤ Embroidery (by hand or machine). Start with monogramming and progress to other designs. Can purchase an embroidery attachment for your sewing machine or purchase an embroidery machine, which can cost from $2,499 to $7,000. Contact Sew & Serg Co., 9789 Florida Blvd., Baton Rouge, LA 70815; (504) 923-1285 for information.

Also contact the Embroiderers' Guild of America, Inc., 335 W. Broadway, Suite 100, Louisville, KY 40202. They publish Needle Arts, offer correspondence courses, and hold seminars.

The following books are good resources for embroidery information:

Celebrating the Stitch: An Embroiderer's Workshop of Design Techniques and Strategies. Sterling Publishing, New York.

Contemporary Machine Embroidery, by Deborah Gonet. 1996, Chilton Book Co., 1 Chilton Way, Radnor, PA 19809.

Reader's Digest Complete Book of Embroidery, by Melinda Coss. 1996, Putnam, New York.

❧ 42 ❧
CUSTOM CUSHIONS AND PILLOWS

In this business, you make custom cushions of all sizes and shapes for the following: dining room chairs, Adirondack chairs, boat seats, window seats, patio furniture, rocking chairs, and benches, to name a few. You can also make pillows to match your client's furniture.

Karen began her business, Karen's Cushions, by selling her pillows at craft shows and flea markets. She had simple business cards printed up, which attracted the attention of an interior decorator. The decorator asked Karen to make samples, which the decorator's customers loved.

She worked for several decorators and perfected her sewing skills so that her pillows did not have a homemade look. Karen says, "I was frustrated that I never had the opportunity to talk directly to the decorators' customers, so I decided to advertise for customers myself." Her husband, a draftsman, helped her work out a price guide, and she began to attract customers.

Today she has a steady business and makes one-of-a-kind pillows sewn from antique materials, beyond-repair old garments, and quilts. These pillows sell for as much as $100+ apiece.

Start-Up Costs and Financing Sources
❖ $2,000 to $5,000, which includes the cost of a good industrial sewing machine.
❖ Personal savings, small business loans.

Pricing Guidelines
Depends on the fabric used, the complexity of the designs, and so forth. A handmade quilted pillow can start at $50; pillows made from antique materials can sell for $100 or more apiece and up. For custom-made cushions, factor in the time and materials used in order to come up with a price.

Marketing and Advertising Methods and Tips
❖ Rent a booth at craft shows and flea markets.
❖ Show samples of your work to interior decorators.
❖ Leave your business card and brochures at antique shops and furniture stores.
❖ Place ads in your local newspaper and in home or craft magazines.
❖ Attend home decorating shows and gift shows.

Essential Equipment

Industrial sewing machines—a straight sewer and serger, a button machine, electric knife for cutting foam, work table, contracts for customers to sign, estimate sheets, filing system, fax machine, transportation.

Recommended Training, Experience, or Needed Skills

❖ Enroll in sewing courses at local schools, fabric centers.
❖ Make cushions and pillows for your own home or for friends' and relatives' homes.
❖ Work for an interior decorator.
❖ You need sewing skills to produce professional-quality pillows and cushions.
❖ You also need product presentation skills.

Income Potential

$20,000 to $30,000+ or more a year; $400 or more for pillows made with antique materials.

Type of Business

One-third out-of-the-home, visiting customers' homes for measuring and buying materials; two-thirds in-home for sewing.

Best Customers

Homeowners, decorators, owners of furniture shops and antique shops.

Helpful Tips

❖ Start by buying a used sewing machine and put your first profits into buying a new one.
❖ Have the self-confidence and patience to learn new techniques and skills as your business requires them.
❖ Aim at working with interior decorators and clientele who are looking for unique fabrics.

For More Information

Book

(Also look in Clotilde and Nancy's Notions catalogs.)

Cushions & Covers: A Step-by-Step Guide to Creative Pillow Covers, Tablecloths & Seat Coverings, by Gina Moore. 1997, Reader's Digest, Inc., New York.

Additional Business Ideas

❖ Antique pillows. Hunt antique shops, sales, flea markets, and auctions for vintage materials and patterns. Sell to interior decorators, antique shops, furniture stores. Or offer to make pillows from people's old fabrics (old quilts, needlepoints, etc.).

❖ Quilted and decorative frames made from fabric.

❖ Custom pillows from customers' finished needlework.

❖ Custom canvas covers for outdoor furniture, boats, outdoor vehicles, and so forth.

❖ Fabric photo pillows. Turn photos into pillows with a photocopy-transfer process that does not harm photos. See *Fabric Photos,* by Majorie Croner. 1990, Interweave Press, Loveland, CO.

❧43❧
PATTERNS

In this business, you design and sell sewing patterns to fabric shops and quilting supply stores and to individual customers through the mail. Designs may be for stuffed toys, children's play items, dolls, clothes and accessories, jewelry and lingerie holders, or decorative items for the home.

Check sewing magazines and sewing industry shows to see what kinds of patterns are available and note current trends and styles.

Start-Up Costs and Financing Sources

❖ $400 to $4,000 for supplies, printing, and advertising.

❖ Personal savings, lines of credit on your credit cards, loans from family and friends.

Pricing Guidelines

$8 and up per pattern, depending on complexity of design.

Marketing and Advertising Methods and Tips
❖ Place ads in sewing, doll, quilting, children's, and home decorating magazines.
❖ Attend trade shows.
❖ Have friends and family wear clothing made from your patterns.
❖ Show your finished products to shops.
❖ Sell patterns wholesale through sales representatives.
❖ Give courses and workshops on how to make an item using your pattern and sell additional patterns.

Essential Equipment
Sewing machine, notions, design and work table, computer with design capabilities, telephone, fax, answering machine, copier.

Recommended Training, Experience, or Needed Skills
❖ Take design and pattern-making courses at local technical schools or colleges.
❖ Buy and study patterns to gauge their quality and to see what is offered.
❖ Know your product, how to design it, and how to write easy-to-follow instructions.

Income Potential
$6,000 to $50,000, depending on your range of advertising and the number of stores that carry your patterns.

Type of Business
In-home, except for traveling to shows and shops to increase sales.

Best Customers
People who sew as a hobby.

Helpful Tips
❖ Teach courses using your patterns. This will help you better understand what people need to successfully put together your product.

❖ Develop a line of unique patterns that will appeal to loyal and repeat customers.

❖ Offer your customers the most for their money: an assortment of designs in one pattern package; clear, typeset instructions.

❖ Find out who your best customers are and then focus your advertising on them.

For More Information

Book
How to Make Sewing Patterns, by Donald McCunn. 1997, Design Enterprises, San Francisco, CA.

Pattern-Making Supplies
A.C.S., 447 West 36 St., New York, NY 10018. $3 for catalog.

❧ 44 ☙
UPHOLSTERY

A good upholsterer is always in demand because many people have a favorite piece of furniture they do not want to throw away. Your customers can include individuals as well as small businesses.

Start-Up Costs
$2,500 to $4,000 if you start out with a good, used commercial sewing machine and have a vehicle to transport furniture.

Pricing Guidelines
Call other upholstery businesses to find out what they charge per project. Have customers sign a written estimate.

Marketing and Advertising Methods and Tips
❖ Advertise in newspapers and on cable television.
❖ Place signs on your vehicle, your lawn, or house where permitted by zoning laws.
❖ Encourage word-of-mouth referrals.

❖ Place an ad in the business telephone directory.
❖ Buy ads in coupon books.

Essential Equipment
Industrial sewing machine (contact sewing machine repairmen for good, used machines), air compressor, upholstery staple guns, hand tools, fabrics, vehicle for furniture pick-ups.

Recommended Training, Experience, or Needed Skills
❖ Enroll in upholstery courses at technical schools or through home study.
❖ Work in an upholstery shop.
❖ Practice on used furniture of your own, your friends, or at thrift shops.

Income Potential
$700 to $800 a week; $30,000 to $40,000 a year.

Type of Business
Primarily an in-home business, except for when you go to customers' homes or businesses for estimates and pick-up.

Best Customers
Homeowners, professional offices with waiting rooms, hair salons, motels.

Helpful Tips
❖ Check with local zoning laws about a home-based operation.
❖ Check with state agencies on requirements for stuffing used in furniture.
❖ Develop a good relationship with your upholstery suppliers.

For More Information

Books
Upholstery: A Complete Course, by David James. 1993, Sterling Publishing, 387 Park Ave. S., New York, NY 10016.
Upholstery Basics, by Cowles Creative Publishing. 1997, Minnetonka, MN.

Home Study Course

Foley-Belsaw Co.,
6301 Equitable Rd.
Kansas City, MO 64120-9957.

Offers an upholstery course.

Videos

Videos by Quality Upholstery. 75 Diggs Blvd., Warner Robbins, GA 31093. Do it yourself video for $34.95 + $3.95 shipping and handling.

Upholstery training videos by Verano Upholstery. Box 128PH, El Verano, CA 95433. (707) 996-1059. Call for a free brochure. $49.95 for each video plus $4 shipping each. Also, instruction book for $12.95.

Pet Services

PET GROOMING

Pet grooming is a service needed by people who want their pets to look their best, yet do not have the time or expertise to regularly bathe, clip, and trim their pets. Grooming and care requires physical stamina, skill, and a love of animals.

One woman, Pam, a mother and substitute teacher, started out by clipping her own poodles to save money. She then moved on to the pets of friends and family. When she began to make more money grooming pets than by substitute teaching, Pam decided to turn her garage into a grooming shop and started a full-time business.

Today, she has a thriving dog grooming business and sells supplies and various kinds of pet foods. Many pet groomers sell supplies and/or also offer boarding services for dogs, cats, and even exotic animals.

Start-Up Costs and Financing Sources
✤ $16,000 to $20,000 to set up your shop, workspace, sinks, or tubs; construct runs and cages; and purchase supplies.
✤ Small business loan, home equity loan.

Pricing Guidelines
$30 to $50+ per grooming visit. Charges vary according to breed and the animal's temperament. $9.50 to $11.50 per day to board dogs overnight; $9 for day care. (Charges depend on the

191

size of the dog.) $8.50 per day to board cats overnight; $7.50 for day care. Charges for exotic animals depend on the type and care needed for the animal.

Marketing and Advertising Methods and Tips
- ✤ Encourage word-of-mouth referrals. The best referrals come from the best quality work and care of your customers' pets.
- ✤ Place an ad in the business telephone directory.
- ✤ Advertise in local newspapers and pet publications.
- ✤ Post flyers on community bulletin boards, in veterinarians' offices that do not offer boarding or grooming, and at animal feed and supply centers.

Essential Equipment
Stainless steel crates and cages; grooming table(s) and related equipment; bathing facilities; scheduling, filing, and billing methods (manual or software); bowls, brushes, food, and leashes; business telephone line and answering machine.

Recommended Training, Experience, or Needed Skills
- ✤ Enroll in grooming classes.
- ✤ Work with a professional groomer.
- ✤ Groom friends' and relatives' pets.
- ✤ Study professional manuals.
- ✤ Attend dog and cat shows to see the latest grooming equipment.
- ✤ Subscribe to trade and/or breed publications.

Income Potential
$25,000 to $40,000 for a sole owner. $60,000 and up with an assistant.

Type of Business
An in-home business if you have a shop and/or kennels on your property. Check with zoning officials and neighbors before you open for business. With boarding, it helps to be in a more isolated location because of possible noise complaints.

Best Customers

Pet owners of animal breeds with coats that need regular grooming or clipping, owners of exotic pets.

Helpful Tips

✤ Keep your facilities spotlessly clean and odor-free.
✤ Have a veterinarian on call for any emergencies. Very important to know what shots animals must have before they can be boarded.
✤ Check with your insurance agent and lawyer about liability coverage.
✤ Treat each pet as if it were your own and give it the best possible care.

For More Information

Associations

National Dog Groomers Association of America
Box 101
Clark, PA 16116
(412) 962-2711

Newsletter, seminars, workshops, and certifications; send an LSASE for information and a list of grooming schools.

American Pet Boarding Association
P.O. Box 931
Wheeling, IL 60096

Send an LSASE for membership information.

Books

The All Breed Dog Grooming Guide, Rev. ed., by Sam Kohl. 1995, AARONCO, New York, NY.
The Art and Business of Grooming, by Dorothy Walis. 1986, Alpine Publications, Loveland, CO.
From Problems to Profits: The Madson Management System for Pet Grooming Businesses, by Madeline Bright Olge. 1997, The Madson Group, New York.

Internet Site

< http://www.petgroomer.com >

Publication
Groom and Board, 20 E. Jackson Blvd., Suite 200, Chicago, IL 60604. (312) 663-4040. Write or call for subscription information.

Start-Up Guide
National Business Library's Start-Up Guide, *Pet Sitting & Grooming.* (800) 947-7724. $39.95 + shipping and handling.

Additional Business Ideas
✣ Special tub for dog washing. Install a large, waist-high tub for owners to wash and dry their dogs. Charge $7 to $10 for small dogs, $11 to $13 for medium dogs, $15+ and up for larger dogs. Have the owner bring the towel and shampoo, and you provide the tub, table, and dryer. Include 15 minutes of free drying time. Charge extra for additional dryer time. Installation cost may be about $3,000 or more.
✣ Mobile pet groomer. Professional Mobile Groomers International, 936 Potter Ave., Union, NJ 07083. Send an LSASE for membership information.
✣ Dog training. Contact Association of Pet Dog Trainers, P.O. Box 385, Davis, CA 95617. < http://www.puppyworks.com/apdthomepage.html >

༺ 46 ༻
PET SITTING

This business involves visits to clients' homes to feed and exercise their pets. Your services may also include a home security check, watering plants, or collecting mail or newspapers. Most owners of pet sitting services are bonded.

You will need to set up appointments with your clients in their homes to go over the services requested and to give them cost estimates.

Start-Up Costs and Financing Sources
✣ $5,000 to $11,000.
✣ Personal savings, small business loan.

Pricing Guidelines
$15 to $25 per day per visit with two animals, additional charges for other services.

Marketing and Advertising Methods and Tips
* ❖ Place an ad in the business telephone directory.
* ❖ Post flyers on bulletin boards at veterinarian offices, grooming centers, pet stores, and animal food stores.
* ❖ Send direct mailings to local travel agencies, pet and animal associations and clubs.
* ❖ Advertise on local cable television, in newspapers, and in pet newsletters, especially in the spring and summer months.
* ❖ Rent a booth at pet and animal shows.

Essential Equipment
Animal supplies (food, crates, leashes, travel carriers in case you have to take the animal for medical care), a dependable vehicle to transport animals in case of an emergency, billing and record-keeping systems, a business telephone line and answering machine, a pager or a cellular phone, scheduling book.

Recommended Training, Experience, or Needed Skills
* ❖ Have experience and/or training with the kinds of animals you will care for.
* ❖ Work in a veterinarian's office or a pet store.
* ❖ Need a love of animals and a basic understanding of their needs and behavior.

Income Potential
$25,000 to $50,000+ a year, depending on the number of clients you have and the services you offer.

Type of Business
An out-of-the-home business.

Best Customers
Retired or professional working couples who travel frequently and do not want their pets in a boarding facility, owners of

exotic animals that cannot find boarding for their pets, owners of animals who for some reason are not able to have their animals boarded.

Helpful Tips

✤ Offer to sit for friends' or relatives' pets to get the experience.

✤ Instill trust in pet owners that you will take the best possible care of their pets and homes. Treat each pet and home as if it were your own. If you develop a good reputation for giving quality care, your business will increase from word-of-mouth referrals.

✤ Have a list of available, on-call professionals for both pet and home emergencies, twenty-four hours a day.

✤ Know how to reach your clients while they are away.

Franchises, Distributorships, and Licenses

Franchises
Critter Care, Inc. of America
8261 Summa #F
Baton Rouge, LA 70809

Pets Are Inn
7723 Tanglewood Ct., Suite 150
Minneapolis, MN 55439
(800) 248-PETS (7387)

Boards pets in private homes.

For More Information

Associations
Pet Sitters International
Patti Moran, Coordinator
418 East King St.
King, NC 27021-9163
< http://www.petsit.com >

Accreditation, provides legal services, a referral line, liability insurance. Publishes a networking directory. Send an LSASE for more information.

National Association of Pet Sitters
1200 G. St., NW, Suite 760
Washington, DC 20005
(202) 393-3317; < http://www.petsitters.org >

Book
Pet Sitting for Profit: A Complete Manual for Success, by Patti Moran. 1997, Howell Book House, Macmillan Publishing, New York.

Start-Up Guide
Entrepreneur's Start-Up Guide, *Pet Sitting.* (800) 421-2300. $69 + shipping and handling.

Supplies
See < http://www.petsitproducts.com > for products for pet sitters.
American Pet Products Manufacturers Association, 255 Glenville Rd., Greenwich, CT 06831. < http://www.appma.org >

Additional Business Ideas
✤ Specialize in exotic or large animal care.
✤ Add additional services such as sales of animal-related products: food, stain and odor removers.
✤ Dog-walking, for pets belonging to persons who work during the day.
✤ Yard clean-up.

✑47✒
PET TRANSPORTATION

This business involves transporting dogs, cats, rabbits, birds, and other animals including small livestock such as sheep and goats to veterinarian visits, grooming appointments, boarding facilities, or other destinations the owner wishes. You provide a useful service for people who are not able to transport their animals, have busy work schedules, or who just like the convenience of the service.

Janet Jones, who had worked with all kinds of animals for more than fifteen years, started her "Pet-Mo-Bile" service when friends and family repeatedly asked her to take their animals to one place or another. "They knew I worked at night and that I was free during the day to take their pets to appointments, so I decided to have my own pet taxi and do what I love best—working with animals."

Start-Up Costs
$1,000 to $2,000 if you already own a truck or van.

Pricing Guidelines
$20 to $35 for one-way transportation. Prices vary according to the distance, size of the pet, and the number of pets an owner wants transported.

Marketing and Advertising Methods and Tips
* Post flyers and your business cards on community bulletin boards, in pet grooming shops, veterinarian offices, pet stores, and livestock feed and supply centers.
* Encourage word-of-mouth referrals.
* Place magnetic or painted signs advertising your service on your vehicle.
* Advertise in local newspapers and pet publications.

Essential Equipment
Van or truck equipped with animal crates of different sizes, leashes, harnesses, car phone or pager, business telephone line and answering machine or service, billing and record-keeping systems.

Recommended Training, Experience, or Needed Skills
* Get experience working with animals at a veterinarian's office, animal shelter, or pet store.
* Attend classes at a local technical or agricultural school.
* Understand the types and breeds of animals and how to best handle them.
* Need strength, energy, and an empathy for animals.

Income Potential
$200+ a day or more. Expect more income if you sell or deliver food and supplies. Janet Jones also offers an ambulance service for sick animals, but enjoys the pet taxi part better. She also designs and builds outdoor, enclosed cat yards for places where cats cannot roam free. These cost $3,000 to $8,000.

Type of Business
An out-of-the-home business.

Best Customers
Busy people with full-time jobs, older people who cannot transport their animals, pet owners who do not have a vehicle or do not want their pet in their car.

Helpful Tips
✤ Give efficient, reliable, and good care to the animals, and people will refer others to you.
✤ Check with your auto insurance agent as to what insurance you should be carrying. Janet Jones's agent put a livestock rider on her van insurance so she would be covered when transporting animals.

For More Information

Book
The Portable Pet, by Barbara Nicolas. 1990, Harvard Common Press, Lanham, MD.

Home Study Course
International Correspondence Schools
925 Oak St.
Scranton, PA 18515
Offers animal care specialist course.

Additional Business Ideas
✤ Animal hauling. Take horses, cows, sheep, or other animals to 4-H, horse or farm shows, or to new owners when sold.

Need a sturdy truck or trailer and a good driving record. Must know how to load and unload certain animals.

One woman who owns a horse trailer charges $25 for one animal and $35 for two animals for a one-way trip within twenty miles of her home. Beyond twenty miles, she charges an additional $1 per mile for one animal and $1.50 a mile for two animals.

❖ Sell or make custom animal transportation carriers.

Business-to-Business Services

〜48〜
ANSWERING SERVICE

This is an excellent niche for home-based businesses. Even though answering machines, cellular phones, voice mail, and call forwarding abound, many businesses still prefer a personalized answering service.

Some successful answering services that were started in the home moved to larger offices when they needed more space. Others still operate from their homes because their owners prefer to stay small. The physically challenged find this a good business to fit their special needs.

Start-Up Costs
$27,000 to $47,000. You can start, however, by having your clients use call forwarding to your home business telephone number.

Pricing Guidelines
Charge according to a set number of calls per month, say 100 calls, for $80 per month. Add a surcharge of 50 cents for each call beyond the 100 calls. Rates may vary from state to state and community to community: Find out what other answering services in your area charge.

Marketing and Advertising Methods and Tips
+ Advertise in the business telephone directory.
+ Place classified ads or small display ads in the weekly business section of local newspapers.
+ Send direct mailings to small businesses, individual contractors, and professionals.

Essential Equipment
Telephone lines or switchboard, computer with billing and bookkeeping software, fax machine, promotional materials for direct mailing, and business cards.

Recommended Training, Experience, or Needed Skills
+ Work for an answering service, or as an operator or telemarketer.
+ Have a pleasant and professional phone manner.
+ Keep accurate records of calls received for your clients.

Income Potential
$30,000 to $55,000+ .

Type of Business
An in-home business.

Best Customers
Professionals, independent contractors, salespersons, repair persons.

Helpful Tips
+ Be efficient and accurate in taking and then relaying messages to your clients.
+ Check with local zoning laws to see if you need special permits.

For More Information
Association
Association of Telemessaging Services International (ATSI)
1200 19th St., NW, Suite 300
Washington, DC 20036
< http://www.atsi.org >

ATSI is not for home-based telemessagers, but their kit, trade magazine, and newsletter may be of interest. Send an LSASE for information.

Start-Up Guides
How to Start and Manage an Answering Service Business, by Leslie Renn and Jerre G. Lewis. Order from Lewis & Renn Assocs., 10315 Harmony Drive, Interlochen, MI 49643. $14.95 + $3 for postage and handling.

National Business Library's Start-Up Guide, *Telephone Answering Service.* (800) 947-7724. $39.95 + shipping and handling.

Additional Business Ideas
❖ Add additional services: make appointments, give referrals, take orders, provide information.
❖ Rent cellular phones or pagers.
❖ Be a home office communications consultant. See *Computer Telephoning: Automating Home Offices and Small Businesses,* by Ed Tittel and Dawn Roder. 1996, Academic Press, San Diego, CA.

❦49❧
BILLING SERVICE

Many small businesses do not have the time or organizational skills necessary to send out bills or past-due notices. In addition, many businesses often procrastinate in sending out notices or fail to keep a systematic check on customers who have not paid. Your billing service will help these business persons focus on their work while you get them money owed for services rendered.

Services could include invoice preparation and accounts receivables; processing and preparing for mailing of invoices; and printing up receivable reports for your customers to keep them informed.

Start-Up Costs
$3,000 to $5,000.

Pricing Guidelines

Some charge a certain amount per invoice (not including postage). Others charge monthly rates. Check with other office support service professionals in your locale for an idea of the going rates, as well as what your trade association recommends.

Marketing and Advertising Methods and Tips

❖ Send direct mailings to small businesses in your area, especially those for whom you have worked or had previous contact with.

❖ Make direct calls to selected businesses and follow up with a personal presentation.

❖ Place ads in the business section of local newspapers.

❖ Advertise in the business telephone directory.

Essential Equipment

High-quality laser printer; business computer with capability to handle a multicompany billing software program to include income analysis, customer service history, billing records tracking, account review, and statements; business telephone line, answering service or voice mail, fax machine.

Recommended Training, Experience, or Needed Skills

❖ Work in a bookkeeping and/or billing department of a large company.

❖ Need to provide accurate, on-time, monthly invoices for clients.

❖ Courses at business schools, colleges.

Income Potential

$50 to $80 an hour; $14,000 part-time, $30,000 to $80,000 full-time annual income, depending on the number of clients you have.

Type of Business

An in-home business except for marketing and personal presentations to potential customers.

Best Customers

Small businesses and professionals with offices (not including medical offices—see "Medical Billing Services" entry, page 231), small businesses in which you are familiar with their expertise (such as photography), or businesses that have at least 25 to 30 bills per month.

Helpful Tips

✦ Offer businesses a month's trial period to see if you can increase the percentage of bills paid.

✦ Present yourself and your work in a professional manner and give the best service you can for each of your clients.

✦ Research the market well to determine the best small businesses you wish to target.

For More Information

Software

Sage U.S. Inc.,*Timeslips*. 17950 Preston Rd., Suite 800, Dallas, TX 75252. (972) 818-3900. < http://www.timeslips.com > *Timeslips* is a popular time and billing program. Has versatile invoicing capabilities and includes a variety of billing arrangements and full customizable bill formatting.

Additional Business Ideas

Offer additional office support services as your customers need them.

⊷⊱ 50 ⊰⊶

BOOKKEEPING

If you took basic bookkeeping and/or accounting courses in high school or have worked in the bookkeeping department of a company, you may already have the basic skills and knowledge needed to start your own bookkeeping service.

Many smaller businesses or independent contractors often dump bookkeeping responsibilities on their spouses, who may hate this job and will welcome you to take it off their hands.

These are just the customers who hire Pam to do their book-keeping.

Pam started her bookkeeping business from her home part-time when she discovered she was only clearing $20 per week from her company bookkeeping job after paying day care expenses, keeping up her business wardrobe, and buying gas for her commute. Her first client was a friend who owned an antique business. That friend then referred her to another contractor. That was seven years ago. Today, her business grosses more than $40,000 per year.

Many of Pam's clients are in seasonal lines of work, which works out great for her. "When one business is slow, another may be busy, which enables me to have steady work year-round," she says. She likes, too, the way she can manage her business hours around her children's school and other activities. "I like being my own boss," she says. "I can never picture myself working for anyone else again."

Start-Up Costs
$250 for basic home office supplies. $3,000 to $5,000 for a computer, software, and other equipment. Start out with good used equipment or rent and then buy your equipment from your first earnings.

Pricing Guidelines
$65 for a first meeting and evaluation of a business's bookkeeping records. Charge $50 to $70 an hour after that. Also go by your trade association's rate recommendations.

Marketing and Advertising Methods and Tips
+ Encourage word-of-mouth referrals from your customers.
+ Look in the classified or business sections of local newspapers to find small businesses. Call to make an appointment with them.
+ Place classified ads in the business section of newspapers.

Essential Equipment
You can start with just a typewriter and a calculator, but most bookkeeping and accounting businesses use a computer and

bookkeeping software. You'll also need a separate business telephone, answering machine or service, fax, copier.

Recommended Training, Experience, or Needed Skills
* Work in a bookkeeping department of a company.
* Take a home study course or courses at a local business school or college.
* Volunteer to help a friend or relative with a small business do their bookkeeping.

Income Potential
$20,000 to $40,000 or more a year.

Type of Business
One-half in-home; one-half out-of-the-home at your clients' businesses.

Best Customers
Small businesses that gross between $100,000 to $500,000 a year. Often these are seasonal businesses such as concrete contractors, landscapers, and pool cleaners.

Helpful Tips
* Be honest with your customers. Know what resources can help you and your client.
* Work with your customers' accountants to make sure you have the right tax forms, and so forth. Accountants may often refer other customers to you because you will make their jobs easier.

For More Information

Association

American Institute of Professional Bookkeepers (AIPB)
60001 Montrose Rd., Suite 207
Rockville, MD 20852
(301) 770-7300

Write or call for membership information.

Bookkeeping System
Safeguard Business Systems, P.O. Box 158, Souderton, PA 18964. Packages start at $75.

Books
Bookkeeping & Tax Preparation: Start & Build a Prosperous Bookkeeping, Tax & Financial Services Business, by Gordon P. Lewis. 1996, Acton Circulation, Ukiah, CA.
Keeping the Books: Basic Recordkeeping & Accounting for the Small Business, by Linda Pinson and Jerry Jinnet. 1998, Upstart Publishing, Dover, NH.

Home Study Courses
Write for the latest catalog.

International Correspondence Schools
925 Oak St.
Scranton, PA 18515

Offers diploma in bookkeeping, computer-assisted bookkeeping.

Lifetime Career Schools
101 Harrison St.
Archbald, PA 18403

Offers course in bookkeeping.

NRI Schools
4401 Connecticut Ave., NW
Washington, DC 20008

Courses available in bookkeeping and accounting.

USDA (U.S. Dept. of Agriculture) Correspondence programs, Accounting courses. Write to:

Graduate School USDA
Stop 9911, Room 1112 S.
1400 Independence Ave., SW
Washington, DC 20250-9911

Software
Peachtree Bookkeeping software. (800) 247-3224. < http://
www.peachtree.com >

Start-Up Guide
How to Start and Manage a Bookkeeping Service Business, by Leslie
D. Renn and Jerre G. Lewis. Order from Lewis & Renn Associ-
ates, 10315 Harmony Dr., Interlochen, MI 49643. $14.95 +
$3 for postage and handling.

Additional Business Ideas
Add services such as billings, mailings, correspondence, pay
rolls, collection calls, and preparation of tax forms.

∾ 51 ≫

BUSINESS CONSULTANT/COACH

Right now may be a good time for you to become a consultant—
businesses are downsizing and laying off workers. For many
companies, it is less expensive to purchase a consultant's services than to pay a full-time staff member.

If you have business management training—overall or a
specialization—you may want to offer your services to existing
businesses in your industry as a *business consultant.* A *business
coach* will give assistance and guidance to new entrepreneurs
and/or to owners of home-based and other small ventures. Experts recommend holding onto your present job while starting
your consulting business. Network with former employers and
friends. Keep your ears open to any prospective customers in
your industry or trade. Potential clients could be former employers, customers, or even competitors. These are ideal clients to
start with since they are already familiar with your work.

Work out a complete and thorough business plan and consider your insurance and credit needs. Get any additional training or information before you quit your job.

A consultant can make a good living and have the independence of working for him- or herself. Plenty of research and planning will only help to ensure your success.

Start-Up Costs and Financing Sources
+ $5,000 to $20,000. You should have savings equivalent to three to six months' of your present salary to cushion you while you search for clients.
+ Personal savings, small business loan.

Pricing Guidelines
Network with other consultants in your trade or industry and/or follow any related trade association guidelines. Average billing rate for all consultants is approximately $1,000 per day. This will vary with your specialty.

Marketing and Advertising Methods and Tips
+ Place ads in business and trade publications.
+ Rent a booth at your industry's trade show and distribute promotional materials.
+ Offer talks, seminars, and workshops in your field.
+ Encourage word-of-mouth referrals from clients.
+ Network with other consultants.
+ Make your promotional materials professional and dynamic-looking.

Essential Equipment
Computer with word processing, database, and spreadsheet software; modem; business telephone line; answering machine, answering service, or voice mail; fax machine, copier.

Recommended Training, Experience, or Needed Skills
+ Have broad enough experience to serve the varied needs of your clients.
+ Have confidence in your expertise.

Income Potential
$25,000 to $100,000+ per year.

Type of Business
Approximately one-half in-home and one-half out-of-the-home, depending on whether work needs to be done at your client's place of business.

Best Customers
Businesses who need an expert, but not on a full-time basis.

Helpful Tips
❖ Be flexible. Expect the worst and plan for it.
❖ Be professional, ethical, and honest with your clients.
❖ Be prepared to put in long hours, especially in getting your business started.
❖ Keep up-to-date with your specialty.
❖ Charge what you are worth.
❖ Continue marketing and advertising no matter how many clients you have at the moment.
❖ Check with the IRS for tax guidelines on professional consulting.
❖ Have your lawyer draw up business contracts.

For More Information

Association
The Institute of Management Consultants
521 Fifth Ave., 35th Fl.
New York, NY 10175-3598
< http://www.imcusa.org >

Maintains a free referral service for certified management consultants who have completed the Institute's professional accreditation program, finished an ethics exam, signed a code-of-ethics agreement, and undergone a screening process.

Books and Publications
The Complete Guide to Consulting Success, 3rd ed., by Howard Shenson and Ted Nicholas. 1997, Upstart Publishing Co., Dover, NH. A step-by-step handbook complete with agreements and forms. Also includes a listing of online databases, consulting newsletters and journals.

The Consultant's Kit: Establishing and Operating Your Successful Consulting Business, by Dr. Jeffrey Lant. Jeffrey Lant Associates, P.O. Box 38-2767, Cambridge, MA 02238.

The Consultant's Survival Guide, by Marsha D. Lewin. 1997, John Wiley & Sons, New York.

Contract and Fee-Setting Guide for Consultants and Professionals, by Howard Shenson. 1990, John Wiley & Sons, New York.

Going Solo: Developing a Home-Based Consulting Business from the Ground Up, by William J. Bond. 1998, McGraw-Hill, New York.

Million Dollar Consulting: The Professional's Guide to Growing a Business, by Alan Weiss. 1997, McGraw-Hill, New York.

The Portable Coach: 28 Sure-Fire Strategies for Business and Personal Success, by Thomas J. Leonard and Byron Laursen. 1998, C. Scribner's, New York.

Software
Consulting ReadyWorks, Round Lake Publishing Co., 31 Bailey Ave., Ridgefield, CT 06877. Contact for more information.

Start-Up Guide
How to Start & Manage an Independent Consulting Practice, by Jerre G. Lewis and Leslie D. Renn. Order from Lewis & Renn Associates, 10315 Harmony Dr., Interlochen, MI 49643. $14.95 + $3 for postage and handling.

Additional Business Ideas
Start a newsletter for other consultants in your field or on the area of your specialty. (See "Newsletter" entry, page 327).

⟡ 52 ⟡
BUSINESS AND OFFICE SUPPORT SERVICES

More and more, businesses are using business and office support services. Business and office support services often include typing, letter writing and mailing, transcription, general bookkeeping, dictation, copying, customer service, research assistance, proofreading and editing, dictaphone work and transcription, data entry, publicity writing reports, and other office-support services.

Your business can start by offering a wide range of business and office support services. Then, by seeing which services are most in-demand and/or profitable for you, you can determine in which areas to specialize. Your work history, training, and expertise will also help determine areas of specialization. Joining professional associations (see "For More Information," later in this section), reading trade publications, and networking with other owners of business and office support services will keep you up-to-date with the industry.

Start-Up Costs and Financing Sources
* $5,000 to $23,000.
* Personal savings, small business loan, lines of credit on credit cards, loans from friends, family.

Pricing Guidelines
$20 to $30 per hour. Some word processors charge per 1,000 characters or by the job. See the Association of Business Support Services International's *Pricing Manual*, listed under "Books and Publications" in this section.

Marketing and Advertising Methods and Tips
* Advertise in the business telephone directory.
* Network with business owners at local conferences.
* Join the local chamber of commerce; attend their meetings.
* Print business cards and brochures describing the exact services you offer.
* Offer fast service and free pick-up and delivery.
* Send direct mailings to small businesses that do not have a secretarial staff.
* Ask printers, copy centers, and satisfied customers to refer other clients to you.

Essential Equipment
You can start with a typewriter, word processor, and manual file system, but it's best to have a computer with a modem, laser

printer, desktop publishing and word processing software, database and a simple spreadsheet program that downloads addresses, charts, and graphs to documents. Also need a business telephone line; an answering machine, service, or voice mail; a fax; and a dependable vehicle if you make pick-ups or deliveries.

Recommended Training, Experience, or Needed Skills

✦ Need secretarial, word processing, and business writing skills obtained through business school or college courses. It is also helpful to have worked in an office.

✦ Project a professional image, be fast and accurate with your assignments.

Income Potential

$20,000 to $60,000 or more.

Type of Business

In-home except to pick up and deliver work.

Best Customers

Small firms who cannot afford to have a full-time office support staff.

Helpful Tips

✦ Start out taking a variety of assignments until you have enough clients to handle and to see which are the most fun and profitable for you.

✦ Talk to friends or acquaintances to see if they know of any potential clients who might need your services.

Franchises, Distributorships, and Licenses

Franchise

The Letter Writer
9357 Haggerty Rd.
Plymouth, MI 48170
(734) 455-8892

Note that you should clear it with your local officials to ensure that it is permissible to have clients come to your home office. You may find that you will have to move your office to a commercial district if you get too much traffic to your home office with this franchise. Write or call for information.

For More Information

Associations
Midwest Secretarial Services Network (MSSN)
12015 Manchester, Suite 102
St. Louis, MO 63131
(314) 957-9280

Holds monthly meetings in St. Louis, seminars, office tours, networking. Publishes a monthly newsletter available separately or included with membership. Write or call for membership information.

Assn. of Business Support Services International, Inc. (ABSSI)
22875 Savi Ranch Parkway, Suite H
Yorba Linda, CA 92887-4619
(800) 237-1462; < http://www.nass.com >

Publishes a monthly newsletter (available to nonmembers for $48 per year) as well as *Industry Production Standards* and various manuals on running a secretarial service.

Books and Publications
(See also related associations above.)
The Complete Typing Business Guide: Everything You Need to Know to Start & Successfully Operate a Home Typing Business, by Frank Chisenhall. 1990, Super TextPublishing, New York.
How to Open and Operate a Home-Based Secretarial Service, by Jan Melnik. 1996, Globe Pequot Press, Old Saybrook, CT.
How to Start a Secretarial and Business Service, by Mary Temple. Order from Pilot Books (800) 79-pilot (see "Books Through the Mail" in Part III).
Pricing Manual, Association of Business Support Services International (address listed under "Associations"). $39.95 for nonmembers, plus $5 for shipping and handling.

Start & Run a Profitable Office Service Business from Your Home: Secretarial Support, Word Processing, Desktop Publishing, Your Step-By-Step Business Plan, by Louise Hogan. 1995, Self-Counsel Press, Bellingham, WA.

Home Study Courses
(See "Home Study Courses" in Part III for addresses.)

International Correspondence Schools, diploma: Secretary.

NRI Schools, Word Processing Home Business.

Magazines and Newsletters
Keyboard Connection, Nancy Malvin, editor, Troy IL 62294-0229; (618) 607-4666. Quarterly newsletter for owners of secretarial and office support services. Call or write for information and for a sample copy.

SOS Quarterly, Kay Young, editor, 1431 Willow Brook Cove #4, St. Louis, MO 63146; (314) 567-3636. Offers low-cost marketing ideas and practical advice for running your business. $3 for a sample issue, $25 for a one-year subscription.

See also "Associations," listed earlier in this section, for ABSSI and MSSN newsletters.

Software
See the ABSSI recommendations (address listed earlier in this section).

Start-Up Guides
Entrepreneur's Start-Up Guide, *Secretarial/Word Processing Service.* (800) 421-2300. $69 + shipping and handling.

National Business Library's Start-Up Guide, *Secretarial Service.* (800) 947-7724. $39.95 + shipping and handling.

Additional Business Ideas
❖ Stenographic service.

❖ File preparation and organization and/or public notary services may be offered in addition to your regular services.

↪53↩
BUSINESS PLAN CONSULTANT

People who want to start a business or small businesses and want to expand need a business plan to get loans or additional financing. As the consultant, you write a formal business plan that can be presented to potential lenders.

A typical business plan includes a description of the business, current assets and income, present and potential markets, and a financial projection of the business's earnings. You can type up the plan or use one of the many computer software programs available.

Your fee is based on the complexity and length of the plan your customer needs.

Start-Up Costs and Financing Sources
* $1,000 to $6,000 to start, depending on whether you have a computer with software.
* Personal savings, small business loan, credit lines on credit cards.

Pricing Guidelines
$500 to $5,000 per plan.

Marketing and Advertising Methods and Tips
* Contact the SBA Small Business Development Center to see if they can refer potential clients to you.
* Send direct mailings to community colleges, adult evening and technical schools that offer business start-up courses.
* Attend workshops and seminars on small business issues.
* Rent a booth at small business development shows.
* Place classified ads in business sections of local newspapers.
* Make presentations describing your business to lending institutions. They may send you referrals.

Essential Equipment
Computer, business planning software, laser printer, telephone, fax machine, answering machine or service, copier.

Recommended Training, Experience, or Needed Skills

✤ Background in banking; experience working at lending institutions.

✤ Enroll in courses on how to write business plans (check with your SBA Small Business Development Office for seminars and workshops).

✤ Ask local lending institutions what they like to see in business plans.

✤ Talk with accountants for tips on what to include in business plans.

Income Potential

From $500 to $5,000 (per plan), depending on your client, the length and complexity of the plan, and your expertise (if you are a certified professional, your rates will be higher than those of someone who is not).

Type of Business

In-home business except for research, interviews, presentations, show exhibits, and so forth.

Best Customers

Entrepreneurs needing start-up money or small businesses needing money for expansion or diversification.

For More Information

Also see consulting books in "Business Consultant/Coach" section.

Books

Anatomy of a Business Plan: A Step-By-Step Guide to Starting Smart, Building the Business, and Securing Your Company's Future, 3rd ed., by Linda Pinson and Jerry Jinnett. 1996, Upstart Publishing Co., Dover, NH.

The Business Planning Guide: Creating a Plan for Success in Your Own Business, 7th ed., by David H. Bangs, Jr. 1992, Upstart Publishing, Dover, NH.

How to Write a Business Plan, 4th ed., by Mike McKeever. 1992, Nolo Press. (800) 992-6656. An easy, step-by-step guide that includes fill-in-the blank financial forms and sample business plans. $21.95.

Software
Jian, 1975 El Camino Real, Mountain View, CA 94040-2218. (800) 346-5426.
Microsoft Corp., Redmond, WA 98052. (800) 426-9400.
Palo Alto Software, Palo Alto, CA 94306. (800) 229-7526.

Start-Up Guides
Entrepreneur's Start-Up Guides, *Business Plan Consultant, Developing a Successful Business Plan, and Writing Effective Business Plans.* (800) 421-2300. $69 + shipping and handling.
How to Write a Successful Business Plan, by Jerre G. Lewis and Leslie D. Renn. Order from Lewis & Renn Associates, 10315 Harmony Dr., Interlochen, MI 49643; $14.95 + $3 for postage and handling.

Additional Business Ideas
Help others fill out SBA loan applications. Order video *Your Guide to SBA Loans and Programs* from IWS, Inc., 24 Canterbury Rd., Rockville Centre, NY 11570. Also read *Free Money from the Federal Government for Small Businesses and Entrepreneurs,* 2nd ed., by Laurie Blum. 1996, John Wiley & Sons, New York.

᎒᎒54᎒᎒
BUSINESS WRITING

Freelance business writing has endless markets. Corporations may need writers for the following: manuals, annual reports, press releases, sales letters, critiques, direct-mail packages, and catalog descriptions. Nonprofit organizations frequently need writers to help them with brochures, press releases, promotional and fund-raising articles and literature.

What you write and for whom depends on your interests, experience, and training. Finding a niche is particularly helpful. One retired real estate agent makes more than $50,000 a year writing brochures for local real estate agencies.

Start-Up Costs and Financing Sources
+ $5,000 to $25,000.
+ Small business loan, personal savings.

Pricing Guidelines
Public relations writing prices can run from $25 to $100 per hour; $300 or more per day; $2,000 to $3000+ for a monthly retainer. The *Writer's Market* (see later in this section) gives pricing suggestions for a multitude of business writing assignments and projects.

Marketing and Advertising Methods and Tips
+ Send introductory letters and follow up with telephone calls to the advertising departments of large companies and to small business owners.
+ Network with other writers for possible writing assignments.
+ Place classified ads in local newspapers to get individual clients.

Essential Equipment
Word processor or computer with word-processing software; ink-jet or laser printer; modem for online research; copier; business telephone and answering machine, answering service, or voice mail; fax machine; promotional materials; home office suitable for meeting with clients (unless you meet with them at their businesses or residences); a few classic suits for business appointments; reference books—*The Chicago Manual of Style* (latest edition), The University of Chicago Press, Chicago, IL— and other publications related to business formats.

Recommended Training, Experience, or Needed Skills
+ Work in an advertising or public relations firm.
+ Take business writing or journalism courses at a local community college.
+ Be able to contact experts when writing about subjects unfamiliar to you.
+ Know how to write clearly and concisely.

Income Potential
$5,000, part-time; $25,000 to $85,000, full-time.

Type of Business
In-home business except when consulting with clients.

Helpful Tips
✤ Take as many assignments as possible when you start out to determine what assignments are most profitable.
✤ Build up your client list gradually until you are able to run your business full-time.

For More Information

Books
The Business Writer's Book of Lists, by Mary A. DeVries. 1998, Berkley Publishing Group, New York.
The Business Writer's Handbook, 5th ed., by Charles T. Brusaw, Gerald J. Alred, and Walter E. Oliu. 1996, St. Martin's Press, New York.
The Complete Handbook of Model Business Letters, by Jack Giffin. 1997, Prentice Hall, Upper Saddle River, NJ.
The Elements of Business Writing, by Robert W. Bly. 1992, Macmillan General Reference, New York.
The Handbook of Business Letters, 3rd ed., (book and disk) by Roy Poe. 1998, McGraw-Hill, Inc., New York.
How to Start and Run a Writing and Editing Business, by Herman Holtz. 1992, John Wiley & Sons, New York, NY.
Writer's Market. Writer's Digest Books. An annual market guide. Writer's Digest Books, Cincinnati, OH.

Start-Up Guide
Entrepreneur's Start-Up Guide, *Freelance Commercial Writing*. (800) 421-2300. $69 + shipping and handling.

Additional Business Ideas
✤ Freelance technical writing. Read the following books:
The Elements of Technical Writing, by Gary Blake and Robert W. Bly. 1995, Macmillan General Reference, New York.

Handbook of Technical Writing, by Charles T. Brusaw, Gerald J. Alred, and Walter E. Oliu. 1997, St. Martin's Press, New York.

✣ Letter writing: consumer complaint letters, letters of appeal, general correspondence. Read *How to Write Complaint Letters That Work! A Consumer's Guide to Resolving Conflicts & Getting Results,* by Patricia Westheimer and Jim Mastro. 1994, Jist Works, Inc., Indianapolis, IN.

❧ 55 ☙
CONSULTANT FOR
HOME-BASED BUSINESSES

In this consulting business, you evaluate the expertise, experience, business ideas, finances, and future business plans of either home-based entrepreneurs or those considering starting a home-based business. You then provide them with financing options, market breakdowns, sources for products and supplies, and advertising strategies.

With the growth of home-based businesses expected to continue, the services of a consultant specializing in this field will be in demand.

Start-Up Costs and Financing Sources
✣ $5,000 to $8,000.
✣ Personal savings, lines of credit on your credit cards.

Pricing Guidelines
You can charge a one-time consultation fee or an hourly fee. Average is $100 to $150 for the one-time consultation and evaluation fee; $55 to $75 per hour for as-needed consulting.

Marketing and Advertising Methods and Tips
✣ Place ads in local publications and on cable television.
✣ Teach courses on business start-ups and offer consulting to your students when the course is over.

❖ Give presentations on starting a home-based business to local women's groups.
❖ Rent a booth at a small business fair.

Essential Equipment
Computer with modem for on-line information about home-based businesses; database of home-based business resources; copier; business telephone line and answering machine or service; fax; books on marketing, writing business plans, and start-up manuals and publications on specific home-based businesses; suitable office or room in which to receive clients.

Recommended Training, Experience, or Needed Skills
❖ Take entrepreneurial courses at business schools or local community colleges.
❖ Attend small business fairs.
❖ Be familiar with home-based businesses and their special requirements or problems.

Income Potential
$25,000 to $45,000 or more.

Type of Business
In-home except when giving talks, courses, or attending shows.

Best Customers
People who are looking to start a business from their homes: young mothers, the physically challenged, recent retirees.

Helpful Tips
❖ Help people become more effective time managers (or recommend a course they can take).
❖ Teach them the tools to find the information they may need in the future and how to make the most of their available money and resources.

For More Information

Associations

See "Home Business (and Related) Associations" in the "Additional Resources" chapter.

Books

Getting Business to Come to You, 2nd ed., by Paul and Sarah Edwards and Laura Clampitt Douglas. 1998, Putnam Publishing Group, New York.

The Home Business Sourcebook: Everything You Need to Know About Starting & Running a Business from Home, by Lou Henry. 1997, Lowell House, Los Angeles, CA.

Homemade Money: How to Select, Start, Manage, Market, and Multiply the Profits of a Business at Home, 5th ed., by Barbara Brabec. 1997, Betterway Books, Cincinnati, OH. (800) 289-0963.

Seminars

Contact your local SBA Small Business Development Center or Women's Business Center for low-cost business seminars. (See "Government Resources" in "Additional Resources" chapter.)

"Traveling Workshops" by Kimberly Stanséll of *Bootstrapper's Success Secrets*. See "Additional Resources" chapter.

Additional Business Ideas

Sell home office supplies, books, planners.

⸎56⸎
INFORMATION BROKER

The right information can often give one business the edge over a competitor. You will search not only the growing number of computerized databases, but also look through library sources, reference books, and publications and interview experts to find the information your clients require. Many information brokers diversify by doing market research, conducting surveys, and scouting out competitors.

Lucy Mundo owns and operates a market research company, Essential Resources Plus, in Livingston, New Jersey. Her customers include companies and institutions, advertising and public relations firms, international corporations, and individuals who need market research for business start-ups. Mundo had worked ten years in the marketing and sales departments of various corporations. When she decided to go out on her own, she took six months off to fully research her business idea.

Mundo has expanded her business to sell information products like "Total Recall," which creates newsletters for her customers based on the topic they choose. She says, "My business is growing and getting better, but I did not set unrealistic goals."

Start-Up Costs
$8,000 to $11,000.

Pricing Guidelines
$60 to $300 per hour or per project (follow industry pricing guidelines).

Marketing and Advertising Methods and Tips
* Directly contact your target clients through letters of introduction, personal appointments, or presentations.
* Place advertisements in business publications and magazines.
* Attend and network at trade conventions, meetings, and conferences.

Essential Equipment
An updated computer with the latest speed modem, CD-ROM drive, and capability to run software programs for accounting/ billing, database management, word processing; laser or ink jet printer; business telephone line, fax machine, and answering system; subscriptions to your needed online information resources.

Recommended Training, Experience, or Needed Skills
* Need expertise in operating computers and accessing online information.
* Take computer courses at local schools, colleges; business seminars at colleges, schools, SBA Small Business Development Centers.

❖ Work in a research firm.
❖ Take one- or two-day courses offered by database vendors; or various courses sponsored by the industry (found in recommended books in this section).
❖ Be willing to spend longer than eight-hour days to keep your business growing.
❖ Have tenacity and persistence in finding the information your client needs.

Income Potential
$25,000 to $75,000+ if your business is a sole proprietorship; more, if you hire part-time researchers.

Type of Business
In-home except for any presentations or attendance at meetings, and so forth.

Best Customers
Companies that do not have either the employees or the time to do the research they need. Individuals who need specific information for personal or business reasons.

Helpful Tips
❖ Decide what kind of clients and research you wish to specialize in and target your marketing techniques in that direction.
❖ Provide fast, accurate service.
❖ Diversify your research services by offering more than one information service (for example, market research reports), and specialize in one or two areas.

For More Information

Association
Association of Independent Information Professionals (AIIP)
234 W. Delaware Ave.
Pennington, NJ 08534
< http://www.aiip.org >
Contact for membership information.

Books and Publications

The Information Broker's Handbook, 2nd ed., by Sue Rugge and Alfred Glossbrenner. 1997, McGraw-Hill, New York.

Information for Sale, by John Everett and Elizabeth Crowe. 1994, McGraw-Hill, New York, NY.

Secrets of the Super Net Searchers: The Reflections, Revelations and Hard-Won Wisdom of 35 of the World's Top Internet Researchers, by Reva Basch and Howard Rheingold. 1996, Independent Publishing Group, Chicago, IL.

Start Your Own Information Broker Service, by Susan Rachmeler. 1997, Prentice Hall Trade, Englewood Cliffs, NJ.

CD-ROM

Fast Reference Facts, by Gale Research, Detroit, MI.

Seminars

The Information Professionals Institute
3724 F.M. 1960 W., Suite 214
Houston, TX 77068

Contact for dates and locations.

Start-Up Guides

Entrepreneur's Start-Up Guide, *Information Broker.* (800) 421-2300. $69 + shipping and handling.

National Business Library's Start-Up Guide, *Information Broker.* (800) 947-7724. $39.95 + shipping and handling.

Additional Business Ideas

❖ Researching public records.

❖ Health information specialist. Janice Guthrie's medical information service, The Health Resource, Inc., in Conway, Arkansas, helps clients find health information, such as the latest cancer research and treatments. Her reports run 50 to 250 pages and cost from $275 to $375, plus shipping.

❖ Research birth dates. Charge $50 to compile the news events that happened on people's birthdays, anniversaries, or other special dates.

∞57∞
JANITORIAL SERVICE

Cleaning buildings and offices is a competitive business. It is predicted to be one of the faster-growing services in the next few years. You will have to study the industry and then aggressively market your business. Maybe you can find a particular style of service that other, larger janitorial services are not covering.

If you hire others, you will have to combat the high turnover rate. Maybe you can offer babysitting services or job-sharing with any single parents you hire. Getting one contract at a time and doing high quality work may be the best way to success.

Start-Up Costs and Financing Sources
❖ $5,000 to $12,000.
❖ Personal savings, small business loan, lines of credit on your credit cards.

Pricing Guidelines
Most janitorial services charge so many cents per square feet (follow industry standards, see "For More Information," later in this section); call offices and other services to see what the going rate is in your area.

Marketing and Advertising Methods and Tips
❖ Advertise in the business telephone directory.
❖ Look for new buildings being erected and call their owners to see if they have signed a janitorial contract yet.
❖ Send direct mail and make calls to owners of shopping centers, malls, industrial parks.
❖ Find out what type of interiors a building has, then pitch to the owners that you specialize with those types of floors or fabrics (furniture, carpets, drapes, etc.).

Essential Equipment
Cleaning supplies, power equipment (can rent at first).

Recommended Training, Experience, or Needed Skills
✤ Work part- or full-time in one or more janitorial services.
✤ Need stamina, strength, energy, and attention to detail.

Income Potential
$25,000 to $50,000 is about the maximum if you are a sole proprietor. If you are able to expand and manage the business, much more is possible.

Type of Business
Out-of-the-home if you are a one- or two-person business. Many husbands and wives start this business together.

Best Customers
For a one-person business, look for those small or unusual businesses that need professional cleaning.

Helpful Tips
✤ Combine other services—carpet, window, upholstery-cleaning.
✤ Tackle the companies that bigger janitorial services often overlook.

Franchises, Distributorships, and Licenses

Franchise
Also see many listings in the "Franchise and Distributorships" chapter for books.

Coverall Cleaning Concepts
3111 Camino Del Rio, Suite 950
San Diego, CA 92108
(619) 584-1911; (800) 537-3371
< http://www.coverall.com >

Offers a turn-key business with training, equipment, supplies, accounts, billing, and collection services. Investments vary from $7,738 to $76,190. Partial financing is available.

For More Information
(Also see "Cleaning," page 81.)

Association

Building Service Contractors Association International
10201 Lee Highway, Suite 225
Fairfax, VA 22030
< http://www.bscai.org >

Publications, seminars.

Books

Cleaning Up for a Living, by Don Aslett and Mark Browning. Betterway Books, Cincinnati, OH. (800) 289-0963.

Inside the Janitorial Business: How to Start from Scratch & Succeed in Professional Cleaning, 2nd ed., by Frederick R. Massey. 1989, MBM Books.

Consultant Service

Cleaning Consultant Services
P.O. Box 1273
Seattle, WA 98111

Contact for listings of books, videos, and software related to cleaning and self-employment.

Home Study and Seminars

Cleaning Management Institute
National Trade Publications
13 Century Hill Dr.
Latham, NY 12110-2197
(518) 783-1283

Videos, handbooks, seminars; membership includes industry publications, discounts on education and informational products. Write or call for brochure.

Magazine

Cleaning Business, 1512 Western Ave., P.O. Box 1273, Seattle, WA 98111. Geared toward self-employed cleaning professionals. $20 for one year.

Software

Rimrock Technologies, 1919 Montana Ave., Billings, MT 59101. (406) 248-3511. < http://www.rimrocktech.com >

Start-Up Guides

Entrepreneur's Start-Up Guide, *Janitorial Service.* (800) 421-2300. $69 + shipping and handling.

How to Start & Manage a Janitorial Service Business, by Jerre Lewis and Leslie D. Renn. Order from Lewis & Renn Associates, 10315 Harmony Dr., Interlochen, MI 49643. $14.95 + $3 for postage and handling.

National Business Library's Start-Up Guide, *Janitorial Service.* (800) 947-7724. $39.95 + shipping and handling.

Supplies

EGH Corporation
P.O. Box 2055
Tupelo, MS 38803-2055
(601) 840-0022
< http://www.eghcorporation.com >

Sells wholesale cleaning supplies, office supplies, etc. Write, call, or visit the Internet site for ordering information and conditions.

Additional Business Ideas

❖ Cleaning office ceilings. Contact Coustic Glo International Inc., 7111 Ohms Lane, Minneapolis, MN 55439 (franchise).

❖ Window washing. See chapter in *More 101 Best Home-Based Businesses for Women,* by Priscilla Y. Huff. 1998, Prima Publishing, Rocklin, CA.

❖ Sell light bulbs, paper, and soap as a side-line.

ᑫ58ᕠ
MEDICAL BILLING SERVICES

A medical billing service works directly with doctors, health agencies, clinics, and so forth, to process private insurance and Medicare claims on behalf of their patients. Medical training, experience, or background or a familiarity with medical terminology are assets in this business. Research the need for this service, how patients pay for services (some states require patients to pay immediately for services rendered), and whether medical professionals are willing to use an outside billing service.

Start-Up Costs and Financing Sources
+ $5,000 to $20,000.
+ Personal savings, small business loan.

Pricing Guidelines
$20 to $50+ an hour or a price per billing or number of billings.

Marketing and Advertising Methods and Tips
+ Send direct mailings to physicians and medical groups. Make a presentation and show them how you can save them money using your service.
+ Make inquiries at clinics and hospitals, especially those that are having medical office staff cutbacks.
+ Advertise in the business telephone directory.

Essential Equipment
Computer and medical billing software, modem, printer, business telephone line, answering machine or service.

Recommended Training, Experience, or Needed Skills
+ Take medical office management courses at a local community college or through home study.
+ Work in a medical billing department or medical office for the work experience and to make contacts with potential clients.

Income Potential
$6,000+ or more a month is possible if you are near a number of local hospitals and medical complexes.

Type of Business
Two-thirds in-home; one-third out-of-the-home at the offices.

Best Customers
Physicians, other medical professionals who need medical billing services, human services agencies.

Helpful Tips

+ Know your clients' billing procedures and preferences. Make sure your billing software is appropriate for the billing you do for your clients.
+ Be professional, efficient, fast, and accurate.
+ Keep up-to-date on changes in the health-care industry.
+ Network with other billing service professionals.

Franchises, Distributorships, and Licenses

Franchise

Island Automated Medical Services, Inc.
5999 Central Ave., Suite 300
St. Petersburg, FL 33710
(800) 322-1139, ext. 001

"IAMS provides the opportunity for home/office electronic billing and claims processing for medical, dental, and chiropractic providers. The IAMS software also allows the entrepreneur to achieve and provide full practice management for their clients."

Licensing

Infinity Software
27636 Ynez Rd., L-7, #143
Temecula, CA 92591
(909) 699-9581

Provides training through videotapes, software, support, and materials. Send an LSASE for fees and cost of materials.

For More Information

Associations

International Billing Association (IBA)
7315 Wisconsin Ave., #434E
Bethesda, MD 20814
< http://www.biller.com >

Write or call for membership information. $450 to $950 for annual membership. Membership prerequisite: You must have been in business at least two years and have at least two clients in order to join.

The National Electronic Biller's Alliance (NEBA)
2226-A Westborough Blvd., S., #504
San Francisco, CA 94080
< http://www.nebazone.com >

Newsletter, membership discounts, also a self-study course on medical billing procedures and terminology. $129 for an annual membership.

Books

Health Services on Your Home-Based PC, 2nd ed. (book and CD), by Rick Benzel. 1997, McGraw-Hill Computing, Berkeley, CA.

Medical Billing Service: A Survival Guide for the 21st Century. 1997, Sounding B. Order through Barnes & Noble < barnesandnoble.com >

Understanding Health Insurance: A Guide to Professional Billing, 4th ed. (book and disk), by Jo Ann C. Rowell. 1997, Delmar Publishers, Albany, NY.

Software

The Computer Place, Inc., *MediSoft Patient Accounting.* (602) 892-5120.

༒59༒
MEDICAL TRANSCRIBING

If you are a medical transcriptionist, you type up physicians' and other health professionals' dictation. You must be able to edit and rewrite from the audio tapes; know medical terms, English grammar, and spelling; be able to operate transcription equipment; and write clearly without changing the medical professionals' meaning or directions.

Many transcriptionists specialize in different fields of medicine. As a professional, you must stay abreast of the changing terminology and medical techniques. It is a challenging career, but one that can provide steady work once your business is established.

Start-Up Costs

$1,700 to $5,000 or less if you already own a computer.

Pricing Guidelines

Follow the industry standards (see "Association," later in this section). Some charge 14 to 28 cents per line or charge by the character. Hourly rates run from $30 to $70.

Marketing and Advertising Methods and Tips

✤ Contact transcriptionist services for overflow work.

✤ Make direct contact with physicians, health professionals, and hospitals.

Essential Equipment

Computer, modem, printer, transcriber or transcribing unit with conversion capabilities to different sizes of audio tapes, word processing software, business line with answering capabilities, fax. A personal reference library is advisable: journals, medical books, and dictionaries.

Recommended Training, Experience, or Needed Skills

✤ Take medical transcription courses at local business schools or through home study (see "Home Study Courses," later in this section).

✤ Work for a hospital, doctor, or a transcription service to get experience and make contacts.

✤ Be attentive to detail; be accurate.

Income Potential

$25,000 to $100,000 or more a year.

Type of Business

In-home.

For More Information

Association

American Association for Medical Transcriptionists (AAMT)
P.O. Box 576187
3460 Oakdale Rd.
Modesto, CA 95357-6187
< http://www.aamt.org >

Publishes the *Journal of the American Association for Medical Transcriptionists*.

Books
Health Service Businesses on Your Home-Based PC, by Rick Benzel. Contact AAMT for information.
The Independent Medical Transcriptionist, by Donna Avial-Weil and Mary Glaccum. 1998, Rayve Productions, Windsor, CA.
The Medical Transcriptionist's Handbook, 1992, South-Western Publishing, Sun Lakes, AZ.
Saunders Manual of Medical Transcription, by Sheila B. Stone. 1994, W. B. Saunders, Philadelphia, PA.

Home Study Courses
International Correspondence Schools
925 Oak St.
Scranton, PA 18515

Offers diploma for medical transcription.

At Home Professions
2001 Lowe St.
Ft. Collins, CO 80525

Start-Up Guides
Entrepreneur's Start-Up Guide, *Medical Transcription Service*. (800) 421-2300. $69 + shipping and handling.

Additional Business Ideas
Medical records specialist (organizes health records in doctors' offices and hospitals; can freelance).

ᏝᏙ60ᏗᎦ
PROCESS SERVER

A process server delivers legal documents to individuals and business entities involved in court cases. A process server is hired by lawyers, collection agencies, banks and financial institutions, and by some state and federal agencies. State laws govern who may serve state court papers, so be aware of the regulations covering your delivery area.

In 1981 the U. S. Marshal's office was relieved of much of its process-serving duties. Since then, most federal civil processes have been served by private process servers (any person over the age of 18 and not a party to the lawsuit). Sheriffs and constables serve in state courts. Funding cutbacks in many counties, however, have left sheriffs with fewer personnel and more work. This has opened the door for private process servers (where permitted by law) to step in and compete with the sheriff for those services.

Start-Up Costs and Financing Sources
✤ $6,000 minimum (not including the price of a reliable vehicle).
✤ Private savings, small business loan, credit cards.

Pricing Guidelines
$35+ and up per service (rate will vary from state to state—follow industry pricing guidelines).

Marketing and Advertising Methods and Tips
✤ Call lawyers, collection agencies, and others who use process servers.
✤ Call other process servers who may have overflow work.

Essential Equipment
Computer with filing and bookkeeping software (Quicken is one of the best low-cost bookkeeping/check writing programs available; MyInvoices is an excellent program for preparing invoices.), business line with an answering service or voice mail saying you will get back to your caller within 15 minutes, car phone, pager, a reliable vehicle.

Recommended Training, Experience, or Needed Skills
✤ Call a process serving business and ask if they need your services. Try it for a time to see if it is something you can see yourself doing.

✤ Be persistent at tracking people down.
✤ Be professional and reliable.

Income Potential
Check with local lawyers for standard rates for servers' fees.

Type of Business
One-fourth in-home, conducting business matters; three-fourths out-of-the-home, picking up and delivering papers.

Best Customers
Lawyers, who are notorious for waiting until the last minute to file or serve papers and need a lot of immediate personal attention for which process servers can charge extra fees.

Helpful Tips
This business is more profitable part-time in a rural rather than an urban setting. Call a larger agency located in an urban area and tell them you are available to serve papers in your vicinity. Otherwise, provide services full-time and be available for your clients at all times.

Franchises, Distributorships, and Licenses
Franchise
Serving By Irving, Inc.
233 Broadway, Suite 1036
New York, NY 10279

For More Information
Association
National Association of Process Servers (NAPS)
P.O. Box 4547
Portland, OR 97208-4547
(503) 222-4180; (503) 222-3950 fax
< http://www.napps.com >

Publishes a bimonthly newsletter (annual subscription $35) and a membership directory twice a year, plus other publications. This is a not-for-profit organization of some 1,100 members worldwide. To join NAPS, a person must have worked at least two years as a process server or be affiliated with the profession/industry. Call or send a large self-addressed envelope with two first-class stamps for additional membership information and fees.

Additional Business Ideas

❖ Courier services. Many process serving companies in larger cities provide courier services for delivery of business documents in downtown areas and between local communities.
❖ Private investigators. Many private investigators do process serving as part of their work. They frequently are hired to serve subpoenas upon witnesses who are called to testify at trials. (See "Private Investigator" in *101 Best Small Businesses for Women*, by Priscilla Y. Huff. 1996, Prima Publishing, Rocklin, CA.)

৯৫61৯৯
PROFESSIONAL PRACTICE CONSULTANT

As a professional practice consultant, you help new lawyers, doctors, accountants, chiropractors, psychologists, and other independent professionals learn the basics of running an independent business. For already-established practices, you can be a professional evaluator and adviser to help keep their practices running smoothly.

You need a background in business management, especially independent practices, and a working knowledge of the profession of each client so you can keep them updated with the latest information. You can recommend related business services, software, and so forth, that will help run their practices more efficiently.

Start-Up Costs and Financing Sources

❖ $6,000 to $12,000.
❖ Personal savings, small business loan, lines of credit on your credit cards.

Pricing Guidelines
From $60 to $300 per hour, depending on your clients and expertise.

Marketing and Advertising Methods and Tips
+ Send direct mailings, make calls and presentations to newly opened or expanding professional practices with which you have expertise.
+ Network with professionals and consultants in your field of expertise for tips on clients who might need your services.
+ Place ads in trade publications and journals.
+ Advertise in the business telephone directory.
+ Attend talks at professional conferences and meetings on effective management.

Essential Equipment
Computer and accessories, especially modem to get online information, business phone with answering capabilities, professional wardrobe, filing and billing system (manual or computerized), reference library of books and trade publications.

Recommended Training, Experience, or Needed Skills
+ Apprentice in a professional practice consultant service.
+ Enroll in business management and entrepreneur courses held at business schools, institutes, or local colleges.
+ Work in various professional offices to understand standard procedures for that profession(s).
+ Need business management expertise.
+ Have an accounting, business, or financial background as well as some expertise in health-care requirements and law.

Income Potential
$60,000 to hundreds of thousands a year.

Type of Business
About one-third in-home for writing up evaluations, presentations, reports, and so forth; about two-thirds out-of-the-home, meeting and working with clients and staff in their offices.

Best Customers
New professionals, established professional practices that are moving, expanding, or adding staff.

Helpful Tips
This is a relatively new business field. You must have business acumen and know which sources to tap to get your client the best information needed.

For More Information

Associations
Send an LSASE for membership information.

The Society of Medical-Dental Management Consultants
3646 E. Ray Rd., #B 16-45
Phoenix, AZ 85044

National Association of Healthcare Consultants
1255 23rd St., NW
Washington, DC 20037-1174

Books
The "I Hate Selling" Book: Business-Building Advice for Consultants, Attorneys, Accountants, Engineers, Architects, and Other Professionals, by Allan S. Boress. 1994, AMACON, New York.
Managing the Professional Service Firm, by David M. Maister. 1997, Maister Associates, Boston, MA.
Marketing Your Consulting and Professional Services, 2nd ed., by Richard A. Connor, Jr., and Jeffrey P. Davidson. 1990, John Wiley & Sons, New York.

Business Kits
Professional Practice Builders Kit, by Tyler Hicks. See Hicks's book, 199 Great Home Businesses You Can Start (and Succeed in) for Under $1,000. 1993, Prima Publishing, Rocklin, CA.
See also "Business Consultant/Coach" entry, page 209, for more resources.

༂62༂
TEMPORARY HELP SERVICE

With the economy swinging in periodic ups and downs, as well as the increasing cost of employee benefits, businesses turn to temporary help agencies to supply them with staff to adapt to these conditions. Many temporary agencies used to offer only clerical and secretarial workers, but today's agencies also supply professionals in health care, business, law, and other areas.

Start-Up Costs and Financing Sources
+ $40,000 to $80,000. Costs will be less if you are starting with small businesses and more if you plan on a larger number of temps. You need this amount for your payroll since you pay your employees and you bill the businesses—which may not pay you for thirty days or more.
+ Bank loan until the businesses that hire your temps pay you, line-of-credit to cover your payroll.

Pricing Guidelines
40 percent to 50 percent of the going salary for that position—mostly less for clerical and general workers and more for professionals. Keep up with the going pay rates for the positions you fill.

Marketing and Advertising Methods and Tips

For Clients
+ Advertise in the business telephone directory and in the business section of local newspapers and publications.
+ Make calls and presentations to potential business clients.
+ Conduct surveys. Contact the businesses in the area(s) you plan to concentrate on and ask them what times in their fiscal year they need help to fill-in for or back up their employees.
+ Network with the local chambers of commerce.

For Employees
+ Advertise in the business telephone directory.

❖ Place want ads in employment sections of newspapers and on cable television.

❖ Give talks to retirees' groups.

❖ Contact local schools, technical schools, and colleges for student help and recent graduates.

❖ Print professional-looking brochures and advertising literature.

Essential Equipment
Home office suitable for interviewing employees (unless you rent a conference room periodically (once a week or so) to conduct interviews; computer with billing, payroll, temporary help software, modem; desktop publishing capabilities to create forms you need; business telephone line with answering service or voice mail; fax machine.

Recommended Training, Experience, or Needed Skills
❖ Work in a temporary employment office (the management part of it) to see how business is conducted.

❖ Have basic business management skills—from previous work experience and/or from taking courses at colleges or business schools.

❖ If you specialize in certain types of employee placements (nannies, medical professionals, etc.), have training in that same field.

Income Potential
$10,000 to $100,000 and up.

Type of Business
About two-thirds in-home, scheduling employees, billing, recordkeeping; about one-third out of the-home, making presentations to clients, interviewing employees if you rent a conference room.

Best Customers
Companies, practices, and so forth, that need short-term labor.

Helpful Tips

* Research to see if there is a market for your services in your area and enough workers to supply it.
* Requires strict and constant organization at all times, both to keep marketing your business in order to find clients and to recruit (and keep) reliable and qualified temporary employees.
* Hold periodic training for updating employees' skills so that they will be qualified to work for your clients.
* Make sure you have enough start-up money to meet your payrolls, especially until your business is established.
* Check with your business professionals: lawyers, insurance agents, accountants, and tax experts for procedures on reporting taxes, paying employees, contracts, etc.
* Start small and concentrate at first on getting the best employees and best clients possible.
* May be a business to start with a relative or friend.

Franchises, Distributorships, and Licenses

Franchises
Look for additional ones listed in the franchise magazines, in the "Franchise and Distributorships" chapter. Check to see if those that interest you are suitable for home-based operations or not.

Ace Personnel
6400 Glenwood, #309
Overland Park, KS 66202

Send LSASE for information and a listing of states in which they are licensed to operate.

For More Information

Association
National Association of Temporary and Staffing Services
119 S. Saint Asaph St.
Alexandria, VA 22314
< http://www.natss.org >

Quarterly journal, member benefits. Send LSASE for membership information.

Books

How to Start & Manage a Temporary Help Services Business, by Jerre Lewis and Leslie D. Renn. Order from Lewis & Renn Associates, 10315 Harmony Dr., Interlochen, MI 49643. $14.95 + $3 for postage and handling.

Start Your Own Temporary Help Agency. 1996, Prentice-Hall Trade, Upper Saddle River, NJ.

Start-Up Guides

Entrepreneur's Start-Up Guide, *Temporary Help Agency.* (800) 421-2300. $69 + shipping and handling.

National Business Library's Start-Up Guide, *Temporary Help Agency.* (800) 947-7724. $39.95 + shipping and handling.

Additional Business Ideas

Placement services for nannies, day care workers, nurses, home health-care workers.

∾ 63 ∾
VIDEO PRODUCTION SERVICES/ MULTIMEDIA PRODUCTION SERVICES

With little more than a home video camera and an idea, you can either produce your own educational and training tapes for schools and businesses, or make and sell one (or more, if it's a series) yourself on a topic in which you have expertise or interest. Video production services involve scriptwriting, taping, and editing of the video you are producing for a company or business. Multimedia production services involve the video production along with music, graphics, computer technology, etc., to produce presentations for seminars, business meetings, conventions, talks, and training programs.

Just about any how-to topic makes for a good video. Topics for business videos could include safety tips, basic step-by-step training (could be a series), descriptions of new products, or business management techniques. Educational videos could be made in conjunction with textbooks or school classes or for sports instruction or training. Videos for consumers could cover endless how-to topics, such as gardening, sports, crafts, and art instructions.

Once you have basic videotaping knowledge and skills, the possibilities are endless.

Start-Up Costs and Financing Sources
+ From $12,000 to $60,000.
+ Personal savings, small business loan, line of credit.

Pricing Guidelines
Charge per video or project. Follow the industry-suggested rates or survey the rates of video production services.

Marketing and Advertising Methods and Tips
+ Market your services or tapes to the associations, schools, and video distribution companies that sell videos on your topics.
+ Send direct mail to potential customers (send an introductory tape to show samples of your work).
+ Sell to catalog companies that serve customers interested in your specialized topics.

Essential Equipment
Camcorder, at least one (preferably two or three), multimedia computer system and related software, scanner. VCRs, editing equipment, digital switcher, computer, modem, business phone, fax, answering machine or service. You can start out renting your video camera and other necessary equipment, as well as using the services of video reproduction houses.

Recommended Training, Experience, or Needed Skills
+ Take videotaping and production courses at local technical schools or local community colleges.
+ Work in a video reproduction house or for a video production service.

✤ Extensive working knowledge of audio/video hardware and software.

Income Potential
$25,000 to $100,000+.

Type of Business
In-home business except when making a video in a rented studio or on location.

Helpful Tips
✤ Know target markets from your in-depth research.
✤ Try a small test-marketing of your videos to see how they sell and are received.
✤ Try different topics and different markets to find your niche in the industry.

Franchises, Distributorships, and Licenses

Franchise
Video Data Services
3136 Winton Rd. S. #304
Rochester, NY 14623

Send an LSASE for information.

For More Information
Also see "Videotaping Service" section.

Books
Cash in on Your Camcorder, by Eileen Stanton. 1989, Sandia Publishing Group, Albuquerque, NM.
Operating a Desktop Video Service on Your Home-Based PC, by Harvey Summers. 1994, McGraw-Hill, New York.
The Video Camera Operator's Handbook, by Peter Hodges. 1995, Butterworth-Heinemann, Newton, MA.

Internet Site

< http://videouniversity.com >

"Video University"—information for being a professional videographer.

Start-Up Guides

Entrepreneur's Start-Up Guide, *Video Production Service.* (800) 421-2300. $69 + shipping and handling.

National Business Library's Start-Up Guide, *Make Money with Your Camcorder.* (800) 947-7742. $39.95 + shipping and handling.

Additional Business Ideas

❖ Video yearbooks, video portfolios, sports videos.

❖ Video scriptwriting. Read *Video Scriptwriting—How to Write for the $4 Billion Commercial Video Market,* by Barry Hampe. 1992, Penguin Books, New York. Also see *Corporate Scriptwriting,* by Ray Diazzo. 1993, Butterworth-Heinemann, Newton, MA.

❖ Video editing service. Read *Videotape Editing,* by Steven E. Browne. 1996, Butterworth-Heineman.

Entertainment Businesses

CHILDREN'S PARTIES

Birthdays are special days, especially for children. If you enjoy children and have a special skill or talent or are just a "kid-at-heart," then this business may be for you. Here are just a few of the types of parties you can offer in this business:

❖ Character parties. Make up your own costume and character (don't copy any protected well-known, commercial ones). Your character can sponsor such activities as singing, dancing, balloons, pictures, prizes, and a special gift for the birthday boy or girl.

❖ Magic parties. Start with simple tricks and work up to more complicated ones. Teach the children a few simple tricks to do (they love to show their families and friends). Give them each a magic trick gimmick to take home.

❖ Fiesta parties. Have Mexican songs, dances, games, piñatas, and so forth. Bring a sombrero (Mexican hat) for each child. Teach them some simple Spanish phrases.

❖ Western parties. Have square dances, cowboy hats, and pony rides.

❖ Craft parties. Take several simple crafts appropriate for the season or holiday and have the children choose one or more

249

to make. One woman has Sand Art parties—children love it because each work is different.

✤ Music parties. Have an hour of dancing, singing, or playing simple rhythm instruments. You can even have the children make simple instruments to take home.

✤ Puppet shows. Buy or make your own puppets. Write skits or simple plays. Also have the children make their own simple puppets to take home.

✤ Obstacle courses or field day games. Come with your own obstacle course equipment and let the children challenge themselves or one another. Have fun field day events (for ideas, see *The Cooperative Indoor and Outdoor Game Book* listed later in this section).

Also see "Clowning," page 252.

Start-Up Costs and Financing Sources
✤ $500 to $2,000 for advertising, props, supplies, and so forth.
✤ Personal savings, Christmas or Vacation clubs (but use them for your business. You do not get the highest interest, but they can help discipline you to save).

Pricing Guidelines
$50 to $200 or more per hour; add extras for craft supplies, materials, and mileage.

Marketing and Advertising Methods and Tips
✤ Print business cards, flyers, coloring pictures with your name and business number on them.
✤ Have a business stamp made. Stamp paper bags and hand out to each child at the party for them to carry their prizes, candy, and crafts home.
✤ Place ads in local publications, especially parenting newspapers and on cable television.
✤ Hang flyers on bulletin boards in grocery stores and other community gathering places and at party supply stores.

Essential Equipment

Props, party supplies, your own costume(s).

Recommended Training, Experience, or Needed Skills

✤ Work or volunteer in schools or day care centers. Notice the likes and dislikes of different age groups.

✤ Enroll in college child psychology courses.

✤ Be flexible—substitute another game if the one you chose does not go over well.

Income Potential

$600 to $1,000+ a week.

Type of Business

Out-of-the-home.

Best Customers

Families with children in suburban or affluent neighborhoods, schools, churches, day care centers, intermediate units for physically or mentally challenged children, day camps, company family picnics or banquets, scouting banquets.

Helpful Tips

✤ Have a signed contract between you and your client as to payment, date, and time of the party. Confirm this information several days in advance.

✤ Never cancel. Have a stand-by substitute in case of an emergency. No mother wants to have fifteen active children to entertain by herself for three hours!

✤ Check with your insurance agent and lawyer on your liability needs.

✤ Have age-appropriate activities.

✤ Have enough supplies on hand for each child. Always bring extras.

✤ Volunteer to do family or friends' parties to see how your acts go over.

✤ Keep up-to-date on what is popular with children of all ages.

For More Information

Books

Birthday Party Business, by Bruce Fife. 1998, Picadilly Books, Colorado Springs, CO.

The Cooperative Indoor and Outdoor Game Book, by Priscilla Y. Huff, 1992; order from Scholastic Professional Books, Scholastic, Inc., P.O. Box 7502, Jefferson, MO 65102-9968.

Life of the Party, by Betty Bowes. 1998, Crisp Publications, Menlo Park, CA.

Make Money Entertaining Kids, No Experience Necessary, by Keith Johnson. 1998, KMJ Educational Programs. Tells how to earn good money keeping kids entertained at parties, festivals, school events, and malls. Order from KMJ Educational Programs, at (401) 781-6676 (VISA, Mastercard, Discover, money order, or check. U.S. funds only, no COD's). Or order it from your favorite online or real-life bookstore.

Children's Party Business (booklet). Send $7 to P.Y. Huff, Box 286, Sellersville, PA 18960.

Kids' party and craft books. Contact Patty Sachs, 5827 Nicollet Ave., S., Minneapolis, MN 55419. < http://www.geocities. com/ ~ partyexpert > Send an LSASE for list and prices.

Also see "For More Information" in "School Programs and Assemblies" entry, page 258.

Supplies

MeadowLark Party Shoppe, 2 Beistle Plaza, P.O. Box 10, Shippensburg, PA 17257. < http://www.party-here.com > ′Send an LSASE for prices and ordering information.

Additional Business Ideas

Children's cooking classes.

❧ 65 ❧
CLOWNING

For a number of years Donna Huff and Cindy Longacre enjoyed working together as co-directors of a summer day camp for mentally challenged children. They often made up skits to help their campers understand certain educational concepts. A clown they hired to entertain the children invited them to visit a local clown club. The club members gave Donna and Cindy basic clowning tips and suggestions on where they could begin clowning.

Donna and Cindy then enrolled in a high school evening course taught by a former mime. They came up with their duo name, Whoopsie and Daisy, and began to do birthday parties, picnics, and other special events. After attending a clown convention, they came up with the idea to teach educational units as clowns. Being former teachers, this came easily to them—they worked out skits on fire safety, how to clean your room, and other themes.

In addition to parties, they were hired at preschools and elementary schools to perform educational skits. The teachers and children loved it. Donna and Cindy keep files on each party, event, and school at which they perform and what skits they did. They also leave evaluation sheets for both teachers and students. Their clowning career is hectic for their families, but they both say it's given them an income while their children are small. Not only that, it's fun, too.

Start-Up Costs and Financing Sources
✤ $500 to $1,000.
✤ Personal savings, loans from family and friends.

Pricing Guidelines
$75 to $200 per hour, depending on the number of children or people at the event or where you are performing (school, organization, etc.). Network with other clowns, entertainers, and clubs for current entertainment rates.

Marketing and Advertising Methods and Tips
✤ Print business cards. Donna and Cindy had an artist draw their clown faces on colorful business cards, which they hand out to teachers and parents after their performances. They also give away pens with their names and phone numbers on them.

❖ Volunteer to be the clown at a parade or a community event.
❖ Be creative. Donna and Cindy give away pictures for children to color with their names and numbers listed on the bottom.
❖ Approach schools or institutions by personal visits (in your clown suit) or send out brochures. Follow up with phone calls.
❖ Post your business cards and flyers on every community bulletin board you can.

Essential Equipment
Clown make-up supplies (best found in a costume, theater, or dance supply store); gimmicks like oversized sunglasses, kazoos, simple magic tricks (may be found at your costume or magic store); an old suitcase to carry your props (decorate it for your acts); clothes (can buy suits or sew them from patterns or find some at thrift shops and create your own look); hair (use a clown wig, spray your hair, use a hat—whatever you decide your look to be); answering machine; contract to give to your customers; promotional materials; games, related play equipment.

Recommended Training, Experience, or Needed Skills
❖ Take pantomime courses, acting courses.
❖ Work with another clown or clowns in a club.
❖ Volunteer at different events until you decide whether you like this business. It's good practice and will help you decide upon your look and style.
❖ Knowledge and understanding of how to make children laugh and smile.

Income Potential
$500 to $1,000 a week; $50,000 to $125,000 a year.

Type of Business
Out-of-the-home.

Best Customers
Birthday parties (children's and adults), company picnics, opening or sales' days, special community events, fairs, carnivals,

Sunday schools, scouting troops, retirement dinners, roasts, preschools, residential institutions for children with special needs, hospitals, retirement homes.

Helpful Tips

❖ Network with other professional clowns and clubs.

❖ Be professional and keep clown ethics, such as not smoking or doing anything inappropriate while in your clown suit.

❖ Volunteer at different places in your community—everyone needs to laugh now and then!

❖ Make sure you have a signed contract or call in advance to confirm the date, place, time, and payment.

For More Information

Association

World Clown Association
P.O. Box 1413
Corona, CA 91718

Publishes a trade magazine, *Clowning Around,* and offers other information on clowning. Contact with an LSASE for membership information.

Books

Be a Clown: The Complete Guide to Instant Clowning, by Turk Pipin. 1989, Workman, New York.

Creative Clowning, by Bruce Fife. 1992, Picadilly Books, 4841 Ranch Dr., Colorado Springs, CO 80918.

Start-Up Guide

National Business Library's *Rent-a-Clown.* (800) 947-7724. $39.95 + shipping and handling.

Supplies

Clown Supplies: Robert Noel Clarkson, 401 N. Hoback St., Helena, MT 59601. < http://www.clarksonstudio.com/ clowns.htm > Send an LSASE for a listing of the products.

‹ᔕ66ᕈ›
NOVELTY MESSAGE SERVICE

If you are outgoing or have a special talent or product that people would enjoy receiving as a gift or gag, then this unusual and creative business may be for you. You present a gift, card, or bouquet of balloons or flowers with a signed message from the client to the designated person. You may perform a short routine along with it. Here are some ideas for novelty messenger services:

❖ Exotic dancers, belly dancers, tap dancers.
❖ Characters: gorillas, seasonal characters (Santa-grams, witch- or ghost-grams, Easter Bunny-grams), favorite children's storybook characters, clowns, or whatever costumed character you create.
❖ Balloon deliveries, chocolate-grams, teddy bear-grams.

Start-Up Costs and Financing Sources
❖ $1,000 to $3,000.
❖ Personal savings, lines of credit on your credit cards, loans from family or friends.

Pricing Guidelines
$65 to $100 per delivery. Charge more if you provide a short entertainment act.

Marketing and Advertising Methods and Tips
❖ Place ads in the business telephone directory, bridal supplements, and personal sections in newspapers.
❖ Leave business cards where you deliver your messages.
❖ Post flyers on community bulletin boards.
❖ Donate a coupon for one free message for a community auction.
❖ Buy ads on cable television and on local radio stations or national radio stations (if your product is mailed).

Essential Equipment
Business line with answering machine or service, costume, an 800 number for ordering, a dependable vehicle, distinctive

costumes and props, billing and filing system (computerized or manual).

Recommended Training, Experience, or Needed Skills
- Can work in a novelty delivery service.
- Have some dance or acting experience.

Income Potential
$35,000 to $55,000.

Type of Business
Out-of-the-home except for scheduling, marketing, billing.

Best Customers
Engaged couples, recent graduates, new parents or grandparents, new retirees, recipients of awards, those celebrating birthdays, confirmations, bar mitzvahs.

Helpful Tips
- Be professional and tasteful.
- Confirm dates, times, and places a few days before you deliver the service.
- Describe your service accurately so your clients know what they will be getting.
- Have an entertaining answering voice mail or machine message.
- Do your own market research to determine who are your best customers and how you can reach them.

For More Information

Start-Up Guide
National Business Library's *Rent-a-Clown.* (800) 947-7724. $39.95 + shipping and handling.

Additional Business Ideas
Messenger service. See National Business Library's, *Messenger Service.* (800) 947-7724. $39.95 + shipping and handling.

∾67∾
SCHOOL PROGRAMS, ASSEMBLIES, AND PRESENTATIONS

If you are an author or an expert in history, animals and nature, science, environmental sciences, different cultures, and so forth, you have a market to bring your knowledge to public and private schools, institutions, and nursery and day care centers. These institutions are always looking for high quality, educational programs for their students to add to their standard programs.

Donna Weiss Hill, a musician/composer who is blind, takes along her guide dog, Curly Connor, and plays a variety of music on her acoustic guitar. She performs at schools, youth groups, family concerts, and churches. She also answers questions about her blindness and Curly Connor.

You can choose to limit your presentations to your immediate area or you can take your program across county and state lines. Most presenters offer rates for one-hour, two-hour, or all-day presentations. Set your prices according to your expertise (are you certified or a professional in your subject?), the distance traveled, and according to what other presenters charge.

Here are some of the programs offered by various presenters:

❖ Science: Space programs, fun and exciting science experiments.
❖ Animals: Endangered animals, odd or unusual animals (bats, snakes, reptiles).
❖ History: Reenactments, pioneer life (food, customs, dress, tools, crafts), folktales.
❖ Environment: Recycling, earth in danger.
❖ Music: Unusual instruments and their history.

Start-Up Costs
$1,000 to $5,000, depending on your needed supplies, cost of your promotional materials and postage to mail them, transportation costs.

Pricing Guidelines
$175 to $375 for an hour presentation; $400 to $700 for a two-hour program; $800 to $1,200 for a full-day presentation.

Often, your time at a full-day program will be divided to accommodate different age groups. For example, one hour will include grades K–3; second hour, grades 4–6. Some presenters visit individual classrooms to answer questions and show additional information.

Marketing and Advertising Methods and Tips

* Get a copy of the directories of a state's private and public schools and institutions and send direct mail advertising to the person(s) responsible for scheduling special programs.
* Contact school parents' groups who often provide the funding for special programs.
* Have an Internet site and/or get listed on sites that list persons for school programs.

Essential Equipment

Audio-visual equipment, extension cords, cages and crates if you have animals, dependable transportation, promotional materials.

Recommended Training, Experience, or Needed Skills

* Start giving your presentations to small groups for free or for a low fee until you feel your program is ready for a larger audience.
* Know children's interests at different age levels.
* Be familiar with the school's curriculum and see if you can relate your program to a part or part(s) of it.

Income Potential

$1,000 to $3,000+ a week.

Type of Business

Out-of-the-home.

Best Customers

Private, public, and nursery schools; institutions and/or group homes; churches; youth, scouting groups; museums, nature centers; local cable television programs; summer camps.

Helpful Tips

✤ Involve your audience in your presentation to keep up their interest.

✤ Keep your program lively and fun. Stay within the time allotted.

✤ Have a signed contract with terms stated (space needed, electrical requirements, time allotted, grade levels, etc.). Several days in advance, call to confirm times, dates, and locations.

✤ If showing wild or endangered animals, make sure you are following regulations and/or have the licenses required by state or federal departments.

✤ Check with your insurance agent and/or lawyer as to insurance coverage and liability concerns.

✤ Relate your topic to education. Do not just provide entertainment.

Book

See Keith Johnson's, *Make Money Entertaining Kids, No Experience Necessary* in "Children's Parties" section.

Additional Business Ideas

✤ Make your own videos and sell them to educational catalogs or advertise in parent and/or teacher trade publications.

✤ Publish your own regional, state, or national directory of professional presenters and sell to schools, libraries, and other institutions.

ເ⅏68⅏

TOUR SERVICES

If you live in or near historic or interesting places, you may want to start your own local tour service. If you live in a town or a major city, you could give walking tours. Offer interesting facts or places not covered in standard tours or guidebooks. One woman who writes about ghost stories in her historic town gives walking tours to the ghosts' haunts, ending the tour with dinner at one of the local restaurants (also a "haunt" location). She has copies of her book for sale for additional profits.

You could charter a bus or rent a van and specialize in tours like visiting caves in your county or state, nature preserves, or public gardens.

Start-Up Costs
$7,000 to $25,000, depending on whether you need transportation.

Pricing Guidelines
$20 to $40 per person for a one- or two-hour tour. Charge more if the tour is by van or bus.

Marketing and Advertising Methods and Tips
* Contact historic places, travel agencies, restaurants, museums, and bus companies that regularly bring tourists to your town or city.
* Place ads in travel and family magazines.
* Place ads in local publications. Post flyers on community bulletin boards.
* Buy ads on local radio or cable television stations.
* Send out press releases to the travel section editors of local newspapers.
* Print brochures describing your tour and rates. Place them in local hotels, motels, and bed and breakfast establishments.

Essential Equipment
Business line with answering capabilities, promotional materials, van or rental bus if needed.

Recommended Training, Experience, or Needed Skills
* Work as a tour guide or in a travel agency.
* Be an expert in the area of your tours.

Income Potential
$50,000 to $80,000 + or more a year, depending on the length of your tours and the tourist season. Follow industry suggestions and guidelines.

Type of Business
One-third in-home for booking and arranging tours; two-thirds out-of-the-home for conducting the tours.

Best Customers
Tourists, local senior citizens' groups, youth and small school groups or classes, special clubs or hobbyists, companies that attend conventions or seminars in your area.

Helpful Tips
+ Follow licensing, bonding, and tax laws.
+ Check with your insurance agent and lawyer for insurance and liability needs.
+ Offer a variety of tours.
+ Sell souvenirs, booklets, books, and videos for additional profits.
+ Make the history interesting with little known tidbits of information not found in the usual tourbooks.

Franchises, Distributorships, and Licenses
Franchise
Travel Network Ltd.
560 Sylvan Ave.
Englewood Cliffs, NJ 07632
(201) 567-8500; < http://www.travelnetwork.com >

A recognized global chain of full and home-based travel agencies. Call for information.

Look for others in the franchise publications listed in the "Franchises and Distributorships" chapter.

For More Information
Books
The Business of Tour Operations, by Pat Yale. 1995, TransAtlantic Publications, Inc., Philadelphia, PA.
Start and Run a Profitable Tour Guiding Business: Part-Time, Full-Time, at Home or Abroad: Your Step-By-Step Business Plan, by

Barbara Braidwood, Susan M. Boyce, and Richard Cropp. 1996, Self-Counsel Press, Bellingham, WA.

Additional Business Ideas

✤ Lead overnight adventure tours—camping, wagon train, rafting, hiking, mountain climbing.

✤ Make videos of your areas of interest and sell them to travel agencies that book tours in your area.

✤ Home-based travel agency. Have an office suitable for meeting with clients. Provide a relaxed environment and give individual attention. Resources follow:

Entrepreneur's Start-Up Guide, *Specialty Travel and Tours.* (800) 421-2300. $69 + shipping and handling.

Home-Based Travel Agent by Kelly Monaghan. 1997, Intrepid Traveler, New York.

See also "Independent Travel Sales Rep" in *More 101 Best Home-Based Businesses for Women,* by Priscilla Y. Huff. 1998, Prima Publishing, Rocklin, CA.

ᔔ69ᔕ
TOY AND GAME INVENTOR

If you love playing games and are always modifying games and toys or thinking up new ones, you may want to investigate selling your ideas to toy companies. To start your own game company could cost thousands of dollars, even millions. A more practical way to start is to sell the manufacturing and marketing rights to your game or toy to a large toy company that already has distributorships in the United States and around the world. It takes quite a bit of persistence to get your game noticed by a company—but if it is purchased, you receive a percentage of the gross revenues.

Here are a few guidelines:

1. Develop your idea. Make it original, simple, and direct. Games where players work together toward a common goal are most popular.

2. Decide whether your game is for a specific age group or for general entertainment.

3. Test market your game with many people and get their reactions.

4. Make a prototype closely resembling the finished product. It should look professionally designed and be easy for the consumer to tell what kind of game it is from the box.

5. Decide which toy companies would be the best buyers for your game. Research them to find out what games they carry, and then select several to contact for a presentation of your game. If possible, attend toy company trade shows and talk to company representatives.

6. To protect your game idea from being copied, you may have to obtain a patent. Seek advice at your local SBA Business Development Center.

7. It helps to have some design training and to be familiar with manufacturing costs.

8. Read the *Toy Inventor Guide* and check the background and references of what all is involved.

Franchises, Distributorships, and Licenses

Licensing
Louis C. Fernandez
Community Benefits Corporation
Game-O-Poly
131 Deerfield Dr.
Tenafly, NJ 07670

Send an LSASE for more information. Licensees publish their own hometown game-o-poly board games featuring local, hometown advertising businesses.

For More Information

Books

The Game Inventor's Handbook, by Stephen Peek. 1993 (out of print, but look in your local public library listings).

The Inventor's Desktop Companion: A Guide to Successfully Marketing and Protecting Your Ideas, by Richard Levy. 1995, Visible Ink Press, Detroit, MI.

Toy & Game Inventor's Guide, 2nd ed., by Gregory J. Battersby and Charles W. Grimes. 1996, Kent Communications, Stamford, CT.

Also, for more information, see: *Toy Industry Fact Book; TMA Guide to Toys and Play;* and *Toy Inventor Design Guide*—obtain from the Toy Manufacturers of America (TMA) (see address below). Contact TMA for costs and availability.

Government Assistance

Small Business Development Centers or Women's Business Centers.

Patent and Trademark Office, U.S. Dept. of Commerce, Washington, DC 20231. Will send you information about patents and trademarks. (703) 308-HELP [4357]; (703) 305-8600.

Magazine

Playthings, Geyer-McAllister, 51 Madison Ave., New York, NY 10010-1675. Monthly magazine covering toys and hobbies aimed mainly at mass-market toy retailers. Publishes annual issue, *Playthings Buyers' Guide.*

Trade Shows

International Toy Fair (trade only, not for consumers). Contact Toy Manufacturers of America, 1115 Broadway, Suite 400, New York, NY 10010. (212) 675-1141. Held each February, attended by buyers from ninety-three countries.

Green Businesses

Green Resources

Association

American Horticultural Society
7931 East Boulevard Dr.
Alexandria, VA 22308-1300
(800) 777-7931

Journal, gardening information for gardeners.

Books

Backyard Market Growing: The Entrepreneur's Guide to Selling What You Grow, by Andrew W. Lee, et al. 1995, Good Earth Publications, Columbus, NC.

Building Your Own Greenhouse, by Mark Freeman. 1997, Stackpole Books, Mechanicsburg, PA.

Christmas Trees: Growing and Selling Trees, Wreaths, and Greens, by Lewis Hill. 1989, Storey Books, Pownal, VT.

The Flower Farmer: An Organic Grower's Guide to Raising and Selling Cut Flowers, by Lynn Byczynski. 1997, Chelsea Green Publishing Company, White River Junction, VT.

Flowers for Sale: Growing and Marketing Cut Flowers—Backyard to Small Acreage: A Bootstrap Guide, by Lee Sturdivant. 1994, San Juan Naturals, P.O. Box 642, Friday Harbor, WA 98250.

The Four-Season Landscape: Easy-Care Plants and Plans for Year-Round Color, by Susan A. Roth. 1996, Rodale Press, Emmaus, PA.

Herbs for Sale: Growing and Marketing Herbs, Herbal Products, and Herbal Know-how, by Lee Sturdivant. 1994, San Juan Naturals, Friday Harbor, WA.

Indoor & Greenhouse Plants, Vols. 1 and 2, by Roger Phillips and Martyn Rix. 1997, Random House, New York.

Lawn Care and Gardening: A Down-to-Earth Guide to the Business, by Kevin Rossi. 1996, Acton Circle, Ukiah, CA.

The New Organic Grower, by Sherri Amsel and Elliot Coleman. 1995, Chelsea Green Publishing Co., White River Junction, VT.

Successful Small Scale Gardening, 2nd ed., by Karl Schwenke. 1991, Storey Books, Pownal, VT.

Wreath Magic, by Leslie Dierks. 1996, Lark Books, Ashville, NC.

Gardening Book Publishers

Send an LSASE for a listing or catalog of publishers' current books.

Better Homes and Gardens Books, 1100 Walnut St., Des Moines, IA 50309-3400.

Rodale Books, 33 E. Minor St., Emmaus, PA 18099-0229.

Storey/Garden Way Publishing, Pownal, VT 05261. Write for catalog, with many booklets also for sale.

Government Assistance—Cooperative Extension Service.

The U.S. Department of Agriculture has an extension office in every county in the United States. Originally formed to assist farmers, these offices operate in conjunction with state universities and are good sources for information on plants and insects. In recent years, they have also assisted in forming crafts cooperatives and providing information on small business start-ups. Call your local directory assistance for the number of the extension office nearest you. Or try this Web site < http://www. reeusda.gov >

Internet Site

< http://www.hsny.org >
Horticulture on the Net

Magazine and Publication

(See the many consumer and industry publications.)

Lawn Maintenance Pro, Helping Lawn Maintenance Firms Operate Profitably, Johnson Hill Press, 1233 Jamesville Ave., Ft. Atkinson, WI 53538.

Lawn & Landscape Magazine. < http://www.lawnandlandscape.com >

Miscellaneous

To establish a backyard habitat, order the packet from the National Wildlife Federation, 8925 Leesburg Pike, Vienna, VA 22184. (800) 477-5560. < http://www.nwf.org >

Gardening by Mail: A Source Book, 5th ed., by Barbara J. Barton. 1997, Houghton Mifflin, Boston, MA. A comprehensive directory of mail-order sources for gardeners.

ᦉ 70 ᦉ
ENVIRONMENTALLY CONCERNED BUSINESSES

Air and water pollution, accumulation of toxic chemicals and wastes, and overflowing landfills are just some of the environmental problems we face. If you can come up with a unique business or an original idea to fix an ecological problem, you will not only help the earth, but you can also make some handsome profits in the process.

There are a number of existing businesses, franchises, and other opportunities in which you can invest and operate. Or look at your community to see what environmental problems exist and come up with your own ecologically based business to handle them.

Here are just a few of the kinds of businesses that presently exist:

✤ Ecotourism. There are two kinds of ecotourism—one is termed "soft," in which people take hiking, mountain biking, photo, rafting, or other nontraditional excursions and do not disturb the ecosystems; and the other is termed "hard," in which people work toward common goals such as restoring habitats or working at archaeological sites. You may live in a special area in which you can offer such tours.

❖ Selling natural products. These include non-animal-tested cosmetics and environmentally safe home cleaning and pet care products.

❖ Recycling materials. Collect materials for industries and "green" businesses.

❖ Recycling consultant broker. Help communities set up and implement or improve their recycling programs.

❖ Recycling inventor. Come up with a unique way to use recycled materials in a product you devise.

❖ Grower of organic produce and herbs. Sell to healthfood stores, grocery stores, and restaurants.

❖ Natural garden service. Offer chemical-free lawn and garden care service and products.

Start-Up Costs and Financing Sources

❖ $2,000 to $50,000 or more, depending on whether you start a service business or need an inventory.

❖ Personal savings, small business loan, grant from the government if your business qualifies.

Pricing Guidelines

Compare your business to a similar commercial business's prices to give you a starting point. Consider, too, your time and cost of materials involved. Talk to an SBA expert at your local SBA Small Business Development Center (see "Federal Government" in Part III).

Recommended Training, Experience, or Needed Skills

❖ Work in a business similar to one you want to start.

❖ Read environmental publications.

Income Potential

$10,000 to $100,000+ depending on the market and demand for your products or services.

Type of Business
Can be either in-home or out-of-the-home.

Best Customers
Middle- to upper-income people, businesses that want to save money through recycling and want to use recycled products.

Franchises, Distributorships and Licenses
There are a number of franchises that are concerned with the environment. Research them thoroughly before you invest any money. See "Franchise Resources" in "Franchises and Distributorships" chapter, page 44.

For More Information

Association
National Recycling Coalition
1727 King St., Suite 105
Alexandria, VA 22314

Books and Publications
101 Best Small Businesses for Women, 1996, and *More 101 Best Home-Based Businesses for Women*, 1998, for additional "green" resources.

Choose to Reuse: An Encyclopedia of Services, Businesses, Tools & Charitable Programs That Facilitate Reuse, by Nikki & David Goldbeck. 1995, Ceres Press, Woodstock, NY.

Ecopreneuring: The Complete Guide to Small Business Opportunities from the Environmental Revolution, by Steven J. Bennett. 1991, John Wiley & Sons, New York. Order from the New Careers Center's *Whole Work Catalog* (see "Books Through the Mail" in Part III). Highly recommended.

The Recycler's Manual for Business, Government, and the Environmental Community, by David and Melinda Powelson. John Wiley & Sons, New York.

Internet Site
< http://www.recycle.net >
Recycler's World

Additional Business Ideas

+ Papermaking. Recycle junk mail and other paper. Write: Paper Chase/Ann Crume, Sheet and Cast Papermaking Kits, P.O. Box 16555, Kansas City, MO 64133. (816) 455-8753.
+ Create fashion jewelry from paper. Contact Joyce Chambers, Paper Art Originals, 2526 Lamar Ave., Suite 231, Paris, TX 75460.

∽ 71 ∾
FLOWERSCAPING SERVICE

In this business, you buy flowers from a wholesaler or raise them yourself, then plant them in your clients' flower beds. Give advice on what kind of flowers should go where. After you plant the flowers, you can either let your client maintain them, or, for a weekly fee, you can do the weeding, watering, and pruning.

You can specialize in flowers or small bushes (leave the planting of trees and large shrubs to the bigger landscapers in your area).

Start-Up Costs
$3,000 to $8,000.

Pricing Guidelines
Charge an additional 50 percent to 100 percent of the wholesale price of the flowers plus your hourly wage ($20 to $35 per hour, more if you have a degree in landscape design or horticulture).

Marketing and Advertising Methods and Tips
+ Post flyers and your business cards on community bulletin boards.
+ Make direct calls to landscapers who plant only trees and shrubs and not flowers.
+ Leave business cards at garden centers.
+ Encourage word-of-mouth referrals.

Essential Equipment
Truck, van, or station wagon. Gardening equipment: pruners, edger, clippers, shovels/spade/hoe, rakes, wheelbarrow, trowels,

weed puller, washable gloves, drop cloths (for dirt), scissors, measuring tape, watering can. Office equipment: telephone and answering machine, computer for record-keeping, billing and gardening software, promotional materials. Gardening reference books and publications.

Recommended Training, Experience, or Needed Skills

✤ Work in a nursery, garden center, greenhouse, or for a landscaper.

✤ Take gardening and horticulture courses at local vo-tech schools or colleges.

✤ Volunteer to do your friends' and neighbors' gardens and experiment in your own with various flowers.

✤ Need to have a green thumb and enjoy working long hours in the growing seasons.

Income Potential

$30,000 to $45,000 in a growing season.

Type of Business

Out-of-the-home.

Best Customers

Working couples, local businesses and institutions who have flower beds, homeowners in new developments.

Helpful Tips

✤ Charge an evaluation fee, but credit it toward the customers' bill if they decide to hire you.

✤ Study landscape design books.

✤ Know the best flowers for certain soil, light, and weather conditions.

✤ Constantly learn and try new horticultural techniques.

✤ Attend garden shows, read up on the latest garden advances, give talks and/or courses to gardening clubs or at adult evening schools in the off-season.

For More Information

Book

1001 Questions Answered About Flowers, by Norman Taylor and James MacDonald. 1996, Dover Publications, Mineola, NY.

Additional Business Ideas

❖ Specialize in installing wildflower and native plants in landscapes.

❖ Lawn care service (mow, clip, rake—no chemical applications). Order Entrepreneur's Start-Up Guide *Lawn Care Service*. (800) 421-2300. $69 + shipping and handling. Also contact Professional Lawn Care Association of America, 1000 Johnson Ferry Rd., NE, Suite C-135, Marietta, GA 30068. Send LSASE for membership information.

❖ Raise and sell your own flowers, plants, and shrubs to your customers.

ᝒᝢ 72 ᝢᝒ
GARDEN CONSULTING

You help people plan and design their gardens, suggesting the best flowers, shrubs, trees, and even decorative structures for the area. Clients may also call on you to recommend solutions to insect infestations, plant diseases, and other gardening problems.

You can either supply the plantings yourself or refer your client to a suitable garden center. A client may hire you for a one-time consultation or have you come on a regular or as-needed basis.

Start-Up Costs and Financing Sources

❖ $5,000 to $8,000.

❖ Personal savings, credit cards, small business loan.

Pricing Guidelines

$25 to $45 an hour; $75 to $200 an hour if you have a degree or certification in landscape design, architecture, or horticulture.

Marketing and Advertising Methods and Tips

- ✤ Place signs on your customers' lawns while you are working there.
- ✤ Rent booths at home and garden shows.
- ✤ Write a gardening column for your local paper.
- ✤ Place a magnetic sign or paint a sign on your vehicle.
- ✤ Make direct calls to builders of new housing developments.
- ✤ Place an ad in the business telephone directory, as well as in the home and garden supplement of your local newspaper.

Essential Equipment

Garden reference books, access to online gardening databases, graph paper and drafting tools or computer with garden designing software.

Recommended Training, Experience, or Needed Skills

- ✤ Have a degree or training in ornamental horticulture or attend classes in a local agricultural school or community college.
- ✤ Work for an established landscaper.
- ✤ Be creative.

Income Potential

$35,000 to $80,000 + .

Type of Business

Out-of-the-home except for designing on paper.

Helpful Tips

- ✤ Take the necessary courses or have training or work experience to be properly qualified.
- ✤ Keep up on the latest environmental and organic studies related to gardening, as many homeowners are more concerned about chemicals and their effects on living organisms.
- ✤ Specialize in designs for small gardens or lots because many homes are built on smaller lots these days.
- ✤ Make each one of your customers' properties the envy of their neighbors!

For More Information

Books

The Backyard Landscaper: 40 Professional Designs for Do-It-Your-selfers, by Ireland Gannon Associates. 1992, Home Planner Publications, Tucson, AZ.

The Complete Guide to Landscape Design, Renovation, and Maintenance, by Cass Turnbull. 1991, Betterway Books, Cincinnati, OH. (800) 289-0963.

Easy Garden Design: 12 Simple Steps to Creating Successful Gardens and Landscapes, by Janet Macunovich. Storey/Garden Way Publishing, Pownal, VT.

How to Start a Home-Based Landscaping Business, 2nd ed., by Owen E. Dell. 1997, Globe Pequot Press, Old Saybrook, CT.

Software

Lafayette Landscape Designs, *Home Gardner Package* and *Professional Package*, 6323 Lafayette Rd., Medina, OH 44256. (330) 725-7442. < http://www.ne1.bright.net/lldesign > Landscape software for IBM-compatible (386 or better) computer. Write or call for prices and information.

Additional Business Ideas

✤ Plan natural backyard habitats.

✤ Plan and design decorative, backyard water ponds. See *Waterscaping: Plants and Ideas for Natural and Created Water Gardens*, by Judy Glattstein. 1994, Storey/Garden Way Publishing, Pownal, VT.

❦73❧
GROWING HERBS

In the past few years herbs have become popular for use in home remedies, potpourris, gourmet cooking, and by gardeners who want to grow them for their beauty and practical uses. You can make money growing herbs by selling them wholesale or retail or by making and selling your own herbal products.

You need less space than other cash crops. A small greenhouse (either attached to your house or free-standing) will allow you to grow them all year, or at least get them started for the growing season in your area.

Start-Up Costs and Financing Sources
+ $8,000 to $40,000 for equipment, seeds, greenhouse, drying shed, vehicle, advertising.
+ Personal savings, small business loan.

Pricing Guidelines
$4 to $10 per plant. Check with other growers in the herb industry for pricing recommendations.

Marketing and Advertising Methods and Tips
+ Wholesale. Contact garden centers, nurseries, hardware, grocery stores, and restaurants.
+ Retail. Place classified ads in local publications, give talks to garden clubs and hand out flyers and business cards, rent a table at a flea market or farmer's market.
+ Mail Order. Advertise in gardening and herbal publications. Add shipping and handling costs and taxes for some states. Check with state regulations regarding the transportation of plants.

Essential Equipment
Greenhouse(s), outside area for beds, gardening equipment, lumber for tables, plants, dirt, vehicle for transporting plants, markers, pots, seeds. Office supplies: phone with fax, answering machine or service, billing system.

Recommended Training, Experience, or Needed Skills
+ Work in a nursery, a commercial greenhouse, or apprentice with a person who grows herbs.
+ Take courses, workshops, and seminars on herbs at vo-tech schools or agricultural colleges.
+ Know all the different herbs, their properties and characteristics.
+ Know propagation techniques and have basic gardening skills.

Income Potential
$25,000 to $60,000 + .

Type of Business
In-home business except when out-of-the-home selling.

Best Customers
Weekend gardeners, gardening centers, nurseries, restaurants that use herbs, grocery stores, and farm stands that carry local produce. Growing your own specialty herbs—different and unusual varieties—will help you compete with larger, commercial, and foreign markets.

For More Information
Associations
Send an LSASE for more information.

Herb Growing and Marketing Network
P.O. Box 254
Silver Springs, PA 17575-0245
< http://www.herbworld.com >
< http://www.herbnet.com >
Publishes *The Herbal Connection.*

International Herb Association
P.O. Box 317
Mundelein, IL 60060.

American Botanical Council
P.O. Box 201660
Austin, TX 78720
< http://www.herbalgram.org >
Publishes *HerbalGram.*

Books
(See also books reviewed on herbal Internet sites.)

Growing Your Herb Business, by Bertha Reppert. 1994, Storey/ Garden Way Publishing, Pownal, VT.

Herb Resource Directory. Northwind Farm Publications, 439 Ponderosa Way, Jemez Springs, NM 87025.

Herb Topiaries, by Sally Gallo. 1992, Interweave Press, Loveland, CO.

Pay Dirt: How to Raise and Sell Herbs & Produce for Serious Cash, by Mimi Luebbermann. 1997, Prima Publishing, Rocklin, CA.

The Pleasure of Herbs, by Phyllis Shaudys. 1994, Storey/Garden Way Publishing, Pownal, VT.

Profits from Your Backyard Herb Garden, 2nd rev. ed., by Lee Sturdiant. 1995, San Juan Naturals.

Bookseller

Wood Violet Books, 3814 Sunhill Dr., Madison, WI 53704. Offers hundreds of herb and garden books, will do special searches. $2 for catalog.

Internet Site

See others listed with associations.

< http://www.wholeherb.com >

Magazines and Newsletters

AHA Quarterly, published by the American Herb Assn., P.O. Box 1673, Nevada City 95959.

The Business of Herbs, published by Paula Oliver. Send an SASE to Northwind Publications, 439 Ponderosa Way, Jemez Springs, NM 87025. Excellent for herb businesses.

The Herb Companion, Interweave Press, 201 E. Fourth St., Loveland, CO 80537.

Start-Up Guide

Entrepreneur's Start-Up Guide, *Herb Farm.* (800) 421-2300. $59 + shipping and handling.

Additional Business Ideas

❖ Create and sell herbal vinegars, gifts, or potpourris. Teach how-to classes at adult evening schools or at your home.

❖ Plan and install herbal gardens.

❖ Grow cactus plants for states with desert or arid climates.

~~74~~
PLANT MAINTENANCE SERVICE

In this business, you maintain businesses' or institutions' plants and keep them looking healthy. You may also be called on to be a plant "doctor"—that is, to revive sickly plants.

Recent studies have shown that green plants help filter out air pollutants, including toxic chemicals produced by cigarette smoke. Plants also give banks, restaurants, or offices a welcoming and comforting appeal. Plants can be a major investment. For this reason alone, plant care professionals are needed by establishments to keep their plants alive and looking healthy.

Start-Up Costs and Financing Sources
+ $1,000 to $5,000.
+ Personal savings, small business loan, loan from family or friends, lines of credit on your credit cards.

Pricing Guidelines
Plant maintenance: $2 to $3.50 per plant, but charges are determined by the number and size of the plants and can be bid separately with each client. Time at each location can range from 10 to 30 minutes or more. Plant "doctoring": $2.50 per plant.

Marketing and Advertising Methods and Tips
+ Send direct mail and place calls to business offices, restaurants, banks, and other institutions.
+ Place classified ads in local newspapers and magazines.
+ Post flyers on community bulletin boards.
+ Buy ads on local cable television or radio stations.
+ Encourage word-of-mouth referrals.

Essential Equipment
Small ladders, watering devices, soil, pruners, scissors, fertilizer, filing and billing systems (manual or computerized), business phone and answering machine or service, maintenance contracts, plant care reference books.

Recommended Training, Experience, or Needed Skills

- Work in a commercial greenhouse specializing in house plants.
- Enroll in horticultural courses at local vo-tech schools or agricultural colleges.
- Study your own plant reference books or the many available in public libraries.
- Volunteer to take care of friends' house plants.

Income Potential

$9,000 to $65,000.

Type of Business

Out-of-the-home.

Best Customers

Institutions, banks, museums, hospitals, restaurants, offices, persons with higher incomes who have little time to care for plants.

Helpful Tips

- Offer free replacement guarantees if plants die but insist that only you care for the plants.
- Keep up-to-date on the latest plant care techniques, reading and attending gardening and plant workshops/courses.

For More Information

Books

Interior Landscape Dictionary, by Joelle Steele. 1997, John Wiley & Sons, Inc., New York.

Interior Plantscapes: Installation, Maintenance, and Management, 3rd ed., by George H. Manaker. 1996, Prentice Hall, Upper Saddle River, NJ.

Additional Business Ideas

- Rent or lease plants that you have grown yourself or purchased from wholesalers. Charge $2 to $3.50 a plant for rental. Charge $80 to $1,000 a month to lease plants to office buildings and institutions.

✤ Work with caterers, event planners, and convention centers to set up seasonal displays or displays for special occasions.

≪ॐ 75 ॐ≫
WREATHS

Once only brought out during the holiday season, wreaths have now become an indoor and outdoor decorative fixture. The "country" look trend has helped to give this craft popularity, but wreaths can be created to fit the decor of even the most contemporary style.

This is a business that can be started easily part-time and then expanded to full-time as you gather more customers and markets. You can purchase wreath supplies from wholesale growers or craft shops or gather natural materials if you live in a rural area. If you choose to do so, you could also grow the materials you need.

Start-Up Costs and Financing Sources
✤ $8 to $25 for materials for a single wreath. $500 to $1,000 for additional supplies, advertising, promotional materials.
✤ Personal savings, credit lines on credit cards, loans from family or friends.

Pricing Guidelines
$25 to $300 per wreath, depending on the materials and whether it is custom-designed.

Marketing and Advertising Methods and Tips
✤ Begin selling at craft shows, then to home and holiday boutiques.
✤ Donate wreaths to a community auction.
✤ Contact interior decorators for referrals.
✤ Rent booths at home shows.
✤ Contact real estate agents and ask to decorate model homes.

✤ Make direct calls to stores, businesses, and institutions that are being built or redecorated.

Essential Equipment

Glue, glue gun, pruning shears, wreath frames, dried flowers, vines, weeds, other natural materials, decorative accessories, drying shed (if drying your own materials), work room, display rack, large cardboard boxes for carrying and storing wreaths, flexible wire, hangers, telephone with answering machine.

Recommended Training, Experience, or Needed Skills

✤ Take wreath-making courses at craft shops, craft centers, or adult evening schools.
✤ Work in a dried flower or wreath shop.
✤ Know various dried flowers and weeds.
✤ Have a creative flair for design.

Income Potential

$600 to $1,500 or more at a weekend craft show.

Type of Business

About one-half in-home making the wreaths; one-half out-of-the-home selling, delivering, and marketing.

Best Customers

Business offices, interior decorators.

Helpful Tips

✤ Develop your own styles and designs.
✤ Be active marketing your wares and seek out as many places to show your work as possible.
✤ Keep a list of the people who buy from you. Mail them brochures and notify them of shows where you will be selling your wreaths.
✤ Join a craft guild for networking information.

For More Information

Books

Everlasting Flowers: Making and Arranging Dried, Preserved, and Artificial Flowers, by Patricia Crosher. 1997, Dover Publications, Mineola, NY.

How to Do Wreaths Even If You Think You Can't, by *Leisure Arts* Staff. 1997, Leisure Arts, Palm Coast, FL.

Natural Crafts from America's Backyards: Decorate Your Home with Wreaths, Arrangements, and Wall Decorations Gathered from Nature's Harvest, by Ellen Spector Platt. 1997, St. Martin's Press, New York.

Wreath-Making Basics, by Dawn Cusick. 1993, Sterling Publishing, New York.

Supplies

I.F.A.R., Inc.
2917 Anthony Lane
Minneapolis, MN 55418
(800) 578-4327

Offers supplies for wreath makers—frames, decorations, bow-making machine (no dried flowers). Call for free product catalogue.

Additional Business Ideas

Make and sell grapevine wreaths, undecorated, to craft shops. Read *Making Grapevine Wreaths*, by Gayle O'Donnell. 1996, Storey Books, Pownal, VT.

Craft Businesses

Craft Resources
Craftspersons advise trying a variety of ways to market your items. Here are a few:

Craft Mall or Barn
These first opened in Texas and have since spread out over the country. In a craft mall you rent spaces with shelves for a set period of time—one, three, or six months, during which you can decorate and set-up your display as you wish. Craftspeople often share the space and rent with another crafter-friend. The mall's owner sells your items and sends you your profits, minus an advertising fee. The mall's owner pays any sales taxes.

The advantage of this method is that you do not have to be present for the sale of your crafts. A disadvantage is that you do not get a chance to talk to your customers.

To open a craft mall yourself in a busy shopping center, for example, can cost as much as $150,000 for rent, advertising, equipment, and displays. You might start on a smaller scale by remodeling and using a barn or other structure on your property. To be successful, though, you must be open at least six days a week and be near an area frequented by shoppers. (See *Directory of Craft Malls* in "Books," later in this section.)

Craft Mall Software is available. Order from Custom Data Solutions, P.O. Box 3002, Fort Lee, NJ 07024.

Craft Home Parties

If you make a variety of crafts and know others who do, too, you may want to sell items through a craft home-party business. You have to enjoy talking to and meeting new people and working afternoons and evenings.

If you want to start a craft home party business, first see if there are any others in your area, and find out what types of crafts are the most profitable to sell. Then, check with an accountant for tax advice, hire craft demonstrators if needed, and have your lawyer draw up a contract for the demonstrators that supply you with crafts. You make money by selling your own crafts. Or you take a percentage, say 25 percent, of the demonstrator's selling price for their crafts.

You may want to just sell your crafts through someone else's home party business. You will usually have two weeks to fill orders given to you. Make sure you have a contract if you are the supplier. (See *Marketing Crafts Through a Home-Party System,* in "Books," later in this section.)

Crafts Retail

Selling your crafts retail entails face-to-face selling to customers. Most craftspersons start out by selling their crafts at the following places: shopping mall kiosks and carts (temporary or seasonal); craft shows, fairs, and festivals; holiday boutiques and home parties; custom orders from promotional materials, ads, referrals; or your own home shop. (See "Books," later in this section.)

Crafts Wholesale

This involves selling your crafts in large quantities to retail outlets. You set a wholesale price, and the buyer adds on her price to come up with the retail selling price. You have to be able to produce enough of your craft in a certain time period to fill the orders you receive. Some wholesale markets include the following: trade shows—take a booth or hire sales reps (can be expensive, but if you receive enough orders, you may only have to attend one or two a year); sales representatives; galleries or shops (often come to trade shows); mail order catalog houses. (See "Books," below.)

Books

See "Craft Businesses and Resources" in *101 Best Small Businesses for Women*, 1996, and *101 Best Home-Based Businesses for Women*, 1998, by Priscilla Y. Huff. Prima Publishing, Rocklin, CA.

50 Ways to Sell Your Crafts, by Janice West. The Summit Group, 1227 W. Magnolia, Suite 500, Fort Worth, TX 76104.

The Basic Guide to Selling Arts and Crafts, by James Dillehay. 1997, Warm Snow Publishers, Torreon, NM.

The Crafter's Guide to Pricing Your Work, by Dan Ramsey. 1997, Betterway Publications, Cincinnati, OH.

Crafting As a Business, by Wendy Rosen. 1994, Chilton Books, Radnor, PA.

The Crafts Business Answer Book & Resource Guide, by Barbara Brabec. 1998, M. Evans & Co., New York.

The Crafts Supply Sourcebook, by Margaret Boyd. 1996, Betterway Books. (800) 289-0963.

Creative Cash: How to Profit from Your Special Artistry, Creativity, Hand Skills, and Related Know-How, 6th ed., by Barbara Brabec. 1998, Prima Publishing, Rocklin, CA.

Directory of Craft Malls and Rent-a-Space Shops. Front Room Publishers (see address under "Book Publishers").

Directory of Craft Shops/Galleries. Front Room Publishers.

Directory of Wholesale Reps. Front Room Publishers.

Handmade for Profit: Hundreds of Secrets to Success in Selling Arts and Crafts, by Barbara Brabec. 1996, M. Evans & Co., New York.

How to Sell Your Homemade Creations. Success Publications (address in "Book Publishers").

The Learning Extension Catalog. Front Room Publishers. Lists books on selling your crafts, buying supplies wholesale, and creating your own catalog.

Marketing Crafts Through a Home-Party System. Front Room Publishers.

Selling Arts and Crafts by Mail Order. Success Publications.

Selling to Catalog Houses. Front Room Publishers.
Selling to Catalog Houses. Success Publications.
Profitable Crafting (booklet). Send $6.95 + $1 for postage to Priscilla Y. Huff, P.O. Box 286, Sellersville, PA 18960.
The Potters Shop, 31 Thorpe Rd., Needham Heights, MA 02194. (617) 449-7687. Carries many pottery books, videos, and tools. Also sponsors "The Potters School." Send an LSASE for book catalog and brochures.

Book Clubs
Crafter's Choice with Better Homes and Gardens Craft Club
P.O. Box 8823
Camp Hill, PA 17011-9557

Leisure Arts, P.O. Box 2463, Birmingham, AL 35201

Book Publishers with Mail Order Catalogs
(Books, Booklets, Reports)
Write for their current book catalogs. Some may charge a fee.

Chester Book Co., 4 Maple St., Chester, CT 06412.
Dover Publications, Inc., 31 E. 2nd St., Mineola, NY 11501-3582. Many books, stencils, copyright-free designs. Write for current catalog.
Front Room Publishers, P.O. Box 1541, Clifton, NJ 07015-1541. < http://www.intac.com/ ~ rip >
Success Publications, 3419 Dunham, Box 263, Warsaw, NY 14569.

Internet Site
< http://www.procrafter.com >

Magazines
Crafts, P.O. Box 56010, Boulder, CO 80322-6015
Crafts 'n Things, P.O. Box 5026, Des Plaines, FL 60017-5026.
The Crafts Report: The Business Journal for the Crafts Industry, P.O. Box 1992, Wilmington, DE 19899. (800) 777-7098. < http://www.craftsreport.com > Highly recommended for the professional craftsperson and artist. Also reviews art and craft-related books

Show Guides

Arts 'n Crafts Showguide. ACN Publications, P.O. Box 104628-Q, Jefferson City, MO 65110-4628.

A Step Ahead, Ltd. Ronay Guides, 2090 Shadow Lake Dr., Buckhead, GA 30625. (706) 342-7878. Lists in separate guides more than 2,800 arts and crafts shows, fairs, festivals, competitions, and art exhibits for GA, FL, AL, TN, NC, SC, and VA. Each guide is sold individually. Send an LSASE for prices of each guide.

Start-Up Guides

Entrepreneur's Start-Up Guide, *Crafts Business.* (800) 421-2300. $69 + shipping and handling.

Supplies

Dick Blick's Art Materials Catalog, P.O. Box 1267, Galesburg, IL 61402-1267. (800) 828-4548.

❧ 76 ☙

AIRBRUSH ART

In airbrush art, an atomized brush is used to create the pictures, which can be applied to windows, walls, vehicles, t-shirts, and other surfaces.

Start-Up Costs

$2,000 to $8,000 for basic equipment, promotional materials, advertising.

Pricing Guidelines

$100 to $200+ per hour and/or per project.

Marketing and Advertising Methods and Tips

✤ Airbrush a design and business number on your vehicle(s).
✤ Leave business cards at custom van shops and auto centers.
✤ Place ads in local auto publications.
✤ Post flyers on community bulletin boards.

Essential Equipment

An atomizer operated by compressed air that propels paint or ink as a fine spray (a low-line brush is not recommended); business telephone with answering capabilities; billing, filing and record keeping systems.

Recommended Training, Experience, or Needed Skills

♣ Take courses at art schools.
♣ Apprentice with an airbrush artist.
♣ Need basic artistic talent and training.

Income Potential

$35,000 to $80,000+ a year.

Type of Business

Out-of-the-home.

Best Customers

Businesses that have store-front windows, individuals' vehicles, mailboxes, walls, motorcycle helmets, and so forth.

Helpful Tips

♣ Keep a photo record of each job, along with data on the supplies used and the time it took. This will help you calculate your costs and subsequent profits so that you can give accurate estimates to future customers.
♣ Give estimates. It's up to you whether to charge for the estimate. Ask questions like what type of paint(s) will be needed? Is the project for indoors or outdoors? How large an area is to be painted? How much detail work is involved? On what type of surface will you be painting?
♣ Keep track of business records to make sure you are charging enough to cover your expenses, time, and costs for running the business.
♣ Network with other freelance artists.

For More Information

Books

Airbrush: The Complete Studio Handbook, by Radu Vero. 1997, Watson-Guptil, New York.

Big Book of Airbrush: Basic Techniques & Materials, by Miquel Ferron and Jose Maria Parramon. 1990, Watson-Guptil, NY.
Getting Started in Airbrush, by David Miller and Diana Martin. 1993, North Light Books.

Magazine
Airbrush Action, Airbrush Action, Inc., P. O. Box 2052, Lakewood, NJ 08701-8052. (800) 232-8998; < http://www.airbrushaction.com >

Supplies
Badger Air-Brush Co., 9128 W. Belmont Ave., Franklin Park, IL 60131. (847) 678-3104. < http://www.badger-airbrush.com >
Dick Blick's Art Materials Catalog (see "Supplies" in "Craft Resources," page 288).
Paache Airbrush Co., 7440 W. Lawrence Ave., Harwood Heights, IL 60656.

Video
Bob Ross's Art-Video series, *Airbrush.* Bob Ross Co., P.O. Box 946, Sterling, VA 20167. < http://www.bobross.com >

∞ 77 ∞
CALLIGRAPHY

Calligraphy is used on invitations, certificates, envelopes, place cards, and wherever beautiful penmanship is needed. If you are skilled in calligraphy or have elegant handwriting, you may have an opportunity to start a unique business.

Start-Up Costs and Financing Sources
$500 to $2,000 for supplies, materials, advertising, courses.

Pricing Guidelines
8" × 10" documents: $10 to $50 + ; party invitations (preprinted): 75 cents each; place cards, name tags: 40 cents each (for the first 75), 30 cents each (over 75); envelopes: outer mailing—75 cents each, inner—50 cents each (for the first 75), outer mailing—$1

each, inner—45 cents each (over 75). Also check with a local chapter of a calligraphy guild for pricing. Some calligraphers charge by the hour or by so many cents per word.

Follow the recommendations by related associations and what your market will bear.

Marketing and Advertising Methods and Tips
- ✤ Print business cards with a sampling of your work on them.
- ✤ Leave your brochures and business cards at art and/or craft shows and shops.
- ✤ Place classified ads in local publications.
- ✤ Encourage word-of-mouth referrals.
- ✤ Teach calligraphy at workshops.

Essential Equipment
T-square, calligraphy pens, selections of inks, tubes of designer's gouache (water soluble paint), scissors, protractor, plastic transparent ruler, selection of metal nibs, adjustable set square, cutting mat and mat cutter if you also frame your work.

Recommended Training, Experience, or Needed Skills
- ✤ Take courses and workshops in calligraphy.
- ✤ Apprentice with a master calligrapher.

Type of Business
In-home.

Best Customers
Brides, recent graduates, new parents, grandparents, businesses holding special promotions, persons who want their family trees personalized.

Helpful Tips
- ✤ Take the time to perfect this craft. Master the basics before moving on to more complex lettering.
- ✤ Practice, practice, practice.

For More Information

Association

Society for Calligraphy (SFC)
P.O. Box 64174
Los Angeles, CA 90064

Nonprofit; publishes a newsletter, journal, and calendar of events. Send an LSASE for information.

Books and Publications

Calligraphy School, by Gynor Goffe and Anna Ravenscroft. 1994, Reader's Digest, New York.

The Encyclopedia of Calligraphy Techniques: A Comprehensive A–Z Directory of Calligraphy Techniques and a Step-by-Step Guide to Their Use, by Diana Hardy Wilson. 1990, Running Book Publishers, Philadelphia, PA. (Check in your local library's holdings.)

How to Become a Professional Calligrapher, by Stuart David. 1991, Taplinger Publishing Co., New York.

Home Study Course

The Lettering Design Group
3520 W. 75th St., Suite 100
Prairie Village, KS 66208
Contact: Michael Sull

Offers home courses and week-long workshops. Also sells supplies, instructional materials, and videos. Send an LSASE for information.

Internet Site

< http://www.calligraphycentre.com >
Calligraphy Centre. Also has information about workshops.

Magazine

Letter Arts Review and *Upper and Lower Case,* 1624 24th Ave. SW, Norman, OK 73072. (405) 364-8794. < http://www.letterarts.com > $42 per year.

Supplies
ACP Inc., 3875 Statesville Blvd. Salisbury, NC 28147-7457. Send an LSASE for the cost of the catalog.
Fascinating Folds, P.O. Box 10070, Glendale, AZ 85318. < http://www.fascinting-folds.com >

Video
Calligraphy by Ken Brown. Order from *Dick Blick's Art Materials Catalog.* (800) 447-8192. $22.95.

Additional Business Ideas
❖ Sell calligraphy supplies.
❖ Teach calligraphy courses.
❖ Offer to frame your work.

❧ 78 ❧
CANDLES

Candlemaking is a popular home-based business. Some of these craftspeople have home shops for the public. Others sell their candles at craft shows, malls, or through sales representatives or retail outlets.

Start-Up Costs and Financing Sources
❖ $1,000 to $10,000 for supplies, to set up a work room, and for home office supplies and equipment.
❖ Personal savings, small business loan, credit cards.

Pricing Guidelines
Prices depend on the materials and scents used and the size of the candle. They range from $15 to $40 for simple candles, $38 to $62 for more elaborate ones. Network with other candle artisans for guidelines (see "Associations" in "For More Information," later in this section).

Marketing and Advertising Methods and Tips
❖ Print business cards, flyers, and brochures.

❖ Attend home and/or gift shows.
❖ Place classified ads in local publications.
❖ Buy ads in trade publications such as *Giftware News* and *Gift and Decorative Accessories* to attract buyers and sales reps.

Essential Equipment

Wax (paraffin or beeswax), stearin (adds hardness), wax dyes, perfumes, wick holder and wicks, thermometer, equipment to melt and hold waxes, molds and mold seal, enameled containers for dipped candles, knives, stirrers. Home office supplies: phone with answering machine, computer for recordkeeping and billing.

Recommended Training, Experience, or Needed Skills

❖ Work in a candlemaking shop.
❖ Take classes or workshops in candlemaking.
❖ Experiment to develop your individual technique and style.

Income Potential

$40,000 to $90,000+ a year (with sales representatives). As much as $4,500 a weekend at a busy mall or large craft show.

Type of Business

About one-half in-home making the candles; one-half out-of-the-home selling the candles.

Best Customers

Gift shops, bridal accessories shops, craft show attendees, mall shoppers, New Age and aromatherapy shops.

For More Information

Association
International Guild of Candle Artisans
c/o Marie Davis, Membership Chair
Candles & More
103 Park Rd., RD3
Aliquippa, PA 15001

Holds annual convention. Publishes a listing of candle wholesalers—candlemakers can list here to sell candles. Also publishes *The Candlelighter* (a trade publication). $50 membership. Send an LSASE for membership information.

Books

The Candlemaker's Companion: A Comprehensive Guide to Rolling, Pouring, Dipping & Decorating Your Own Candles, by Betty Oppenheimer. 1997, Storey Communications, Pownal, VT.

Candles That Earn: Starting and Operating a Candle Business, by Don Olsen. 1991, Peanut Butter Press, Seattle, WA.

Carvings, by Julie Hodges. Order from Barker Enterprises. This is a candle-carving instruction book.

The Complete Candlemaker: Techniques, Projects & Inspirations, by Norma J. Coney. 1997, Lark Books, Asheville, NC.

Ye Old Candle Instruction Book. Order from Barker Enterprises.

Internet Site

< http://www.candlelady.com >

Supplies

Barker Enterprises, Inc., 15106 10th Ave. SW, Seattle, WA 98166. (206) 244-1870. < http://www.barkerco.com > $3 for catalog.

Candlecraft, 14929 Old Manor Way, Lynwood, WA 98037-2427.

The Wax House, P.O. Box 103, Mequon, WI 53092. (Has a book, *Starting a Candle Business*—$12.) Send $3 for catalog.

Additional Business Ideas

✤   Make paperweights or other objects out of wax.

✤   Add dried flower overlays to your candles.

❧ 79 ❧
CHAIR CANING, RUSHWORK, AND WEAVING

In this business, you revive the traditional craft of caning, doing rushwork on, or weaving the seats and backs of old and new chairs. Antiques and reproductions are always in demand by collectors and early American furniture makers, as well by individuals who want to restore and preserve family heirlooms.

Start-Up Costs
$300 to $3,000 for equipment and supplies, promotional materials, advertising, and set-up of a work area or home shop.

Pricing Guidelines
Usually charged by the hole, 50 cents to a $1 each, depending on the technique used. Compare your prices with others in your area. The following equation may also be used:

$$(Your\ hourly\ wage \times the\ number\ of\ hours) + cost\ of\ supplies + overhead$$

Marketing and Advertising Methods and Tips
✤ Leave your business cards and flyers at antique shops, folk fairs, folk museums, and historical societies.
✤ Place ads in antique trade publications and country lifestyle magazines.
✤ Exhibit or demonstrate at folk and craft fairs. Have your brochures available.
✤ Teach chair caning classes at adult evening schools, craft shops or centers, or community colleges.
✤ Encourage word-of-mouth referrals.

Essential Equipment
High quality cane—buy from a specialty craft or caning store or order from mail order suppliers. Various tools according to technique used: bucket, pliers, pick or awl, wooden pegs, scissors, glue, chisel, hammer.

Recommended Training, Experience, or Needed Skills
✤ Take courses or private lessons in chair caning.
✤ Practice on old furniture or frames you find at flea markets and thrift shops.

Income Potential
$100 for a chair that has 100 holes.

Type of Business
In-home business, except for exhibiting at fairs and crafts shows, or when teaching courses.

Best Customers
Antique shops, antique collectors (professional and amateur), museums, historical societies that have collections of furniture.

For More Information

Books
Also check your local and/or historical libraries for out-of-print books on chair caning and weaving.

The Caner's Handbook, by Bruce W. Miller and Jim Widess. 1992, Lark Books, Asheville, NC.

Chair Seat Weaving, by George Sterns. 1990, Interweave Press, 201 E. Fourth St., Loveland, CO 80537.

Making Chair Seats from Cane, Rush, & Other Natural Materials, by Ruth B. Comstock. 1989, Dover Publications, Mineola, NY.

Supplies
GH Productions, 521 E. Walnut St., Dept. EM-Box 621, Scottsville, KY 42164. Basket making and chair seating supplies. Send an LSASE for prices.

Additional Business Ideas
❖ Make and sell unique baskets (especially research the heritage of your area to see what baskets were made and used a century or two ago—i.e., Native American, African American, European).

❖ Collect old wicker furniture, old baskets, old chairs, to repair and refinish them for resale.

❖ Make twig furniture or miniature twig furniture for country-style decor. Read *Willow Chair: How to Build Your Own*, by

Joseph S. Stone and Carollyn Wolff. 1992, Genesis Publications, North Andover, MA.

∽80∾
DOLLHOUSES

You can build dollhouses from kits, create replicas of customers' homes or businesses, or design and build your own unique dollhouses. As a sideline to this business, you can sell commercial or handmade miniature furniture and/or accessories. Though many of your dollhouses will be ordered as gifts for children, others will be made for adults who will display them for their own pleasure.

Start-Up Costs
$6,000 to $15,000, depending on whether you have a home retail shop on your property or not.

Pricing Guidelines
Go by industry standards. Join MIAA (see "For More Information") and attend dollhouse and miniatures trade shows to check out prices. Handmade, innovative, and original houses and accessories are more expensive than those that are mass-produced. A dollhouse can sell for $300 to $4,000 or more, depending on its size and detail.

Marketing and Advertising Methods and Tips
* Donate a replica of a historic building in your town for a charity auction or work with a local school's shop or vo-tech students to make a dollhouse to give to a day care center.
* Place your business cards in toy shops.
* Attend craft and mall shows: show samples, take orders.
* Teach dollhouse-building classes in your home shop, at local crafts shops, or at adult evening school.
* Place ads in national trade publications (see "For More Information") and magazines. Buy display ads (when you can afford it) in doll and children's magazines and catalogs.

❖ Rent booths at trade shows (see MIAA in "For More Information").

❖ Keep a mailing list of customers, and send out a small newsletter or sales flyer on new miniatures or dollhouses you have made.

❖ Display your dollhouses in your local library's showcase in October, which is National Dollhouse and Miniatures Month.

Essential Equipment
Assorted woodworking and hand tools and supplies: hammers, hand saws, scroll saw. Sewing machine and notions for making miniatures and decorating; paints, odds and ends of materials. Basic drafting tools and graph paper for drawing up designs, plans.

Recommended Training, Experience, or Needed Skills
❖ Have experience in sewing, carpentry, woodworking, interior decorating.

❖ Enroll in dollhouse-building courses or take woodworking, sewing, and other related courses at adult evening schools or vo-tech schools.

❖ Practice building and decorating dollhouses from kits. Then try your own designs.

Income Potential
$20,000 to $75,000.

Type of Business
Two-thirds in-home, building, creating; one-third out-of-the-home, marketing, exhibiting at shows, giving classes.

Helpful Tips
❖ Keep in touch with loyal customers.

❖ Recycle throwaway materials into unusual miniatures.

❖ Keep current with the latest trends in the field (see "For More Information").

For More Information

Association

Miniatures Industry Association of America (MIAA)
1100-H Brandywine Blvd.
P.O. Box 2188
Zanesville, OH 43701-2188
(740) 452-4541

Publishes a newsletter with industry and marketing information, and show dates.

Books

Also check your library's shelves for out-of-print books on building dollhouses and furniture.

The Complete Guide to Remodeling and Expanding Your Dollhouse, by Nola Theiss. 1993, Sterling Publishing Co. Inc., New York.

The Doll's House Do-It-Yourself Book, by Venus A. Dodge. 1993, Sterling Publishing.

Making Doll House Furniture, by Patricia King. 1993, Sterling Publishing.

Making Miniatures, by Venus and Martin Dodge. 1991, Sterling Publishing.

Magazine

Dollhouse Miniatures. Kalmbach Publishing Co., 21027 Crossroads Circle, P.O. Box 1612, Waukesha, WI 53187-1612.

Additional Busines Ideas

✤ Make dollhouse furniture and accessories.

✤ Put together dollhouses for people who buy kits and neither have the desire nor the time to assemble them.

❧81❧
FRAMING

Cindy Smith opened her professional framing and matting service in conjunction with a small art gallery on the lower floor of her house. She also sells original artwork, prints, and posters, framed or just matted.

Smith says, "I began to think of opening up my own framing shop when my husband and I were given an estimate of several hundred dollars to frame two prints." She took a course on framing and assisted her photographer husband in framing his work for shows. She also gained experience by working part-time in two framing shops.

Start-Up Costs and Financing Sources
✤ $30,000 to $50,000, but costs can be less if you buy good, used equipment.
✤ Small business loan, personal savings, refinancing your home.

Pricing Guidelines
Follow the guidelines of the Professional Picture Framers Association (see their listing later in this section). Cindy Smith, however, says that "you have to charge the going rate for your community. You can charge more for your service in affluent neighborhoods where art is supported and art enthusiasts live."

Marketing and Advertising Methods and Tips
✤ Place classified ads in local publications and in the business telephone directory.
✤ Offer an art contest for local high school students with local artists as judges. Frame the winning entry.
✤ Network with various artists' groups.
✤ Send flyers to and/or contact local art instructors.
✤ Join your local chamber of commerce.

Essential Equipment
Mat cutter, knives, wood for frames. You will need a work area that you can screen off to receive clients.

Recommended Training, Experience, or Needed Skills
✤ Take framing courses at art schools or institutes.
✤ Work in framing shops for experience.
✤ Practice framing friends' and relatives' work.

Income Potential
$25,000 to $45,000 is possible in a small community, $90,000 to $115,000+ or more is possible in a larger, art-conscious community.

Type of Business
In-home.

Best Customers
Art enthusiasts, art collectors, artists, photographers, calligraphers, graduates, people wanting to preserve old photographs, those who want their wedding or baptism certificates framed, needlework hobbyists.

Helpful Tips
✤ Work in a framing shop before you open one.
✤ Specialize in different types of matting—French, gold leaf, etc.—depending on the demand for it and your training. Cindy also learned conservation and archival processes to preserve old paper, paintings, and prints.
✤ Follow professional standards in your work and pricing.

For More Information

Association
Professional Picture Framers Association
4305 Sarellen Rd.
Richmond, VA 23231

Send an LSASE for membership information.

Books
The Art of Framing, by Piers and Caroline Feetham. 1997, Clarkson-Potter, New York.

The Encyclopedia of Picture Framing Techniques, by Robert Cunning. 1998, Running Press, Philadelphia, PA.

Home Book of Picture Framing: Professional Secrets of Mounting, Matting, Framing, and Displaying Artworks, Photographs, Posters, Fabrics, Collectibles, by Kenn Oberrecht. 1998, Stackpole Books, Mechanicsburg, PA.

Matting & Framing Made Easy, by Janean Thompson. 1996, Watson-Guptil, New York.

Matting, Mounting, and Framing Art, by Max Hyder. 1986, Watson-Guptill, New York.

Supplies

Art Supply Warehouse Express (ASW), 5325 Departure Dr., North Raleigh, NC 27616-1835. (800) 995-6778. Art and framing supplies. Write or call for a catalog.

Dick Blick's Art Materials Catalog (see "Supplies" in "Craft Resources"). (800) 447-8192.

Additional Business Ideas

❖ Sell local artists', artisans', and craftspersons' work.

❖ Make your own unique frames—sell them to artists, art galleries, framing shops. Resources follow:

Making and Decorating Fantastic Frames, by Thom Boswell. 1994, Sterling Publishing

Making & Decorating Picture Frames, by Janet Bridge. 1996, F & W Publications, Cincinnati, OH.

Making Picture Frames in Wood, by Manly Banister. 1981, Sterling Publishing Co., New York

ᨓ82ᨑ
FURNITURE ART

In this business, old or used furniture and household items are decorated with original art. Pieces you find for a few dollars at garage sales, flea markets, or auctions, can be refinished and/or decorated to sell for ten or more times that amount. If you are not skilled in free-hand painting, there are stencils and other techniques to use that make your work look like a master's. Think of this business as turning junk into someone else's treasure and helping to recycle items that would just be tossed away.

Start-Up Costs and Financing Sources

❖ $500 to $1,000.

❖ Personal savings, loan from friend or family.

Pricing Guidelines

*Your time (total hours to complete) × your rate per hour +
the cost of the piece of furniture + cost of supplies =
total × 2 or 3 (for profit) = Final price*

Prices also depend on what your customers are willing to pay in your selling area. For example, a $5 table might sell for $75 finished.

Marketing and Advertising Methods and Tips

✤ Post business cards and flyers on community bulletin boards.
✤ Make presentations to owners of small furniture or used furniture shops to sell your items.
✤ Rent a booth at a craft mall or home show.
✤ Give a demonstration at a paint or hardware store.
✤ Donate a piece of furniture art to a community charity auction.
✤ Contact interior decorators.

Essential Equipment

Refinishing supplies, paints, good brushes, tracing paper, paper towels, rags, well-ventilated work space, promotional materials.

Recommended Training, Experience, or Needed Skills

✤ Know how to recognize good, used furniture and other salvageable pieces.
✤ Know basic refinishing and painting techniques.
✤ Take courses at vo-tech schools or work in a refinishing shop.
✤ Practice on old pieces you find.
✤ Have to have an artistic eye.

Income Potential

Your profits will vary with each piece, from $30 to $800 or more. Annual earnings can average $30,000 to $50,000, depending how much custom work you do for customers.

Type of Business

Two-thirds in-home refinishing and painting the furniture; one-third out-of-the-home looking for pieces and marketing.

Best Customers

People who love original art and handpainted pieces, people who like nontraditional and accent pieces, people who want a new look for a piece of furniture, small antique furniture shops, certain interior decorators who may want you to do custom pieces for their clients.

Helpful Tips

❖ Take the time to look for customers and markets for your pieces.

❖ Network with friends and family—they can refer people to you who may want custom work.

❖ Let the piece you are painting "guide" you as to what design to use.

For More Information

Association

National Society of Tole and Decorative Painters
P.O. Box 808
Newton, KS 67114
(316) 283-9665

Send LSASE for membership information. Publishes bimonthly publication, semiannual sourcebook, and design books. Holds an annual convention, participates in the Smithsonian Christmas Exhibit, has local chapters.

Books

Folk Art and Tole Painting: New Designs for Decorative Paintwork, by Kate Coombe. 1993, Sterling Publishing Co., Inc., New York.

Master Strokes: A Guide to Using Decorative Paint Finishes, by Jennifer Bennell. 1997, Rockport Publishers, Rockport, MA.

Painting & Decorating Furniture, by Sheila McGraw. 1997, Firefly Books, Buffalo, NY.

Priscilla Hauser's Book of Decorative Painting, by Priscilla Hauser. 1997, F & W Publications, Cincinnati, OH.

Book Clubs

Decorative Artist's Book Club, 1507 Dana Ave., Cincinnati, OH 45208. (800) 289-0963. Books on decorative and tole painting.

North Light Book Club, 1507 Dana Ave., Cincinnati, OH 45208. (800) 289-0963. Books on painting techniques. Write for information.

Publications

Decorative Artist's Workbook, F & W Publications, 1507 Dana Ave., Cincinnati, OH 45208. For subscription write to P.O. Box 3284, Harlin, IA 51593.

Decorative Arts Painting, Clapper Publications, P.O. Box 7520, Red Oak, IA 51591-2520. (800) 333-0888. One year/6 issues costs $21.

Painting Magazine, Pack-O-Fun Magazine, 2400 Devon, Suite 375, Des Plaines, IL 60018. (800) 444-0441. < http://www. paintingmag.com > One year/6 issues costs $19.95 (U.S.).

Paint Works, All American Crafts, Inc./MSC Publishing, 243 Newton-Sparta Rd., Newton, NJ 07860. $44.55 per year.

Supplies

Dick Blick's Art Materials Catalog (see "Supplies" in "Craft Resources," p. 288.)

Hofcraft!, P.O. Box 72 Grand Haven, MI 49417. (800) 828-0359. < http://www.hofcraft.com > $5 for catalog. Offers full line of supplies and paints for decorative arts.

Additional Business Ideas

Repairing and refinishing furniture. Check these resources:

National Business Library's Start-Up Guide *Furniture Refinishing.* (800) 947-7724. $39.95 + shipping handling.

How to Recognize and Refinish Antiques for Pleasure and Profit, 4th ed., by Jacquelyn Peake. 1997, Globe Pequot Press, Old Saybrook, CT.

⊷83↬
GREETING CARDS

In the past few years there has been an explosion of variety in the greeting card market. The Greeting Card Association says that over 7 billion greeting cards were purchased by American consumers, resulting in $7.1 billion in U.S. retail sales. Greeting cards now cover themes ranging from the sentimental and poetic to the humorous, sometimes to the point of being almost off-color.

One woman, Kathy Davis, is an artist who started her own line of greeting cards and products, called Kathy Davis Designs. She sells them in her own gift shop and also to various shops around the country. Davis sends out flyers to customers on her mailing list, including a calendar of events advertising contests, specials, and other activities she holds at her store. This designer, illustrator, and writer says, "Work hard and love your work."

You can contact her at her Web site, < http://www.kathy-davis.com > .

Start-Up Costs
$8,000 to $15,000.

Pricing Guidelines
Printed packs of cards with your designs—20 cards for $13 to $19. Add other items with your designs: mug—$7.95; recipe cards—$6.50; canvas tote bag—$19.95; sweatshirts (preshrunk)—$39.95. Individual printed cards (stamped, embossed, hand-colored)—$3 to $4 each.

Follow industry suggestions.

Marketing and Advertising Methods and Tips
✤ Design your own line and market directly to shops and companies.
✤ Attend trade shows to show your portfolio (see "For More Information").
✤ Sell your cards at craft and art shows, to gift stores or small, unique shops (big shops already have cards).

❖ Design your own promotional materials to send out to greeting card companies.

❖ Mail a periodic flyer with your new line of cards and products. Have customers buy through mail order (get names at craft and art shows).

Essential Equipment
Art and graphic arts supplies, computer with graphic arts design capabilities and laser printer, telephone with answering machine or service.

Recommended Training, Experience, or Needed Skills
❖ Take courses or get training in graphic arts and/or design.

❖ Research what types of greeting cards are on the market and what greeting card companies look for in submissions. See if you can come up with your own distinctive cards.

Income Potential
Depends on your materials, your reputation as a designer, the contract you sign (a percentage). Network with others in the industry for the going rate paid.

Type of Business
In-home.

Helpful Tips
❖ Kathy Davis says, "Believe in yourself. Do the work you want to do, and do not give up. Take satisfaction in every job you do, however small."

❖ Stay current with industry news.

For More Information
Associations
The Greeting Card Association
1200 G St., NW, Suite 760
Washington, DC 20005
< http://www.greetingcard.org >
Write for information.

The Graphic Artists Guild
(See "Graphic Artist" entry in "Computer Businesses" chapter, page 323.)

Books
(See also "Graphic Artist" entry in "Computer Businesses" chapter, page 323.)

The Artist's and Graphic Designer's Market. Writer's Digest Books, Cincinnati, OH. An annual listing of markets for your art and designs.

Card Crafting: Over 45 Ideas for Making Greeting Cards and Stationery, by Gillan Souter. Sterling Publishing Co., New York.

The Complete Guide to Greeting Card Design and Illustration, Rev. ed., by Eva Szela. 1994, North Light Books, Cincinnati, OH.

How to Make Money Publishing from Home: Everything You Need to Know to Successfully Publish Books, Newsletters, Greeting Cards, Zines, and Software, by Lisa Shaw. 1997, Prima Publishing, Rocklin, CA.

How to Write and Sell: Greeting Cards, Bumper Stickers, T-Shirts and Other Fun Stuff, by Molly Wigand. 1992, Writer's Digest Books, Cincinnati, OH.

Write Well & Sell Greeting Cards, by Sandra M. Louden. 1998 Jam-Packed Press, Dept. TF, P.O. Box 9701, Pittsburgh, PA 15229. $9.95 (send check or money order). Sandra M. Louden has written for a number of years in the greeting card industry.

Home Business Opportunity
Gardening Greetings features cards with the Garden Lady™ character. For prices and information about the *Home-Based Greeting Card Kit,* send an LSASE to Gardening Greetings, 189a Paradise Circle, Woodland Park, CO 80863. < http://www.gardeninggreetings.com >

Trade Show
National Stationery Show
10 Bank St.
White Plains, NY 10606-1954

Held each May at the Jacob Javits Center in New York City. Attendance is for those in the industry only, but you may register at the door as an artist if you have a business card and artwork to show. Great opportunity to see companies' greeting cards first-hand and possibly meet with their creative directors. Call George Little Management, Inc. for show dates and times: (914) 421-3200.

~84~
JEWELRY

Today jewelry can be made of anything from gold and silver to clay and cloth, with styles ranging from formal to funky. Research where and to whom you will sell your pieces, based on your style of design and materials. Your potential markets will also depend on your expertise and what people are willing to pay. By attending craft and trade shows, reading trade publications, and networking with other jewelry makers, you will be able to determine where your pieces can sell best.

The jewelry crafts referred to here pertain to pieces made from a variety of materials: metal, glass, ceramics, wood, paper, leather, fabric, plastic, stones, and recycled items.

Start-Up Costs and Financing Sources
❖ $3,000 to $8,000 for supplies and advertising.
❖ Personal savings, loans from friends and family.

Pricing Guidelines
Depends on the cost of materials, cost of running your business, the time it takes to make your pieces, and the demand for your jewelry. Check out other jewelry prices at craft and trade shows.

Marketing and Advertising Methods and Tips
❖ Rent a booth at jewelry and/or gift trade shows.
❖ Place a classified or color display ad in craft marketing publications.
❖ Offer to make custom orders.
❖ Take samples of your work to jewelry and gift shops.
❖ Wear your jewelry and have friends and relatives wear it, too.
❖ Send direct mailings to customers from a mailing list gathered from show attendees or past customers.

Essential Equipment
The tools needed depend on the type of jewelry you are making, for example, metalworking requires files, cutters, clamps, pliers, solders. Materials—new or recycled, clasps, fasteners, strings, display equipment.

Recommended Training, Experience, or Needed Skills
* Study jewelry making at art centers.
* Apprentice with a jewelry maker or work as an assistant in a small jewelry-making business.
* Need an artistic flair for design and a mastery of the technique you use.

Income Potential
$500 to $1,000 a week ($25,000 to $50,000+ a year), depending on your reputation, your customers, and your markets.

Type of Business
In-home except when at shows or marketing your pieces.

Best Customers
Shops selling fine handcrafts, jewelry show attendees, craft show attendees, jewelry catalogs, galleries.

Helpful Tips
* Try to develop a following and keep a list of customers who buy your jewelry.
* Establish your own individual style.
* Keep up-to-date with the fashion and style trends.
* Develop new markets wherever you can.

For More Information
See also "Jewelry" in *101 Best Small Businesses for Women,* by Priscilla Y. Huff. 1996, Prima Publishing, Rocklin, CA.

Books
The Art and Craft of Jewelry, by Janet Fitch. 1994, Chronicle Books, San Francisco, CA.

The Book of Jewelry, by Joo Moody. 1994, Simon & Schuster, New York.

The Encyclopedia of Jewelry-Making, by Jinks McGrath. 1995, Running Press, Philadelphia, PA.

Jewelry Concepts and Technology, by Oppi Untracht. 1982, Doubleday, New York.

Jewelry Making, by David Rider. 1994, Order from Chester Book Co. (See "Book Publishers" in "Craft Resources," page 287).

Jewelry Making Manual, by Sylvia Wicks. 1990, The Bookshelf, P.O. Box 6925, Ventura, CA 93006.

Home Study Course

Gemological Institute of America
5345 Armada Dr.
Carlsbad, CA 92008

Offers gemology and jewelry design courses.

Magazine

Jewelry Crafts, 5000 Eagle Rock Blvd. #105, Los Angeles, CA 90041. < http://www.jewelrycrafts.com >

Features techniques and styles of popular jewelry making. Contains ads for jewelry-making suppliers.

Supplies

Alpha Supply, Inc.
1225 Hollis St., #2133
Bremerton, WA 98310
(800) 257-4211; (206)373-3302

Thousands of supplies, items for jewelry making, faceting, and lapidary needs. Offers a large selection of books on jewelry making. Catalog costs $5, with a $10 certificate toward your order.

Trade Show

Check listings of show dates in trade publications such as *Jewelry Crafts.*

Tucson's Gem and Mineral Society Show (held every February), P.O. Box 42543, 3727 E. Blacklidge Dr., Tucson, AZ 85733. Send an LSASE for information on retail and wholesale sections.

Video
The Complete Metalsmith, The Brookfield Craft Center, P.O. Box 122, Brookfield, CT 06804.

Additional Business Ideas
* ❖ Design jewelry for large people or extremely thin people.
* ❖ Sew cloth jewelry.
* ❖ Make clay jewelry. See *Creative Clay Jewelry,* by Leslie Dierks. 1994, Lark Books, Asheville, NC.
* ❖ Use recycled materials. Send an LSASE to Joyce Chambers, Paper Art Originals, 2526 Lamar Ave., Suite 231, Paris, TX 75460.

✺ 85 ✺
PHOTOGRAPHY

Here are just some of the business opportunities open to photographers:

* ❖ Pet photographs. People love their pets—you can specialize in taking pet photos at their homes or contact pet and feed stores to hold an annual pet photo day. Owners of purebred and registered animals also need photos of their pets for promotion or on show days when their animals receive awards. Many photographers make a full-time living following horse, dog, and livestock shows.
* ❖ Portraiture. One woman photographer specializes in wedding and children's portraits. She had a home studio built onto her house for indoor portraits and also had a decorative gazebo and a bridge built over a small stream for outdoor photos. Her sister, who lives nearby, is a make-up artist and hairdresser and she adds her services if a customer wishes.
* ❖ Newborn pictures. Take infants' photos at the hospital.
* ❖ Children's sports photos. Market them to schools and sports associations.

❖ Photos of people's houses and cars. Sell this service to individuals, real estate companies, auto clubs.

❖ Photos of community's events. Contact your local chamber of commerce, historical associations.

❖ Photos of crafts and artworks. Many artists and craftspeople need professional slides/photos of their work to qualify for entry into shows and contests. Contact local and state craft guilds.

❖ Children's photos for identification purposes.

❖ Restored and tinted photographs.

❖ Sell stock photos to publishers, writers, and so forth.

You may come up with other ideas such as photographing people's gardens, family reunions, baptisms, or confirmations. You can also sell to greeting card and postcard companies, or do photos for attorneys' and insurance investigations. Whatever kind of photography you do, you must (1) get adequate training, either by enrolling in formal courses or working as an apprentice and (2) decide upon your special area of practice. Then you can decide which potential customers you want to target in your marketing plan.

Start-Up Costs
$5,000 to $15,000.

Essential Equipment
Cameras, assorted lenses, dark room access, and so forth.

Franchises, Distributorships, and Licenses
The Sports Section, Inc.
B & H Products, Inc.
3871 Lakefield Dr., Suite 100
Suwanee, GA 30024

Provides sports photography memorabilia for youth and amateur athletic teams. No photographic experience necessary. Write for information.

Ident-A-Kid
2810 Schere Dr., Suite 100
St. Petersburg, FL 33716
(813) 577-4646

Markets identification service to schools. Franchisers sell laminated photographs to parents for I.D. purposes.

For More Information

Books and Publications
Guide to Literary Agents and Art/Photo Reps. Writer's Digest Books. (800) 289-0963.
How to Start a Home-Based Photography Business, by Kenn Oberrecht. 1996, Globe Pequot Press, Old Saybrook, CT.
Photographer's Market (Annual). Writer's Digest Books.

Home Study Courses
American School, 850 E. 58th St., Chicago, IL 60637.

International Correspondence Schools
925 Oak St.
Scranton, PA 18515

Offers career diploma in photography.

Trade Magazines
Popular Photography, P.O. Box 54912, Boulder, CO 80322-4912.
Shooter's Rag, The Practical Gazette for Silver and Digital Photographers. Havelin Communications, P.O. Box 8509, Asheville, NC 28814.

Start-Up Guide
National Business Library's Start-Up Guide, *Photography Services.* (800) 947-7724. $39.95 + shipping and handling.

ᑋ86ᕋ
SILK AND FABRIC FLOWER
AND PLANT ARRANGING

Although fresh flowers are beautiful, many individuals and home and business owners prefer silk or fabric floral arrangements to the real thing. Artificial arrangements are more practical for those who don't have the money or time to care for live plants or flowers. In this business, you make up arrangements to order as well as have a stock of premade floral and plant arrangements.

You can buy the silk plants and flowers from wholesalers or make them yourself (if you have the time and skill).

Start-Up Costs and Financing Sources
✤ $3,000 to $5,000.
✤ Personal savings, small business loan, loans from family and friends.

Pricing Guidelines
Compare prices with others in a similar business. Price according to the cost of supplies, your hourly wage, total time it takes to make an arrangement, plus a percentage of overhead.

Marketing and Advertising Methods and Tips
✤ Print business cards and flyers to hand out at shows and post on bulletin boards.
✤ Rent booths at home, bridal shows, or craft shows.
✤ Invite people to sign a mailing list at craft and other shows and send periodic mailings of your specials or places and dates where you will be exhibiting.
✤ Sell to home accessory or gift shops, also garden centers.
✤ Contact interior decorators.
✤ Let your local chamber of commerce members know you are available to decorate offices.
✤ Contact bridal shops, churches, banks, and hospitals. They often want plants in lounges or public areas.

Essential Equipment
Telephone with answering machine; billing and bookkeeping systems; photo portfolio of arrangements you've done; promotional materials. Fabric flowers (cotton, silk, etc.), scissors, standard craft and floral supplies, flower parts, ribbon, and sewing notions.

Recommended Training, Experience, or Needed Skills
✤ Take flower arranging courses at craft shops or through adult education or at horticultural centers.
✤ Work in a flower shop or at a silk flower distributor.

❖ Have a good sense of color and balance; know flower arranging.

Income Potential
$18,000 to $45,000 a year.

Type of Business
In-home business except when doing shows or promotions.

Best Customers
Brides, homeowners, businesses, restaurants, institutions, customers at craft shows and craft home parties, boutiques, parents of girls being confirmed (flower-covered headbands are
popular), interior decorators.

Helpful Tips
❖ Keep a notebook listing the supplies needed for each arrangement, as well as the suppliers, your wholesale and retail
   price, and a photo. This will help you give accurate estimates
   to future customers.
❖ Keep up with trends—attend floral trade shows, study catalogs, trade publications.
❖ Network with other floral and silk plant designers and pro-
   ducers.

For More Information

Books
*Decorating with Silk & Dried Flowers: 80 Arrangements Using Floral
   Materials of All Kinds,* by Cowles Creative Publications. 1993.
   Minneapolis-St.Paul, MN.
Leisure Arts Books. (Check to see if their books are carried in your
   local craft supply shops.)
*The New Silk Flower Book: Making Stylish Arrangements, Wreaths &
   Decorations,* by Laura Dover Doran. 1997, Lark Books,
   Asheville, NC.
Silk Flowers, by Anne Hamilton and Kathleen White. 1988, David
   R. Godine Publishers, Boston, MA.

Home Study Course
Lifetime Career Schools
2251 Barry Ave.
Los Angeles, CA 90064

Offer courses in floral arrangement.

Publication
Crafts 'n Things, P.O. Box 5026, Des Plaines, IL 60017-5026. Call (800) 444-0441 for subscription information. A good source for general craft project ideas.

Supplies
North American Floral & Packaging Supply
P.O. Box 342 Forest Rd.
Greenfield, NH 03047
< http://www.nafps.com >

Sells goods wholesale. Send an LSASE for ordering information.

Also try your local craft supply shop for flower parts (leaves, buds) to make your own fabric flowers.

Videos
Three videos on making silk flower arrangements for a wedding. Send an LSASE for information to Personal Touch, 2108 Honeysuckle Rd., #234, Dothan, AL 36301

Additional Business Ideas
Make dried flower arrangements. See *The Flower Arranger's Encyclopedia of Preserving and Drying*, by Maureen Foster. 1992, Sterling Publishing Co., Inc., New York. (See also "Wreaths" section.)

Computer
Businesses

Computer Resources

Books

121 Internet Businesses You Can Start from Home: Plus a Beginner's Guide to Starting a Business Online, by Ron Gielgun. 1997, Actium Publishing, Santa Rosa, CA.

Computer Resources for People with Disabilities: A Guide to Exploring Today's Assistive Technology, by Stephen Hawking and the Alliance for Technology Access. 1996, Hunter House, Inc., Alameda, CA.

How to Earn More Than $25,000 a Year with Your Home Computer: Over 140 Income-Producing Projects, by Phil Wilcox. 1997, Citadel Press, New York.

Make Money with Your PC!: A Guide to Starting and Running Successful PC-Based Businesses, Rev. ed., by Lynn Walford. 1994, Ten Speed Press, Berkeley, CA.

Making Money with Your Computer at Home, by Paul and Sarah Edwards. 1993, Perigee, New York.

Book Club

The Computer Book Club, McGraw-Hill Book Clubs, 860 Taylor Station Rd., Blacklick, OH 43099-0007.

Home Study Courses
International Correspondence Schools
925 Oak St.
Scranton, PA 18515
Offers career diploma for personal computer specialist.

Magazines
Look in your local bookstore, newsstand, or large library.
Home Office Computing/Smart Business Computing, Scholastic, Inc.,
411 Lafayette, New York, NY 10003. < http://www.smalloffice.com >
Smart Computing, Sandhills Publishing, 131 W. Grand Dr.,
P.O. Box 85380, Lincoln, NE 68501. < http://www.smart
computing.com >
Windows® magazine, Box 420215, Palm Coast, FL 32142. < http:
//www.winmag.com >

Start-Up Guides
Entrepreneur's Start-Up Guide, *Making Money with Your PC*,
(800) 421-2300. $69 + shipping handling.

Supplies
CDW® Computer Centers, Inc., 200 N. Milwaukee Ave., Vernon
Hills, IL 60061. (800) 856-4239. < http://www.cdw.com >
Call for catalog.

☜87☞
COMPUTER CONSULTING

As a computer consultant, you help select the best computer
system for your client, including the best software and related
equipment. You follow up by providing instruction in acclimat-
ing the computer system into the client's business. In other
words, you help the individual or business owner learn how to
use a computer system to make more money or gain access to
more information.

Consultants can specialize in PCs or the larger business computer systems used by corporations and large institutions. PC

specialists are most in demand because small- and medium-size firms cannot afford full-time computer specialists. Clients can call you for a one-time consultation or have you back as needed.

With the number of home-based businesses growing each year, most of these business owners will need someone to advise them on their computer needs. That someone could be you.

Start-Up Costs
$800 for simple advising to $10,000 for a home office set-up and equipment.

Pricing Guidelines
$55 to $100+ per hour, depending on your level of expertise, training, experience, and customers. Go by the industry guidelines and recommendations and network with others.

Marketing and Advertising Methods and Tips
* Aim your marketing efforts at those clients who you determine will be the best clients for you. Make appointments and presentations to demonstrate to potential clients how to increase their profits with a computer.
* Place classified ads in local business publications.
* Give talks at business meetings and conferences.
* Contact local chambers of commerce members for referrals.
* Print business cards, flyers, and brochures.

Essential Equipment
Business telephone line with answering capabilities, fax, computer and peripherals, legal contract forms if you will be signed on a retainer.

Recommended Training, Experience, or Needed Skills
* Computer training and education.
* Work as a systems analyst, trainer, or teacher.
* Need a thorough knowledge of computers used for the business and their related software.
* Have to have patience and be able to teach the system to your client.

Income Potential
Can range from $35,000 to $250,000 a year.

Type of Business
One-third in-home, running and marketing your consulting service; two-thirds out-of-the-home, working on-site of the client's office.

Best Customers
Small- and medium-size businesses (many home-based), individuals who need advice on purchasing a computer or are learning computer basics or how to use a software program.

Helpful Tips
+ Market your service constantly.
+ Educate potential clients as to how your computer consulting can help them increase their profits.
+ Know your specialization or, if you are a generalist, have sources you can turn to if you do not know an answer.
+ Consult with a lawyer for the proper wording in your contracts and with the IRS for tax reporting procedures.

For More Information

Associations

Independent Computer Consultants' Association (ICCA)
11131 S. Towne Square, Suite 7
St. Louis, MO 63123
(800) 774-4222; (314) 892-1675
< http://www.icca.org >

Offers support to independent computer consultants and publishes a bimonthly newsletter, *The Independent*. Local chapters around the country.

Women in Computers
41 Sutter St., Suite 10006
San Francisco, CA 94104
< http://www.awc-hq.org >

Association for women in computing. Send an LSASE for membership information.

Books

Computer Consulting on Your Home-Based PC, by Herman Holtz. 1994, Windcrest/McGraw-Hill, Blue Ridge Summit, PA 17294-0850.

Computer Money, by Alan N. Canton. Order from Adams-Blake Publishing, 8041 Sierra St., Fair Oaks, CA 95628. < http://www.adams-blake.com > How-to guide for establishing and running an independent technical consulting business.

Going Solo: Developing a Home-Based Consulting Business from the Ground Up, by William J. Bond. 1997, McGraw-Hill, New York.

How to Be a Successful Computer Consultant, 4th ed., by Alan R. Simon. 1998, McGraw-Hill, New York.

Start-Up Guide

Entrepreneur's Computer Consulting, (800) 421-2300. $69 + shipping and handling.

Additional Business Ideas

Computer trainer. Train other home-based business owners to use their computers and software programs for their business. Resources follow:

The Complete Computer Trainer, by Paul Clothier. 1996, McGraw-Hill, New York.

Computer Repair: Start Your Own Computer Repair Business, by Linda Rohrbough and Michael Hordeski. 1995, McGraw-Hill Computing, New York.

❧88❧
GRAPHIC ARTIST/DESIGNER

Using your computer and basic graphic design training and education, you can have your own graphic design studio. You can produce professionally designed logs, mechanicals, layouts, illustrations, presentations, brochures, direct mail, business cards, and other advertising and marketing materials.

You will need a background in design and computer graphics, and it will be helpful if you have worked as a graphic designer for a firm before you start out on your own.

You can also use two software packages—Print Artist and Gift Maker—to start your own business creating customized graphic output for clients who own small businesses.

Print Artist allows users to create professional-looking signs, greeting cards, banners, posters, certificates, and more in minutes. It grows with the user's ability, offering thousands of combinations of graphics, fonts, and special effects to create advanced custom designs. Gift Maker lets you design one-of-a-kind personalized merchandise—from t-shirts to teddy bears—and order them direct from the factory.

Possibilities using Print Artist include designing and creating letterheads, envelopes, and business cards; and making print advertisements, flyers, banners, and signs that clients can use to promote their businesses. Gift Maker can be used to create a wide range of promotional items, including polo shirts, sweatshirts, coffee mugs, caps, and tote bags.

If you have professional paint software, you can import your original designs into Print Artist and Gift Maker. You can design and sell matching stationery and envelopes, greeting cards, postcards, and paper crafts with Print Artist. With Gift Maker, you can put your artwork on clothing, clocks, coasters, mouse pads, calendars, teddy bears, and more.

Start-Up Costs and Financing Sources
+ $12,000 to $20,000.
+ Small business loan, personal savings, lines of credit on credit cards.

Pricing Guidelines
Go by industry standards (see "For More Information") and compare your prices with those of other graphic design firms.

Marketing and Advertising Methods and Tips

✤ Advertise in the business telephone directory.

✤ Print promotional materials. These are a sampling of what your business can do, so make them look professional and dynamic. Send to your target customers: small businesses, organizations, schools, small ad agencies.

✤ Place ads in business publications.

Essential Equipment

Computer such as a Macintosh LCIII with graphic design software such as PageMaker, QuarkXPress, Print Artist, Gift Maker, or Aldus Freehand. Print Artist and Gift Maker require a 386 PC running Windows software. Other office supplies and equipment: fax machine, printer (preferably a color printer), modem, telephone, answering machine or service, filing and bookkeeping software, promotional materials, graphics art reference books.

Recommended Training, Experience, or Needed Skills

✤ Need a good background or training in basic design principles.

✤ Work in a design or publishing firm.

✤ Need to be creative and be able to communicate with your clients.

Income Potential

$35,000 to $75,000+.

Type of Business

In-home business, except for times when meeting with clients (unless your home office is set up for meetings).

Best Customers

Small businesses, advertising companies, organizations, architects, engineers, brides, companies wanting direct mail promotions.

Helpful Tips

✤ Create unique layouts and communicate well with your clients. This will help bring you repeat business and referrals.

❖ Send out a monthly promotional flyer with marketing and/or business tips to those on your mailing list. This will help keep your business in your clients' minds.

❖ Keep current on advertising and industry trends.

❖ Use Print Artist and Gift Maker to create promotional items for your business or to create sample designs and sample output to show clients.

❖ Come up with a list of ideas on how your clients can use the items you produce to promote their businesses.

For More Information

Association

The Graphic Artists Guild
90 John St., Suite 403
New York, NY 10038-3202
(212) 463-7730; < http://www.gag.org >

A national resource and advocacy organization with local chapters. Provides legal and accounting services and legislative information. Publishes newsletters and members receive *The Graphic Artists Guild Handbook: Pricing and Ethical Guidelines.*

Books

AAIGA Professional Practices in Graphic Design: The American Institute of Graphic Arts, by Tad Crawford. 1998, Watson-Guptil, New York.

Artist's and Graphic Designer's Market. Writer's Digest Books, 1507 Dana Ave., Cincinnati, OH 45207. (800) 289-0963. Annual publication.

The Designer's Commonsense Business Book, Rev. ed., by Barbara Ganin. 1995, North Light Books, Cincinnati, OH.

How to Make Your Design Business Profitable, by Joyce Stewart. 1992, North Light Books.

The Professional Designer's Guide to Marketing Your Work, by Mary Yeung. 1991, North Light Books.

Starting Your Small Graphic Design Studio, by Michael Fleishman. 1993, North Light Books.

Book Club
Graphic Design Book Club, P.O. Box 12526, Cincinnati, OH 45212-0526. Exclusively for graphic design professionals.

Magazine
Dynamic Graphics, bi-monthly, published by Dynamic Graphics, Inc., 6000 N. Forest Park Dr., P.O. Box 1901, Peoria, IL 61614-3592. For desktop designers.
< http://www.dgusa.com >

Software
Go by industry recommendations.

Supplies
Dick Blick's Art Materials Catalog (see "Supplies" in "Craft Resources," page 288).

ൟ89ൟ
NEWSLETTER PUBLISHER (DESKTOP)

Over the past ten years, the newsletter industry has seen phenomenal growth. Newsletters focus on specialized topics, condensing relevant information and providing it to readers. They also give inside tips for certain groups or industries.

In this desktop publishing business you produce newsletters for businesses, for individual clients, or for a particular consumer or special interest group. Unless you have assistance, you have to do both the writing and selling of your newsletter. If you hit the right market and can sell a lot of subscriptions, you can have a lucrative business.

Kimberly Stanséll, owner of the Los Angeles-based business Research Done Write! and publisher of the newsletter *Bootstrappin' Entrepreneur* says that to succeed as a newsletter publisher, "It is important you know the idiosyncrasies of your target audience. For example, if you publish a travel newsletter, your readers will probably be a more stable audience and subscribe regularly as opposed to a newsletter whose readership has a high turnover rate. The editor of the latter example will have to continually market his or her newsletter to get new sub-scribers."

Start-Up Costs
$7,000 to $18,000.

Marketing and Advertising Methods and Tips
* Send direct mail to your target customers (use a mailing list you've compiled or buy one from a direct mail house).
* Attend trade shows and hand out copies of your newsletter.
* Place classified ads in trade and business publications.

Essential Equipment
Updated computer with multi-capablities to handle desktop publishing software; scanner, laser printer, modem, fax ma-chine, business telephone line, answering machine or service, photocopier (or access to one).

Recommended Training, Experience, or Needed Skills
* Study newsletter manuals and books; attend conferences and workshops on newsletter publishing (see "Associa-tions," later in this section).
* Take desktop publishing courses.
* Work or volunteer at a nonprofit organization to produce a newsletter.
* Need desktop publishing expertise. A journalism and graphic design background helps.

Income Potential
$25,000 to $75,000+ depending on the readership.

Type of Business
In-home.

Best Customers
Special interest groups or businesses, your determined target market.

Helpful Tips

✤ Need a mailing list that is effective in bringing in subscriptions.

✤ Be an expert in the field in which you are writing.

✤ Provide valuable, even exclusive information (not easily obtained elsewhere) to help your readers improve themselves, their businesses, or their profits.

✤ Stanséll suggests the following: "To keep costs down, it is important to maximize every resource you have and be aware of expenditures. Balance your newsletter with both helpful resources and information and note where your readership can get free help or ideas. Believe in your newsletter and make it a tool to help you expand your business. Be persistent! There are very few overnight successes."

For More Information

Associations

National Association of Desktop Publishers (NADTP)
462 Boston St.
Topsfield, MA 01983-1232
< http://www.nadtp.org >

Publishes *Desktop Publishers Journal*. Send an LSASE for information.

Newsletter Publishers Association
1501 Wilson Blvd., Suite 509
Arlington, VA 22209
(703) 527-2333; < http://www.newsletters.org >

Publishes *How to Launch a Newsletter, Success in Newsletter Publishing: A Practical Guide,* and their membership newsletter, *Hotline.*

Books

Design Principles for Desktop Publishers, by Tom Lichty. 1994, Wadsworth Publishing Co., Belmont, CA.

Desktop Publishing & Design for Dummies, by Roger C. Parker. 1995, IDG Books, Worldwide, Foster City, CA.

Home-Based Newsletter Publishing, by William J. Bond. 1997, Mc-Graw-Hill, New York.

How to Start a Home-Based Desktop Publishing Business, by Louise Kursmark. 1996, Globe Pequot Press, Old Saybrook, CT.

Start Your Own Newsletter Publishing Business, by Susan Rachmeler. 1997, Prentice-Hall, Upper Saddle River, NJ.

See also Lisa Shaw's book in the "Greeting Card" section.

Newsletters and Magazines

The Newsletter on Newsletters, Howard Hudson, editor. The Newsletter Clearinghouse, 44 W. Market St., P.O. Box 311, Rhinebeck, NY 12572. (914) 876-2081. $192 per year.

Publish, P.O. Box 5039, Brentwood, TN 37024-9816. < http://www.publish.com > Geared to electronic publishers.

Start-Up Guide

National Business Library's Start-Up Guide, *Newsletter Publishing and Desktop Publishing.* (800) 947-7724. $39.95 + shipping handling.

໑ 90 ໑
NEWSPAPER PUBLISHER (DESKTOP)

If you live in a small rural or suburban area or know of a community within an urban setting that does not have a newspaper covering its events, you might just consider using your desktop publishing system to produce your own. Your advertising and subscriptions will provide the income. You will still have to take your master copy to a printer, but your desktop publishing equipment will have saved you thousands of dollars on layout and typesetting costs.

Start-Up Costs and Financing Sources
✦ $14,000 to $55,000.
✦ Personal savings, small business loan, credit lines on credit cards.

Pricing Guidelines

Depends on your circulation and the number of advertisers you carry. Network with other small newspaper publishers (see "Association," further along in this section).

Marketing and Advertising Methods and Tips

❖ Send direct mailings to local community businesses.

❖ Contact the local chamber of commerce.

❖ Send out flyers to residents in your circulation area.

❖ Speak to community groups.

❖ Hand out free issues at local public libraries and community events.

❖ Stage a promotional event to announce the first issue of your paper.

Essential Equipment

Computer with capabilities to handle desktop publishing and graphic design software (see "Essential Equipment" in "Graphic Artist/Designer" entry, page 325), scanner, laser printer, modem, fax machine, business telephone line, answering machine or service, photocopier (or access to one).

Recommended Training, Experience, or Needed Skills

❖ Take newspaper writing and editing courses at local colleges.

❖ Work in a small (or large) newspaper office.

❖ Have an interest in people and the community you write about.

❖ Be persistent in getting publicity.

❖ Be able to meet deadlines.

Income Potential

$50,000 to $100,000+.

Type of Business

One-half in-home, writing; one-half out-of-the-home, getting the news and marketing.

Best Customers
Small businesses, community residents. After you're established, go to advertisers in larger cities who wish to attract people from the surrounding smaller communities.

Helpful Tips
Do not try to be too broad in your news coverage. Customers will come to you for the local angle.

For More Information
See also "For More Information" in "Newsletter Publishing (Desktop)" entry, page 329.

Association
National Newspaper Association (NNA)
1525 Wilson Blvd., Suite 550
Arlington, VA 22209-2434.

Books
How to Start Your Own Underground Newspaper, by Jay Gross. 1995, AmiGadget Press, Box 1696, Lexington, SC 29071.
The Newspaper Designer's Handbook, 4th ed., by Tim Harrower. 1997, McGraw-Hill, New York.
Also see Lisa Shaw's book in "Greeting Cards," *How to Make Money Publishing from Home.*

Additional Business Ideas
✢ Offer graphic printing services.
✢ Publish a newspaper of solely paid ads.
✢ See also "Freelance Writing" entry, page 344.

Food-Related Businesses

CATERING

Catering can mean creating romantic dinners for two or making food for a wedding reception of 500 or more. Many start their catering services from their own kitchens or they rent kitchens by the day. The investment is low, and with good management, the profits can be high. Check with your state health department regarding regulations for preparing food.

Start-Up Costs
$6,000 to $80,000, depending on whether you have to put in a kitchen.

Pricing Guidelines
A set fee per person is usually charged, sometimes two to three times the cost of the food and paper products. Factor in your preparation time, costs of running the business, and any rental fees or commissions to party/event planners you have to pay. Go by industry and expert recommendations (see "For More Information," later in this section).

Marketing and Advertising Methods and Tips

✣ Encourage word-of-mouth referrals from satisfied clients.

✣ Stage a catered party to celebrate your business opening. Invite other small business owners with whom you will be working, such as wedding and event consultants and planners, owners of banquet halls, D.J.s and small bands, balloon decorators and florists, and so forth. Give them a sampling of your best dishes and set-up. Have business cards, flyers, and brochures listing your specialties available to hand out.

✣ Advertise in the business telephone directory.

✣ Rent a booth at bridal shows.

✣ Send direct mail or make presentations to members of the local chamber of commerce.

✣ Place classified ads in local publications.

Essential Equipment

A professional kitchen (one you can rent), necessary culinary equipment.

Recommended Training, Experience, or Needed Skills

✣ Take courses at local vo-tech schools or culinary institutes.

✣ Work for one or more catering businesses.

✣ Need culinary skills and attention to detail.

✣ Be well-organized, yet able to deal with last-minute changes.

✣ Be creative in your food presentation.

Income Potential

$50,000 to $100,000 + depending on the size of the event(s) you cater.

Type of Business

One-half in-home, attending to pre-party preparation; one-half out-of-the-home, overseeing each party and marketing.

Best Customers

Businesses for seasonal parties, meetings, company picnics. Individuals wanting the following events catered: weddings, retirement parties, graduation parties, small dinner parties, anniversary celebrations.

Helpful Tips

✤ Give your best effort with each client—good news travels fast!

✤ Do something special to make your catering memorable; for example, use ice sculptures or other special food presentations.

✤ Do not be afraid to suggest ideas to your clients. Your clients may really appreciate it and this could be reflected in your profits.

✤ Hire help (if needed) with good people skills.

✤ Offer one-stop catering—add rental of china, tents, party supplies, or work with a party rental service to coordinate everything.

For More Information

Books

How to Open and Operate a Home-Based Catering Business, 2nd ed. by Denise Vivaldo. 1996, Globe Pequot Press, Old Saybrook, CT.

How to Run a Catering Business from Home, by Christopher Egerton-Thomas. 1996, John Wiley & Sons, New York.

Start Your Own Catering Business, by Kathleen Deming. 1997, Prentice Hall Trade, Upper Saddle River, NJ.

Home Study Courses

International Correspondence Schools
925 Oak St.
Scranton, PA 18515

Offers career diploma in catering/gourmet cooking.

Lifetime Career Schools
101 Harrison St.
Archbald, PA 18403
Offers courses in cooking.

Software

Schrek Software, *PC-Food II*. 1420 Interlochen Circle, Woodbury, MN 55125. < http://www.schrecksoftware.com >

CaterWARE® Inc. (614) 481-7699. < http://www.caterware. com >
Sells two programs: one for small catering start-ups at $395;
another for larger catering operations at $995. Call or visit
their Web site for ordering information.

Start-Up Guide
Entrepreneur's Start-Up Guide, *Food and Party Catering Service.*
(800) 421-2300. $69 + shipping and handling.

Additional Business Ideas
❖ Romantic dinners for two in a couple's home or apartment.
Clients pick from a menu beforehand, you bring the food,
the china, a rose, and serve the food in a tuxedo. Charge
from $75 to $120 per meal.
❖ Box lunches for company workers.
❖ Personal chef. You (and an assistant, if needed) go to a customer's home and cook a gourmet meal for a small dinner
party or gathering.

❧ 92 ☙
FOOD DELIVERY SERVICE

In this business, you will contract with restaurants to deliver
food for the menu price plus your fee for delivery. Usually, your
customers will be couples and individuals who prefer to stay at
home but want a restaurant menu. Hotels, motels, and businesses sponsoring seminars and workshops may find this service particularly convenient.

Or you can cook and freeze meals to deliver to your clients.
Make sure you check with your state's food regulations in doing
any cooking in your home.

Start-Up Costs
$10,000 to $25,000 (with your own vehicle).

Type of Business
Primarily out-of-the-home.

Franchises, Distributorships, and Licenses

Check the franchise publications listed in the "Franchise and Distributorships" chapter. They list many food-related franchises.

For More Information

Book

Professional Cooking, by Wayne Gissler. 1994, John Wiley & Sons, New York.

Start-Up Guide

Entrepreneur's Start-Up Guide, *Food Delivery Service.* (800) 421-2300. $69 + shipping and handling.

Additional Business Ideas

✦ Start your own restaurant truck. You go to offices, companies, and factories' parking lots or lounges and serve soups, sandwiches, hoagies, coffee, sweet rolls, and so forth. See *From Dogs to Riches: A Step-by-Step Guide to Start and Operate Your Own Mobile Cart Vending Business* by Vera Denise Clark-Rugley. MCC Publishing Co., Los Angeles, CA (310) 323-5557.

✦ Be a personal chef. See *More 101 Best Home-Based Businesses for Women,* by Priscilla Y. Huff. 1998, Prima Publishing, Rocklin, CA.

ເ◈93◈ະ
JUST DESSERTS

Few people have time to bake or prepare special desserts for guests, dinner parties, or special celebrations. If you love doing special desserts, pies, or cakes, you may find your services much in demand. Contact party/wedding planners and caterers and offer a menu and samples of your best recipes. You may also be able to supply restaurants and food delivery services who will order from you. (Check on your state's regulations regarding cooking in your home. You may rent a kitchen from a church or business, instead.)

Type of Business
Primarily in-home.

For More Information
See also "For More Information" in "Catering" entry, page 335.

Association
American Institute of Baking (AIB)
1213 Bakers Way
Manhattan, KS 66502
< http://www.aibonline.org >

Send an LSASE for information.

Books
Also look for ideas in the cookbook section of your local library in good, out-of-print books and in the cookbooks produced by local places of worship.

All-Time Favorite Dessert Recipes, compiled by Jean Wickstrom Liles. 1996, Leisure Arts, Palm Coast, FL.

Dessert: The Grand Finale, by the staff of Sedgewood Press. Order from Better Homes and Gardens Crafts Club, 1716 Locust St., P.O. Box 4724, Des Moines, IA 50336-4724.

The Neighborhood Bake Shop: Recipes and Reminiscences of America's Favorite Bakery Treats, by Jill Van Cleave. 1997, William Morrow & Co., New York.

Turn Your Kitchen into a Goldmine, by Alice and Alfred Howard. 1981, Harper and Row, New York. Out of print—but some public libraries may still have copies.

Additional Business Ideas
❖ Jams and jellies. Grow the fruit and make your own to sell to specialty shops or by mail order.
❖ Breads and muffins. Sell all kinds, including lowfat ones.
❖ Christmas cookies. Sell by the half-pound and whole pound.
❖ Frozen dessert specialties. Read *Ice Cream & Frozen Desserts: A Commercial Guide to Production and Marketing*, by Malcolm Stogo. 1998, John Wiley & Sons, New York.

✤ Cheesecakes. See *Cheesecake Extraordinaire: More Than 100 Sumptuous Recipes for the Ultimate Dessert,* reprint ed., by Mary Crownover. 1997, NTC/Contemporary Publishing, Lincolnwood, IL.

ᘓᑍ94ᕙᔕ
SELLING A FAMILY RECIPE

If people rave over your special condiments (horseradish, mustard, sauce) or brownies, cookies, or cakes made from recipes that have been handed down in your family, you may have a specialty food that will bring you profits. You must, of course, make sure the recipe was not taken from a copyrighted source.

Your food item has to be unique to compete with big companies that can spend millions on research, development, and marketing. If you (and others that you have given samples to) believe your product is the best, then you should go ahead with a business plan.

After perfecting your product, you will need to design (or have someone else design) a food label and packaging. You will also need a food handler's license and other permits, as well as Food and Drug Administration approval if you plan to ship the food via mail order. Your home office must be set up to fill orders by mailing list customers and/or specialty food retailers and suppliers. If you are successful at selling one food product, consider adding additional products later.

Start-Up Costs
$1,000 to $10,000.

Marketing and Advertising Methods and Tips
✤ Rent booths at food trade shows.
✤ Send direct mail with samples to specialty food retailers and suppliers.

Essential Equipment
Kitchen and cooking equipment, computer with billing and order processing/inventory software.

Income Potential
$100,000+ depending on the demand and your market!

Type of Business
Primarily in-home, except when attending trade shows.

Helpful Tips
+ Study the success stories of food specialty entrepreneurs.
+ Attend trade shows. While there, talk to food brokers, retailers, and suppliers to get tips and to see where your recipe would fit in the market.

For More Information

Association
National Association for the Specialty Food Trade, Inc.
(NASFT)
120 Wall St.
New York, NY 10018

Note: You must have had your food products in stores for one year to qualify for membership. Write for details.

Book
From Kitchen to Market: Selling Your Gourmet Food Specialty, 2nd ed., by Stephen F. Hall. 1996, Upstart Publishing, Dover, NH.

Start-Up Guide
Entrepreneur's Start-Up Guide, *Marketing a Family Recipe.* (800) 421-2300. $69 + shipping and handling.

Other Businesses

cC**95**Ccc
ENGRAVING

Engraving is used for both identification and decoration purposes. If you have experience in handling engraving tools (or have the patience to learn), an engraving business may be the venture for you. You could start with a simple electric engraver and take the time to learn the techniques of engraving. Then, when you feel you have the basic skills mastered, take on simple projects and work up to more complicated ones.

Start-Up Costs and Financing Sources
✤ $40 to $80 for a simple electric engraver to $4,000 to $5,000 + for an air-driven, hand-held drill engraver. $1,000 to $7,000 for advertising and office supplies.
✤ Personal savings, credit card financing.

Pricing Guidelines
Check to see what other engravers charge.

Marketing and Advertising Methods and Tips
✤ Place an ad in the business telephone directory.
✤ Place classified ads in the local newspaper.
✤ Print promotional materials—business cards, flyers.
✤ Send direct mailings to shop owners and auto dealers.
✤ Present samples of your work to jewelers and gift shops.

Essential Equipment
Engraving tools. Also products if you sell engraved items.

Recommended Training, Experience, or Needed Skills
+ Practice on your own glass and wood items.
+ Work as an apprentice in a jewelry shop.
+ Practice to be skilled so that your work is of professional quality.

Income Potential
$300 to $500 + a week, more as your skill and reputation increase.

Type of Business
In-home, except for marketing presentations.

Best Customers
Contact insurance companies to find out what items should be engraved for identification purposes, bridal shops, jewelers, trophy shops, hunting shops (engraving of guns), auto shops, gift shops.

For More Information

Book
The Thames & Hudson Manual of Etching & Engraving, reprint, edited by Walter Chambelain. 1992, Thames & Hudson Publishing, New York.

Engraving Tools
Basic electric engravers: Dick Blick's Art Materials Catalog, P.O. Box 1267, Galesburg, IL 61402-1267; (800) 447-8192.

High-tech engraving system: Paragrave Corporation, 1455 W. Center St., Orem, UT 84058. Complete video training, equipment, and supplies. Send an LSASE for full information.

⚛96⚛
FINDING SERVICE

In this business, you find things for people for a fee. What kinds of things? That depends on your background and experience. For individuals, you could look for collectibles, antiques, a lost friend, a job prospect, specific information, or whatever area you'd like to specialize in. For businesses, you might search for loan money, a special software program, a new business site, customers for a new product, and so on. It all depends on what your customers cannot find and what you can.

Start-Up Costs
$1,000 to $8,000 for advertising, office equipment.

Pricing Guidelines
Consult with a lawyer to have a standard contract drawn up to give to clients. The contract will state your fee for finding the object, service, or information requested. You and your client can also agree if there is to be a time limit in which to complete your findings.

Marketing and Advertising Methods and Tips
+ Place classified ads in business and trade publications.
+ Encourage word-of-mouth referrals.
+ Network with friends or business associates for "finding" prospects.
+ Contact your local chamber of commerce. Make them aware of your service.
+ Give talks to community groups about how to find whatever it is you specialize in.

Essential Equipment
Business telephone line, answering machine, fax machine, promotional materials; computer and modem with Internet connection (for online research).

Recommended Training, Experience, or Needed Skills
✤ Work or acquire knowledge in the line of business or businesses in which your clients need things, so that you are familiar with the subject and know how to make contacts that can help you.
✤ Need to be persistent, accurate, and fast.

Income Potential
$25,000 to $80,000 + a year.

Type of Business
Both in-home and out-of-the home.

Best Customers
Businesses that need services, loans, advice, supplies, or market research, to improve profits; individuals who need information, collectibles, or to find other individuals.

Helpful Tips
Be familiar with research techniques and methods.

For More Information

Books
199 Great Home Businesses You Can Start (and Succeed in) for Under $1,000, by Tyler Hicks. 1993, Prima Publishing.
K-1 Success Kit, by Tyler Hicks. Includes how to start a finder service. Order from Prima Publishing, P.O. Box 1260BK, Rocklin, CA 95677. $99.50.
See also "Information Broker" section.

～97～
FREELANCE WRITING

Researching the publishing market (books, magazines, trade publications) and finding out what type of writing is in demand is one of the most important factors in successful freelance writing. You need to know who wants the kind of writing you do.

You also need to study the craft of writing. Take courses, read trade publications and how-to books, and then write and write some more until you've got the best you can produce.

Knowing how to approach an editor is crucial—usually with a query letter—as is knowing manuscript form and submission procedures. There is no guarantee your work will be accepted, but those writers who persist and work at improving their writing skills may eventually get published.

Start-Up Costs and Financing Sources
✤ $4,000 to $8,000.
✤ Personal savings, small business loan, friends, family, credit lines on credit cards.

Pricing Guidelines
The *Writer's Market* (see "For More Information") lists average payments for writing projects. Magazine articles: pay by the word (a few cents per word) or up to $2,000 for a mid-size article. Books: advances can range from $250 to $10,000 (these increase as your writing reputation grows).

Marketing and Advertising Methods and Tips
✤ Send query letters and/or book proposals to publishers on your topic.
✤ Hire an agent to handle your marketing (you pay them a percentage of whatever contract you sign).
✤ Attend writer's conferences and talk to editors about what they look for.

Essential Equipment
Typewriter or word processor, or computer with word processing software that is compatible with publishers'; ink-jet or laser printer, modem with connection to Internet; telephone, answering system; photocopier; fax machine.

Recommended Training, Experience, or Needed Skills
✤ Take writing courses at adult evening schools or colleges.
✤ Work for a newspaper or magazine.

❖ Volunteer to write a newsletter for a nonprofit organization.
❖ Start out writing for local publications—write newspaper features to get practice.

Income Potential
$15,000 to $55,000 + a year, depending on whether you are writing full- or part-time.

Type of Business
In-home.

Best Customers
Start with small publishers, publications, and trade publications, which are more likely to accept your work than the big-name publishers. This does not mean you shouldn't try larger circulation magazines or large publishers at the same time.

Helpful Tips
❖ Know your genre of writing, which publishers publish your type of writing, what the current trends are.
❖ Present your writing in a professional-looking format (readable print, proper margins).
❖ Join related writing associations specific to your writing genre(s).

For More Information

Books and Book Clubs
Children's Writer's and Illustrator's Market. Writer's Digest Books.
Freelance Writing for Magazines and Newspapers, by Marcia Yudkin. 1993, 1st ed., HarperCollins Publishers, New York.
Handbook for Freelance Writing, by Michael Perry. 1998, NTC Publishing Group, Lincolnwood, IL.
How to Write While You Sleep, by Elizabeth Irvin Ross. 1993, Ten Speed Press, Berkeley, CA.

Insider's Guide to Book Editors, Publishers, and Literary Agents, 1997–1998 by Jeff Herman. 1997, Prima Publishing, Box 1260BK, Rocklin, CA 95677.

The Silver Pen: Starting a Profitable Writing Business from a Lifetime of Experience, by Alan N. Canton. 1996, Adams-Blake, Fair Oaks, CA.

Start & Run a Profitable Freelance Writing Business: Your Step-By-Step Business Plan, by Christine Adamec. 1994, Self-Counsel Press, Bellingham, WA.

Writer's Digest Book Club—the latest on every writing topic. Publishes numerous books on all types of writing. Sponsors a book club, offers a home study writing course, and publishes *Writer's Digest* magazine and various annual market books.

Writer's Digest Books, 1507 Dana Ave., Cincinnati, OH 45207. (800) 289-0963.

Writer's Market. Writer's Digest Books. Annual market guide that lists book publishers, magazine publishers, and other markets for your writing. Also gives pricing guidelines for various writing services and projects.

Writing—Getting into Print: A Business Guide for Writers, by Jo Frohbieter-Mueller. 1994, Glenbridge Publishing, 6010 W. Jewell Ave., Lakewood, CO 80232.

Home Study Course

NRI Schools
4401 Connecticut Ave., NW
Washington, DC 20008
< http://www.writersclub.com >

Offers courses in fiction/nonfiction writing; membership in the online Writer's Club.

Magazines and Newsletters

Children's Writer: The Newsletter of Writing and Publishing Trends, 95 Long Ridge Rd., West Redding, CT 06896-1124.

The Writer, 120 Boylston St., Boston, MA 02116-4615.

Writer's Digest, Writer's Digest Books (see address above). < http://www.writersdigest.com >

Online

Many writers' Web sites—look in popular Internet search engines.

Additional Business Ideas

❖ Freelance editing. Pays $25 to $85 per hour. Proofreading can pay up to $20 per hour. Take correspondence courses from the USDA Graduate School in editing and proofreading.

❖ Self-publishing. With the desktop publishing systems available today, more and more people are bypassing the query/proposal route and self-publishing their own booklets, manuals, newsletters, and books. Patricia Gallagher has written and self-published six books. She's promoted her books on nearly 200 radio and television shows, including the *Oprah Winfrey Show* (twice), CNN, and *Sally Jessy Raphael*. This young mother went on a 9,100-mile book tour (with three of her children and pregnant with her fourth). Gallagher was even able to have James A. Michener write an endorsement on the inside cover of her book, *For All the Write Reasons* (see below). Other books that have been self-published are *What Color Is Your Parachute?* (4.3 million copies sold); *How to Keep Your Volkswagen Alive* (2.2 million copies sold); and *Simple Things You Can Do to Save the Earth* (3.5 million copies sold).

The following books will help guide you:

The Complete Guide to Self-Publishing, 3rd ed., by Tom and Marilyn Ross. 1997, Writer's Digest Books.

For All the Write Reasons: Forty Successful Authors, Publishers, Agents, and Writers Tell How to Get Your Book Published, by Patricia Gallagher. Young Sparrow Publishing, Box 265, Worcester, PA 19490. $24.95. Send $2 and an LSASE for *Tips on Self-Publishing* booklet.

How to Self-Publish Your Own Comic Book, by Tony Caputo. 1997, Watson-Guptil, New York.

Small Publishers Association of North America (SPAN), founded by Tom and Marilyn Ross. Write P.O. Box 1306, 425 Cedar St., Buena Vista, CO 81211. < http://www.SPANnet.org >

ᮮ98ᮭ
HOME ART OR MUSIC SCHOOL

If you have training in art, music, dance, and physical education and exercise, you may want to open your own home studio or school like these women did:

❖ Musical kindergarten. One older woman has operated a musical kindergarten from her home classroom for many years. The children start at age two and a half and go for a two-year (weekly) program that teaches them the basics of musical notes, songs, and simple instruments. At the end of two years, there is a "graduation," complete with miniature caps and gowns.

A $40 registration fee is charged as well as a monthly fee ranging from $30 to $55. Class sizes average 10 to 12 students. Classes last about an hour or so, depending on the students' age level.

❖ Art studio. Bonnie, an artist and mother of three, opened her own children's art studio in a former farm outbuilding. It already had a bathroom and sink, so with a few touch-ups and an investment of about $500 in supplies, she opened her business. Her advertising costs were about $750, but she says, "I've never had to advertise again. I get my business through word-of-mouth and have a waiting list."

Bonnie takes students from 6 to 18 years of age and teaches classes four days a week from 2:30 P.M. to 10:00 P.M. She says, "I go to work when everyone else's work day is over, but I love the convenience of having my business near my family." She charges $55 a month, for a weekly 1 1/2-hour lesson; $65 a month for more advanced classes. She averages about 60 students a month. Of course, she checked zoning requirements and has a permit to operate the school on her property.

You may want to open a similar studio or hold other lessons at your home. Do not forget to check with your insurance agent for liability coverage needed and your zoning officer for any permits required.

Franchises, Distributorships, and Licenses

Franchise

Kinderdance, Int., Inc.
268 N. Babcock St., Suite A
Melbourne, FL 32935

Write for information.

For More Information

Books

Growing Artists: Teaching Art to Young Children, by Joan Bouza Koster. 1997, Delmar Publishers, Inc., Albany, NY.
Making Money Teaching Music, by David R. and Barbara Newsam. 1995, Writer's Digest Books, Cincinnati, OH.

∽ 99 ∼
MAIL ORDER

Mail order is a broad term for selling products or information—either a manufacturer's or your own—through the mail. Even though numerous mail-order catalogs show up in your mailbox, there is still room for more! In tune with our modern lifestyles, the mail-order industry has made shopping convenient and easy.

Though many people have made millions of dollars in this business, many have also lost money. Make sure you take the time to study experts' advice and the business methods and tips of those individuals who have had success in their mail-order businesses. It is a good home-based business because of the flexibility in work hours, the ability to work from the home, and the potential to make high profits. The formula for success is to pick a good product or products, find the right customers, and have the money and/or marketing strategy for reaching those customers.

You may want to start your business part-time and on a small-scale, and then build it up as you learn (and earn) more.

Start-Up Costs and Financing Sources
+ Can average anywhere from as little as $200 to $5,000 to as much as $16,000 to $70,000.
+ Personal savings, credit lines on your credit cards, investors.

Pricing Guidelines
Go by recommendations quoted by experts. See "For More Information," later in this section.

Marketing and Advertising Methods and Tips
+ Start with small classified ads in publications (that your own market research reveals are the best to reach your potential customers). These will generate leads to which you can send more promotional materials that more fully describe your product(s).
+ Buy mailing lists from list brokers (investigate to make sure they are worth the money).

Essential Equipment
Promotional materials, computer with mail-order software. Appropriate tools and supplies, if you make your own product. Mailing supplies, mailing permits, area for assembling and packaging, business telephone line, and/or 800 number for ordering.

Recommended Training, Experience, or Needed Skills
+ Study mail-order manuals and books.
+ Attend workshops, seminars on mail-order business management.
+ Work in a mail-order company.
+ Have a carefully planned marketing strategy.
+ Be cost-effective with all aspects of your business.

Income Potential
Can range from a few hundred or thousand dollars to $70,000 or more a year.

Type of Business
In-home.

Best Customers

Those that you gather for your own compiled mailing list; those who respond to "free information" ads; those you sign up at trade shows; those that have already purchased something from you; referrals from customers.

Helpful Tips

❖ Start slowly and build steadily as you begin to make profits. Do not jump into producing your own catalog until you have a reliable mailing list of at least 10,000 names.

❖ Follow local, state, and federal regulations concerning mail-order businesses.

❖ Give your customer the best product for the best price, and offer the best service you can.

For More Information

Associations

Direct Marketing Association
1120 Avenue of the Americas
New York, NY 10036-6700
(212) 768-7277; < http://www.the-dma.org >

Offers professional development, training seminars, workshops, library, and information services. Sponsors an annual conference and exhibition and carries a direct marketing publications catalog.

National Mail Order Association (NMOA)
2807 Polk St., NE
Minneapolis, MN 55418-2924

Federal Government Offices
Department of Commerce
Office of Consumer Affairs
1620 L St., NW #17
Washington, DC 20036

Provides information and booklets on importing/exporting, advertising, packaging, labeling, and product warranties and servicing.

Federal Trade Commission
Division of Legal and Public Records
6th and Pennsylvania Ave., NW
Washington, DC 20580
(202) 326-2222; < http://www.ftc.gov >

Oversees truth in advertising and the mail-order industry. Order their *Mail-Order Rule* booklet.

Books and Booklets

101 Great Mail-Order Businesses, by Tyler Hicks. 1996, Prima Publishing, Rocklin, CA.

Building a Mail Order Business: A Complete Manual for Success, 4th ed., by William Cohen. 1996, John Wiley & Sons, New York.

How to Create Successful Catalogs, by Maxwell Sroge. 1995, NTC Business Books, Lincolnwood, IL.

How to Start a Home-Based Mail Order Business, by Georganne Fiumara. 1996, Globe Pequot Press, Old Saybrook, CT.

How to Start a Home-Based Mail Order Business (The 21st Century Entrepreneur), by Mike Powers and Stephen Pollan. 1996, Avon Books, New York.

Broker

AMERICRAFT—The Gift Brokers, Inc.
210 Lockes Village Rd.
Wendell, MA 01379
(978) 544-7330; (978) 544-2771 fax

Brokers of U.S.-made merchandise to the American mail-order catalog industry.

Business Kit

Mail-Order Business Kit. Order from Success Publications (see "Books Through the Mail" in Part III).

Mailing List Broker

Compiler's Plus Inc.
100 Paragon Dr.
Montvale, NJ 07645-1745

Sales leads and mailing lists.

Magazines and Newsletters

Mail Order Digest, National Mail Order Association (see address in "Associations").

Mail Order Messenger, Box 358, Middleton, TN 38052-0358.

Software

Mail Order Wizard, Haven Corp., 1227 Dodge Ave., Evanston, IL 60202-1008. (847) 869-3434. Write for information about IBM-compatible software for mail-order businesses. Prices start at $495. Help line available.

Mailer's Software, 970 Calle Negocio, San Clemente, CA 92673-6201. (800) 800-MAIL.

Start-Up Guide

National Business Library, *Mail Order*. (800) 947-7724. $39.95 + shipping and handling.

Additional Business Ideas

❖ Mailing list business service.

❖ Selling your items in others' mail-order catalogs. See *Selling to Catalog Houses*. Order from The Front Room Publishers, Catalog Dept. B11/94, P.O. Box 1541, Clifton, NJ 07015-1541. Also read *How to Sell to Catalog Houses*. Order from Success Publications, 3419 Dunham, Box 263, Warsaw, NY 14569. SASE for prices.

❧ 100 ☙
SIGN-PAINTING BUSINESS

This business can be run on a small or large scale. Signs are still being created by artists with sandblasting or carving techniques, but today computers may be used to produce letter stencils for commercial banners, in addition to etching and silk screening techniques.

Having artistic talent and training or sign-painting experience is a plus. You should also be able to communicate well with your customers and help them in planning a design for their sign that will best portray their businesses' unique style.

Nancy Booz, a young mother and artist, has painted signs, logos, and scenes on trucks, a YMCA fitness center, and a stagecoach, to name a few. She first meets with her customers and comes up with a mental picture from the ideas given her. Then she will draw several preliminary sketches until one is approved. Booz says, "My business is seldom boring because I never know what I will be called to do. It's great getting paid for doing what I enjoy!"

Start-Up Costs
$1,000 to $2,000 for basic supplies and advertising (more if you purchase a computer).

Pricing Guidelines
Compare the prices of other sign painting businesses. Go with industry standards and recommendations (see "For More Information"). Some sign painters charge $20 to $25 an hour for a drawing; $35 an hour for lettering; and $45 or more an hour for a mural. Your price will depend on the time involved, the materials, and the size of the project. Work up a written estimate and sketch for your customer. If you do get the job, then charge for the sketch(es)—make sure you keep the sketches.

Marketing and Advertising Methods and Tips
* Advertise in the business telephone directory.
* Leave your business cards at paint stores and office supply centers.
* Place classified and display ads in your local newspaper.
* Send direct mail to new businesses (watch for legal notices publicized in your local papers).
* Join your local chamber of commerce.
* Paint your business name and address on the back of your signs.
* Donate a sign to a community auction or paint a sign for a nonprofit event when you first start to get free advertising.

Essential Equipment
Good set of brushes and other basic art supplies, promotional materials (make sure they illustrate a sampling of your artistic

skills, paints), special tools like an electro pounce or sandblast stencil, computer (as needed).

Recommended Training, Experience, or Needed Skills

❖ Take art and design courses.

❖ Have artistic skill or sense of design, plus a mechanical aptitude.

❖ Apprentice with a master sign painter, if possible.

❖ Work in a sign-painting shop.

Income Potential

$15,000 to $50,000+, depending on the population density in your area, your production methods, and types of signs.

Type of Business

In-home, except for marketing and meeting with customers.

Best Customers

New businesses, satisfied customers who want additional signs or decorations (send them direct mailings of new ideas), non-profit organizations when announcing fundraising events, garage sale holders, seasonal home boutiques.

Helpful Tips

❖ Make sure you calculate your time adequately when figuring out your price quotes.

❖ Keep original sketches and photos of completed projects in a portfolio to show prospective customers. Also keep a record of the time spent, materials used, and the surface you painted to better estimate the costs of future projects.

❖ Buy paints and materials as you need them for each project.

❖ Give your customers a choice of two or more signs (with price differences), a simple one and more detailed one.

❖ Never stop learning new techniques and ways to improve your skills.

Franchises, Distributorships, and Licenses

Franchises

There are a number of custom-made sign franchises with investments ranging from $30,000 to $80,000 or more. If you are thinking of this type of franchise, follow tips on deciding whether a specific franchise is best for you. (See "Franchises and Distributorships" chapter, page 44).

For More Information

Books

Order the following from *Dick Blick's Art Materials Catalog*, P.O. Box 1267, Galesburg, IL 61402-1267. (800) 447-8192.

Practical Sign Shop Operation, by Bob Fitzgerald. 1992, St. Publications, Cincinnati, OH.

Sign Layout Idea Handbook. $14.50 + shipping.

Sign Painting and Graphics Course.

Magazines

Sign Business, National Business Media, Inc., P.O. Box 1416, Broomfield, CO 80038-1416. $45 for a one-year (13 issues) subscription, $70 for two years, $88 for three years. < http://www.nbm.com/signbusiness >

SignCraft, P.O. Box 60031, Ft. Myers, FL 33906. < http://www. signcraft.com > 6 issues for one year costs $28.

Pricing Guide.

Signwork: A Craftsman's Manual, 2nd ed., by Bill Stewart. 1994, Bladwell Scientific Inc., Cambridge, MA.

Additional Business Ideas

* Make wood signs. Take evening woodworking courses at local vo-tech schools to learn basic router machine skills. See *Making Wood Signs*, by Patrick Spielman.
* Rent lawn or yard signs. Create and paint special occasion yard signs and rent to nonprofit organizations or consumers to announce special events or celebrations (births, birthdays, etc.).

❖ Cut out and paint seasonal lawn or yard signs. Create, design, and paint seasonal signs: scarecrows, witches, pump-
kins; Santa Claus and reindeer; Easter Bunny; humorous
characters and figures to decorate lawns and gardens. Sell at
craft shows or from your own lawn.

❦ 101 ❧
TAX PREPARATION SERVICE

Most of us do not look forward to filing our income taxes every
year, but others see it as a part- or full-time income opportunity. If you know income tax filing procedures or are skilled in
accounting and good with figures, this may be a good business
for you. Of course, most of your business will be from January
to April 15th, every year, but many professional tax preparers
work for their clients year-round: They file any necessary ex-
tensions, help clients keep their records in order, and provide
other services that make it easier to file each year's taxes.

If this business venture interests you, talk to professional tax
preparers, study tax preparation manuals, and survey if there is
a need for a preparer in your community.

Start-Up Costs and Financing Sources
❖ $6,000 to $8,000.
❖ Personal savings, lines of credit on credit cards, loans by
family or friends.

Pricing Guidelines
Check with other preparers to see what the going rate per form
is. Begin with basic charges for the simplest forms, and then figure a fee for preparing each schedule and additional form. Your
fees should be based on the number of forms that the IRS requires to be filed, not based on your client's refund or payment.
Some professional preparers charge from $30 to several hun-
dred dollars, depending on the number of forms and the time involved in preparing a client's taxes.

Marketing and Advertising Methods and Tips
* Place an ad in the business telephone directory.
* Post flyers on community bulletin boards.
* Place classified ads in the local newspaper.
* Hand out business cards to family and friends to pass on to others.
* Encourage word-of-mouth referrals.
* Put up road signs (if permitted by zoning) by your home office.
* Send direct mailings to business associates.

Essential Equipment
Calculator, tax forms, tax reference manuals, miscellaneous office supplies and equipment, business telephone line with answering machine or service, fax, computer hardware and software (if filing electronically), home office set up to receive clients (unless you rent office space during the tax season).

Recommended Training, Experience, or Needed Skills
* Enroll in tax preparation courses and seminars.
* Take accounting courses at local schools or community colleges.
* Take home study courses (see later in this section).
* Work for a tax preparation service.
* Need to have attention to detail and be accurate, honest, and patient.

Income Potential
$40,000 to $60,000+ a year.

Type of Business
In-home business, unless you rent a temporary office during the tax season.

Best Customers
Retirees, couples with complex filing schedules (medical expenses, divorced or separated, rental property owners), small business owners.

Helpful Tips

❖ Make sure you have the proper training, experience, and license to be a professional tax preparer.

❖ Be current on each year's tax law changes and new forms to be filed. Check with local accountants and bookkeepers for locations of tax forms or updates.

❖ Contact your local tax and IRS offices and inform them you are a licensed tax practitioner. Ask if they would supply you with the tax forms and instructions.

❖ Make copies of all prepared returns for you and your client. Put copies in your files.

❖ Explain each line on the form to your client and have him or her sign and date it and return it in the proper envelope.

❖ Check and recheck each form you do. Do not be afraid to check with the IRS if you have any questions.

Franchises, Distributorships, and Licenses

Franchise

Triple Check Income Tax Services, Inc.
2441 Honolulu Ave.
Montrose, CA 91020
(800) 283-1040

For More Information

Association

American Society of Tax Professionals
P.O. Box 245
Centerville, IA 52544

Send an LSASE for membership information.

Books

Bookkeeping & Tax Preparation: Start & Build a Prosperous Bookkeeping, Tax & Financial Services Business, by Gordon P. Lewis. 1996, Acton Cir., Ukiah, CA.

Guide to a Successful Tax Practice, by Practitioners Publishing Co., 1992.

Home Study Courses

Federated Tax Service
4638 N. Ravenswood Ave.
Chicago, IL 60618
(773) 561-4400

Offers a tax preparation course, manual and computerized software, and information on electronic filing. Free information packet available.

National Tax Training School
4 Melnick Dr., Box 382
Monsey, NY 10957
< http://www.nattax.com >

Publishes booklet *Building a Successful Tax Practice* and a newsletter.

Internet Site

< http://www.handrblock.com >
H & R Block Tax Web site

Reference Tax Guides

American Express Tax Guide 1998, by American Express Tax, Business Services, Inc. HarperCollins, New York.
H & R Block (1998 Income Tax Guide) [Annual], by H & R Block, Inc., Simon & Schuster, New York.

Tax Offices

IRS
4300 Caroline Ave.
Richmond, VA 23222
(800) 829-1040; < http://www.irs.ustreas.gov >

Write or call for Publication #910, *Guide to Free Tax Services.* You can choose free tax publications concerning the business use of your home and other tax information booklets. Or call your local IRS office.

Look in the white or blue pages of the telephone directory to find your State Department of Revenue, which can provide information on state taxes.

Check with your clients' city, town, borough, or township revenue offices for local taxes to be paid.

Additional Business Ideas

✤ Filing income tax forms electronically. Check with the IRS office nearest you and request publications covering electronic filing procedures. You will need a computer, modem, and tax filing software.

✤ Tax consultant. Help individuals and couples with tax planning for retirement.

Part III

ADDITIONAL
RESOURCES

Additional Resources

Unless otherwise noted, please send an LSASE if you are contacting these organizations through the mail.

Associations for Women Working from Home
American Mothers at Home
914 S. Santa Fe, Suite 297
Vista, CA 92084

Association of Electronic Cottages
Available on CompuServe, type GO WORK (see "Online Services," later in this section).

At-Home Mothers' Resource Center
406 E. Buchanan Ave.
Fairfield, IA 52556
< http://www.at-home-mothers.com >

Information, resources for at-home mothers. Publishes the *At-Home Mother Resource Catalog* and *At-Home Mothering Magazine*.

Formerly Employed Mothers at the Leading Edge (FEMALE)
P.O. Box 31
Elmhurst, IL 60126
< http://female.home.org >

Network helping home-based mothers keep in touch with other professional women. Networking opportunities and newsletter.

Home-Based Working Moms (HBWM)
P.O. Box 500164
Austin, TX 78750
< http://www.hbwm.com >

National organization for moms (and dads) working at home. Newsletter, networking information, and more.

Mothers' Access to Careers at Home (MATCH)
P.O. Box 123
Annandale, VA 22003
< http://www.freestate.ne/match >

Networking, support group for women working from home. Newsletter and resource directory for sale.

Mothers' Home Business Network
P.O. Box 423
East Meadow, NY 11554
< http://www.mhbm.com >

Home business guidance; newsletter and resource guide.

Business Associations

American Women's Economic Development Corporation (AWED)
71 Vanderbilt Ave., Suite 320
New York, NY 10169
(212) 692-9100

The premier national, not-for-profit organization committed to helping entrepreneurial women start and grow their own businesses.

Business Women's Network
1146 19th St., NW, 3rd Floor
Washington, DC 20036
(202) 466-8209

The National Association of Women Business Owners (NAWBO)
110 Wayne Ave., Suite 830
Silver Spring, MD 20910-5603
< http://www.nawbo.org >

"The premier source of information on women-owned businesses . . . worldwide." Its research branch is the National Foundation for Women Business Owners. < http://www.nfwbo.org >

National Chamber of Commerce for Women: The Home-
  Based Business Committee
10 Waterside Plaza, Suite 6H
New York, NY 10010
(212) 685-3454

"Publishes updated job descriptions and pay comparisons for business-owners and for job-holders; also provides Home-Based Business of the Year guidelines for opportunity-seekers."

National Women's Business Council (NWBC)
409 3rd St., SW, Suite 5850
Washington, DC 20034
(202) 205-3850

Their mission is to foster women's business enterprise. They publish a quarterly newsletter, *The Partnership.*

Women Incorporated (WI)
1401 21st St., Suite 310
Sacramento, CA 95814
(916) 448-8444; < http://www.capcon.com/wi/

Women in Franchising (WIF)
53 W. Jackson Blvd., Suite 205
Chicago, IL 60604
(312) 431-1467

Women's Franchise Network (see "Franchises and
  Distributorships" chapter)

Home Business (and Related) Associations
American Association of Home-Based Businesses, Inc.
P.O. Box 10023
Rockville, MD 20849-0023
< http://www.aahbb.org >

"A national, nonprofit association dedicated to the support and advocacy of home-based businesses." Does not sell or endorse any business opportunities.

American Home Business Association
4505 S. Wasatach Blvd.
Salt Lake City, UT 84124-9918
< http://www.homebusiness.com >

Offers many benefits and discounts to members.

Disabled Businesspersons Association (DBA)
9625 Black Mountain Rd., Suite 207
San Diego, CA 92126-4564

Executive Suite Association
438 E. Wilson Bridge Rd., Suite 200
Columbus, OH 43085

Office space to rent for meetings and business support. Write for locations of office suites nearest to you.

Home Office Association of America
909 Third Ave., Suite 990
New York, NY 10022-4731

Member benefits, newsletter.

National Association for the Cottage Industry
P.O. Box 14850
Chicago, IL 60614
(312) 472-8116

Send an LSASE for information. Sells the *Home Office Resource Bibliography*. $6.95; make check payable to Kern Reports.

National Association of Home-Based Businesses
10451 Mill Run Circle, Suite 400
Owings Mill, MD 21117
(410) 363-3698

Send a self-addressed, $8^1/2$" × 11" envelope with appropriate postage affixed for information.

National Association for the Self-Employed (NASE)
2121 Precinct Line Rd.
Hurst, TX 76054
(800) 232-6273

Offers a health insurance plan for members.

National Business Incubation Association
20 E. Circle Dr., Suite 190
Athens, OH 45701
< http://www.nbia.org >

Fosters small businesses and helps them become independent. Write for the location of a business incubator near you.

Small Office/Home Office Association (SOHOA)
1765 Business Center Dr., #100
Reston, VA 20190-5326

Offers a range of benefits for members.

Working Today
P.O. Box 1261,
Old Chelsea Station
New York, NY 10113
< http://www.workingtoday.org >

A national nonprofit membership organization that promotes the interests of people who work on their own.

(Also check the *Encyclopedia of Associations* in your local library for national trade associations in your area of business.)

Government Resources

Federal

Bureau of the Census, Customer Services
Data User Services Division
Suitland and Silver Hill Roads
Washington, DC 20233
(301) 763-8576; < http://www.census.gov >

Provides statistics.

Bureau of Labor Statistics
(202) 606-6378
< http://www.bls.gov >

Also provides statistics.

Bureau of Consumer Protection
Division of Special Statutes
6th and Pennsylvania Aves., NW
Washington, DC 20580

Provides information on the labeling of textile products or wool clothing.

Consumer Information Center
P.O. Box 100
Pueblo, CO 81002
< http://www.pueblo.gsa.gov >

Send for free *Consumer Information Catalog.* You can order free or low-cost information on many topics, including small business information.

Cooperative Extension Service
< http://www.reeusda.gov >

Call your county seat for the phone number and location of the office in your county. Part of the Department of Agriculture, this service usually works in conjunction with a university. Provides information and services in the areas of agriculture and home economics, in addition to small businesses and crafts marketing.

Department of Labor Women's Bureau
(202) 219-6611.

Internal Revenue Service (IRS)
4300 Caroline Ave.
Richmond, VA 23222
(800) 829-1040
< http://www.securetax.com >

< http://www.irs.ustreas.gov > (other state and federal tax forms)

Write for tax publications concerning business use of your home or call your local IRS office.

Office of Women's Business Ownership
Small Business Administration
409 Third St. SW, 6th Floor
Washington, DC 20416
(202) 205-6673; < http://www.sba.gov/womeninbusiness >

Send for a free packet of business information of interest to women.

Register of Copyrights
Copyright Office
Library of Congress
10 First St., SE
Washington, DC 20540

Provides information on obtaining copyrights, patents, trademarks.

Service Corps of Retired Executives Association (SCORE)
409 Third St., SW, 4th Floor
Washington, DC 20024
< http://www.sba.gov/SCORE/program.html >

A nonprofit association funded by the SBA, made up of mostly retired men and women who worked in business management. Services are free and they provide small business counseling. Write for SCORE contacts in your area or call your local SBDC (see page 372).

U.S. Patent and Trademark Office
Washington, DC 20231
(703) 308-HELP [4357]; < http://www.uspto.gov >

U.S. Small Business Administration (SBA)
409 Third St., SW
Washington, DC 20416

This is the primary source for government assistance for small businesses. Their regional and Small Business

Development Centers offer free or low-cost assistance, seminars, and workshops. They also offer many helpful publications.

✤ SBA Answer Desk: (800) 827-5722; (202) 205-7064, fax; (202) 205-7333, TDD for the hearing impaired. Provides referrals to recorded business topics. Ask for a free copy of the *Small Business Directory*, a listing of SBA publications and products, including the comprehensive videotape *Home-Based Business: A Winning Blueprint*.

✤ SBA Financial Assistance: (800) 8-ASK-SBA. Ask for the "SBA's Finance a Business" or log onto http://www.sba.gov/financing >

✤ SBA Online: (800) 859-INFO for a 2400 baud modem; (800) 697-INFO for a 9600 baud modem. A national electronic bulletin board service providing a synopsis of SBA information.

✤ SBA Procurement Assistance: (800) 8-ASK-SBA. Ask about government contracting for the small business. Read Government Prime Contracts Monthly, 1155 Connecticut Ave. NW, Washington DC 20036 about contracting. < http://www.govdata.com > See also *Free Help from Uncle Sam to Start Your Own Business*, by William Alarid. 1992, Puma Publishing, Santa Monica, CA.

Small Business Development Centers (SBDCs)
Small Business Administration
409 Third St., SW
Washington, DC 20416

Write or call for the SBDC nearest you or look in your telephone directory's white pages under "Small Business Development Center." SBDCs are usually at universities and are available in forty-six states, the District of Columbia, Puerto Rico, and the Virgin Islands. They provide free services, counseling, and low-cost seminars to prospective and existing business owners. Read *SBA Hotline Answer Book*, by Gustave Berle.

WNET Mentor Program
USBA, 409 Third St., SW
Washington, DC 20416.

Purpose is to match seasoned women business owners with new business owners in order to exchange ideas or suggestions.

Women Business Centers

(see Office of Women's Business Ownership for address, page 371), (202) 205-6673; < http://www.onlinewbc.org >

New federally funded women's business centers that offer various business start-up programs and guidance. Call, write, see the site online for the center nearest you. Also see *More 101 Best Home-Based Businesses for Women,* by Priscilla Y. Huff, 1998, which has a listing of these centers.

Publications

USBA, P.O. Box 15434, Fort Worth, TX 76119. Write for listing of small business publications.

State

Check with your state representative and/or state senator for free information on state agencies that help promote women's and small businesses within the state.

Also check in your local library or bookstore for latest editions of *Starting and Operating a Business in . . .* (there is one for each state), by Michael D. Jenkins. The Oasis Press, Grants Pass, OR.

Local

Contact your local SBDC, chamber of commerce, home business associations and county extension office for information on business start-up help in your community.

Books

80 + Great Ideas for Making Money at Home, by Erica Barkemeyer. 1992, Walker and Company.

199 Great Home Businesses You Can Start (and Succeed in) for Under $1,000, by Tyler G. Hicks. 1993, Prima Publishing, Rocklin, CA.

Advertising for a Small Business Made Simple, by Bernard Ryan. 1996, Doubleday, New York.

Bootstrapper's Success Secrets: 151 Tactics for Building Your Business on a Shoestring Budget, by Kimberly Stanséll. 1997, Career

Press, Franklin Lakes, NJ. Excellent tips for running a successful business on a budget.

Stanséll also offers a worldwide travel workshop and seminar program based on her book, which includes sessions on customer service, growth strategies, and women's business issues. Contact Stanséll at Suite 306, 6308 W. 89th St., Los Angeles, CA 90045; (310) 568-9861; e-mail: < KmberlyNLA @hotmail.com >

Business Capital for Women: An Essential Handbook for Entrepreneurs, by Emily Card and Adam Miller. 1996, MacMillan General Reference, New York.

Directory of Home-Based Business Resources, by Priscilla Y. Huff. 1995, Pilot Books (see "Books Through the Mail," later in this section).

Finance and Taxes for the Home-Based Business, by Charles and Bryanne Lickson.

Home-Based Business Guide, by Rosalie Marcus. 1997. Send an LSASE to Lasting Impressions, 1039 Wellington Rd., Jenkintown, PA 19046.

Home-Based Business Ideas for Women, by Priscilla Y. Huff. 1993, Pilot Books. $5.95.

Homemade Money, 5th ed., by Barbara Brabec. 1997, Betterway Books, Cincinnati, OH. Excellent source of information.

How To Start and Manage a Home Based Business: A Practical Way to Start Your Own Business, by Jerre G. Lewis and Leslie D. Renn. 1996, Lewis & Renn Associates (see "Books Through the Mail").

The SOHO Desk Reference, by HarperCollins Publishers, 1997, New York.

Teaming Up: The Small Business Guide to Collaborating with Others to Boost Your Earnings and Expand Your Horizons, by Paul and Sarah Edwards and Rick Benzel. 1997, Putnam, New York.

Tips & Traps for Entrepreneurs: Real-Life Ideas and Solutions for the Toughest Problems Facing Entrepreneurs, by Courtney Price and Kathleen Allen. 1998, McGraw-Hill, New York.

The Women's Business Resource Guide: A National Directory of Over 800 Programs, Resources, and Organizations to Help Women Start or Expand a Business, by Barbara Littman. 1997, NTC/ Contemporary Books, Lincolnwood, IL.

Helpful Reference Books/Directories

These can usually be found in college or larger public libraries.

2001 Sources for Financing a Small Business

Book of Business Plans; National Directory of Women-Owned Firms; Small Business Sourcebook, Gale Research.

Directory of Directories, Gale Research, Detroit, MI.

Dun's Business Rankings

Internet Business 500: The Top Essential Sites for Business, by Ryan Bernard. 1995, Ventana Communications Group, Inc., Research Triangle Park, NC.

Thomas's Lists of Manufacturers, < http://www/thomasregister .com >

U.S. Industrial Outlook

See also *A Directory of National Women's Organizations* published by:

The National Council for Research on Women
The Sara Delano Roosevelt Memorial House
47–49 E. 65th St.
New York, NY 10021

Books Through the Mail

Write for catalogs.

Jeffrey Lant Associates, P.O. Box 38-2767, Cambridge, MA 02238.

Lewis & Renn Associates, 10315 Harmony Dr., Interlochen, MI 49643.

The New Careers Center, *Whole Work Catalog,* 1515-23rd St., P.O. Box 339-CT, Boulder, CO 80306.

Pilot Books, 127 Sterling Ave., P.O. Box 2102, Greenport, NY 11944-2102. (800) 79-pilot. < http://www.pilotbooks. com >

Success Publications, 3419 Dunham, Box 263, Warsaw, NY 14569.

Home Study Courses

Distance Education and Training Council (DETC)
1601 18th St., NW
Washington, DC 20009-2529
(202) 234-5100; < www.detc.org >

A trade organization that accredits correspondence schools. Offers free publication, *Accredited Institutions of Post-Secondary Education*. Write or call for a free listing of schools.

ICS Center for Degree Studies
925 Oak St.
Scranton, PA 18515
Offers specialized associate degree programs.

Lifetime Career Schools
101 Harrison St.
Archbald, PA 18403-9982

NRI Schools
McGraw-Hill Continuing Education Center
4401 Connecticut Ave., NW
Washington, DC 20008

Professional Career Development Institute
6065 Roswell Rd.
Atlanta, GA 30328-9894

Stratford Career Institute, Inc.
233 Swanton Rd., Suite 121
St. Albans, VT 05478-9911.

Internet Sites for Women's Home and Small Business Information
(Also see others listed with associations, etc.)

< http://www.anincomeofherown >
An Income of Her Own (a site for teen women to learn entrepreneurship).

< http://www.bizymoms.com >
Resources for work-at-home moms.

< http://www.fodreams.com >
Field of Dreams.

< http://www.ivillage.com >
The Women's Network (work at home forums, chats).

< http://www.momsnetwork.com >
Mom's Network Exchange.

< http://www.tscentral.com >
Trade shows. For trade show consulting contact Trade Show Xpress, 11062 S. Military Trail, Suite 414, Boynton Beach, FL 33436. (515) 733-4888; (515) 733-4841 fax.

< http://www.wisbusuww.edu/homepg/home.htm >
National Home Based Business Virtual Center of the University of Wisconsin Whitewater, College of Business and Economics—valuable links.

< http://www.womenconnect.com >
Women's Connection Online.

< http://www.womweb.com >
Working Woman magazine.

Magazines
(Look in your favorite bookstore or library.)

Business Start-Ups. Subscription Dept., P.O. Box 50347, Boulder, CO 80323-0347. < http://www.entrepreneurmag.com >

Edge magazine, 921 Penllyn Blue Bell Pike, Blue Bell, PA 19422. < http://www.edgeonline.com >

Entrepreneur's Home Office, P.O. Box 53784, Boulder, CO 80323-3784. 6 issues. < http://www.entrepreneurmag.com >

Home Business Connection, Cutting Edge Media, 29 S. Market St., Elizabethtown, PA 17022. 12 issues.

Home Business magazine. (760) 781-5219. < http://www.home-businessmag.com > Call for subscription.

Home Office Computing/Small Business Computing. P.O. Box 53543, Boulder, CO 89323-3543. (800) 288-7812. < http://www.smalloffice.com > 12 issues.

Income Opportunities, P.O. Box 5300, Jenks, OK 74037. (800) 289-7852. 12 issues.

Small Business Opportunities. Harris Publications, Inc., 1115 Broadway, New York, NY 10160-0397. 6 issues.

Working at Home, P.O. Box 5484, Harlan, IA 51593-2984. 4 issues. < http://www.successmagazine.com >

Newsletters
101 Best Home-Based and Small Business for Women Updates: The Latest Facts, News, and Tips for Self-Employed Women, Box 286, Sellersville, PA 18960. Send LSASE for a free sample issue.

Home at Work, P.O. Box 487, Mendon, MA 01756-0487.

ShowcaseNews, Select Entertainment, Inc., 853 Broadway #1516, New York, NY 10003. < http://www.buzznyc.com/ showcasenews > Publication dedicated to new talent and new projects in New York City.

Online Services

CompuServe, Working from Home Forum: (800) 848-8199.

Delphi, Business Forum: (800) 695-4005.

Genie, Home Office/Small Business Roundtable: (800) 683-9636.

Prodigy, Home Office Bulletin Board: (800) 776-3449.

Start-Up Guides

Write or call for catalogs.

Entrepreneur's Start-Up Guides, 2392 Morse Ave., P.O. Box 57050, Irvine, CA 92619-7050. (800) 421-2300.

Lewis & Renn Associates, 10315 Harmony Dr., Interlochen, MI 49643. Write for list of start-up books.

National Business Library's Start-Up Guides, P.O. Box 21957, Santa Barbara, CA 93121. (800) 947-7724.

Software & Forms

Write or call for catalogs.

NEBS, Inc., 500 Main St., Groton, MA 01471-0002. (800) 367-6327. Business and computer forms catalog.

TigerDirect, 8700 W. Flagler St., Miami, FL 33174.(800) 879-1597. < http://www.tigerdirect.com >

Supplies

Write or call for catalogs.

Computer, Office Equipment, and Supplies

Anthro Corp., Technology Furniture, 10450 SW Manhasset Dr., Tualatin, OR 97062. Economical computer carts and work stations.

Damark International, Inc., 7101 Winnetka Ave. N., P.O. Box 29900, Minneapolis, MN 55429-0900. (612) 535-8880. Sells desktop copiers and home office products.

Earth Care Paper, Inc., P.O. Box 3335, Madison, WI 53704. Sells recycled paper and products.

Paper Direct, P.O. Box 742, Long Lake MN 55356-9977.
Pennywise Office Products, 6911 Laurel Bowie Rd., Suite 209, Bowie, MD 20715. (800) 942-3311. Offers a "Welcome Kit" especially for start-up businesses ($24.99).
Power Up!, One MISCO Plaza, Holmdel, NJ 07733. (908) 264-1000. Software and hardware.
Quill Office Products Catalog, Quill Corporation, 100 Schelter Rd, Lincolnshire, IL 60069-3621. < http://www.quillcorp. com > Also has helpful business booklets.

Other
Lefty's Corner
P.O. BOX 615
Clarks Summit, PA 18411

Sells writing supplies, craft equipment, and books specifically designed for lefthanders. $3 for catalog, refundable with first purchase.

MASTERPAK, 50 W. 57th St., 9th Fl., New York, NY 10019. "Archival materials for the packing, shipping, storing, and displaying of fine art, artifacts, and antiques."

Radio Programs
Paul and Sarah Edward's Working from Home show; Business News Network, (719) 528-7040, Sundays from 10 to 11 p.m. E.T.
Success Weekend, a home-based syndicated talk show by Michael Lamp and Jane Beterbing (heard in Reno, NV, and Colorado Springs, CO). Write: Box 1385, Wichita, KS 67201.

Television Programs
Small Business 2000, PBS TV show on small business issues. < http://www.sb2000.com >
Working from Home with Paul and Sarah Edwards, a weekly, half-hour series on the Home & Garden Television network. (423) 694-2700.

Home Shopping Channel
One HSN Dr.
St. Petersburg, FL 33729

QVC/Vendor Relations
1385 Enterprise Dr.
West Chester, PA 19380

Other Resources
Cardservice International
82 North Broadway, Suite 202
Hicksville, NY 11801
< http://www.cardservice.com >

Contact to see if your business qualifies for VISA and MasterCard credit card acceptance.

D-U-N-S, Number
Dun & Bradstreet
899 Eaton Ave.
Bethlehem, PA 18025
(800) 333-0505

Contact for information about getting a D-U-N-S, number for your business (among other things, it is needed to gain a federal contract).

Gebbie Press
P.O. Box 1000
New Paltz, NY 12561
(914) 255-7560; < http://www.gebbieinc.com >

PR data resource of over 22,000 newspapers, magazines, radio and TV stations on disks, mailing labels.

The Kessler Exchange
100 Wilshire Blvd., Suite 1800
Santa Monica, CA 90401
(800) 422-6364

Provides small business research and support. Contact for free catalog.

How to Contact the Author:
If you have any comments, questions, or business ideas you would like to share, please send them to Priscilla Y. Huff, Box 286, Sellersville, PA 18960. Send e-mail to < pyhuff@cynet.net > or visit my Web site at < http:///www.selfemployed woman.com >

Index

381